Christian Ethics and Political Economy in North America

In this religious and moral critique of liberalism, Travis Kroeker analyses how religio-ethical discourse is changed when it is translated into the economic policy discourse of North American liberalism. Focusing on influential representatives of contemporary Christian social ethics, he examines attempts to reconcile prophetic religion and public policy.

Kroeker argues that in trying to make their theological ethics relevant to economic policy Christian social ethicists have accepted assumptions that are incompatible with theological beliefs. Starting with the Social Gospel movement, he discusses the positions of theologian Walter Rauschenbusch and Canadian politician James Shaver Woodsworth. He then turns to Christian Realism and compares the views of Reinhold Niebuhr with those of Gregory Vlastos, the central figure in the Canadian Fellowship for a Christian Social Order. He also examines recent pastoral letters on the economy by the Canadian and U.S. conferences of Roman Catholic bishops.

In conclusion, Kroeker suggests an alternative theological approach based on the classical Christian realism of Augustine that might better address the moral malaise of liberal political economy.

P. TRAVIS KROEKER is associate professor of religious studies, McMaster University.

McGill-Queen's Studies in the History of Religion
G.A. Rawlyk, Editor

Volumes in this series have been supported by the
Jackman Foundation of Toronto.

1 Small Differences
Irish Catholics and Irish Protestants, 1815–1922
An International Perspective
Donald Harman Akenson

2 Two Worlds
The Protestant Culture of
Nineteenth-Century Ontario
William Westfall

3 An Evangelical Mind
Nathanael Burwash and the Methodist Tradition
in Canada, 1839–1918
Marguerite Van Die

4 The Dévotes
Women and Church in Seventeenth-Century France
Elizabeth Rapley

5 The Evangelical Century
College and Creed in English Canada from the Great
Revival to the Great Depression
Michael Gauvreau

6 The German Peasants' War and
Anabaptist Community of Goods
James M. Stayer

7 A World Mission
Canadian Protestantism and the Quest for
a New International Order, 1918–1939
Robert Wright

8 Serving the Present Age
Revivalism, Progressivism, and the
Methodist Tradition in Canada
Phyllis D. Airhart

9 A Sensitive Independence
Canadian Methodist Women Missionaries
in Canada and the Orient, 1881–1925
Rosemary R. Gagan

10 God's Peoples
Covenant and Land in South Africa,
Israel, and Ulster
Donald Harman Akenson

13 Amazing Grace
   Studies in Evangelicalism in the United States,
   Canada, Britain, Australia, and Beyond
   George Rawlyk and Mark A. Noll, editors

14 Children of Peace
   W. John McIntyre

15 A Solitary Pillar
   Montreal's Anglican Church and
   the Quiet Revolution
   Joan Marshall

16 Padres in No Man's Land
   Canadian Chaplains and the Great War
   Duff Crerar

17 Christian Ethics and Political Economy
   in North America
   A Critical Analysis
   P. Travis Kroeker

Christian Ethics and Political Economy in North America

A Critical Analysis

P. TRAVIS KROEKER

McGill-Queen's University Press
Montreal & Kingston • London • Buffalo

ISBN 0-7735-1267-5 (cloth)
ISBN 0-7735-1268-3 (paper)

Legal deposit second quarter 1995
Bibliothèque nationale du Québec

Printed in Canada on acid-free paper

This book has been published with the help of a grant
from the Canadian Federation for the Humanities,
using funds provided by the Social Sciences and
Humanities Research Council of Canada.

McGill-Queen's University Press is grateful to the
Canada Council for support of its publication
program.

Canadian Cataloguing in Publication Data

Kroeker, P. Travis (Peter Travis), 1957–
   Christian ethics and political economy in North
   America : a critical analysis

   (McGill-Queen's studies in the history of religion ; 17)
   Includes bibliographical references and index.
   ISBN 0-7735-1267-5 (bound) –
   ISBN 0-7735-1268-3 (pbk.)

   1. Social ethics – Canada. 2. Social ethics – United
   States. 3. Canada – Social policy – Moral and ethical
   aspects. 4. United States – Social policy – Moral and
   ethical aspects. 5. Canada – Economic policy – Moral
   and ethical aspects. 6. United States – Economic
   policy – Moral and ethical aspects. 7. Sociology,
   Christian. I. Title. II. Series.
   BJ1251.K76 1995   261.8'0971   C94-900730-7

Typeset in Palatino 10/12
by Caractéra production graphique, Quebec City

To my parents

Anna Klassen Kroeker
Peter Lawrence Kroeker

Contents

Preface xi

1 Introduction 3

2 The Cooperative Commonwealth and the Kingdom of
   God: The Social Gospel Quest for a Public Morality 19

3 Christian Realism: Reinhold Niebuhr and the Fellowship
   for a Christian Social Order 45

4 Human Dignity and Labour: The Catholic Bishops and
   Economic Policy 91

5 Conclusion: Toward a Moral Theology of Creation 122

Notes 145

Bibliography 187

Index 199

Preface

This study has grown out of a moral and religious concern about the centrality of the "paradigm of productivity" – the rationality, practices, institutions, and consequences of liberal capitalism – in modern North American public life. It is a public life oriented toward the voracious consumption of material goods, dedicated to the seemingly endless expansion of commodified needs. The efficient management of this process has come to define the very meaning of politics; hence the centrality of "political economy" in our public culture. The problem, as I understand it, is not only or even primarily one of "social justice," understood as a matter of distributional fairness or equal access to goods or democratic participation in economic institutions and processes. Conceptions of justice are closely bound up with visions of reality – of human and non-human nature, society, politics, and so on. This is an especially important consideration for any attempt to relate religious ethics to questions of economic justice, since many modern persons would argue or simply assume that justice is a matter of social contract and formal legal procedures that best maximize individual and group interests and best protect individual and group freedoms. And many people would further argue or assume that justice is therefore primarily a matter of effective social and economic organization and problem-solving based on the most efficient calculation of consequences. In a liberal, pluralistic society, justice must be autonomous from moral and religious values, which remain a matter of individual preference and choice. This is problematic, given the biblical and classical religious understanding of justice as rooted in the goodness of a divinely created order of reality, where social justice is related to the "righteousness" of human agents as they fulfil their created purpose within a "common good." In this view justice is not primarily a matter of external convention, law, or policy (although those are important matters) but a way of life nourished by discernment into the meaningful moral order and truth of things in a spiritual universe. The *root* of injustice is not understood to be faulty organization or external procedure so much as it is a faulty vision of reality.

How we represent the world – the way we envision it or interpret its meaning – makes a crucial difference to the ways in which we respond to it and participate in it. Our attitudes, judgments, and actions are oriented by our symbolic representations. This is not just an individual quest – symbols are public, cultural realities. Political economy as a science and as a public policy concern holds the prominence it does in modern North American society because economic symbols and their institutional embodiments hold great orienting power in our culture. To understand happiness, the good life, and the quest for self-fulfilment in terms of expanded consumer choice, material comfort, and physical health and longevity is a culturally embodied symbol with considerable social and political power.

One of the problems in exploring the relation of religious symbols and traditions to political and social matters in our culture is that those symbols and traditions are often no longer regarded as representing publicly significant and comprehensible, shared experience or meaning. Religious experience and its symbolization has become a private matter, another lifestyle option available in the marketplace of spiritual commodities, which are sometimes called "values." Religious symbols are often treated as preferred opinions that reflect the tastes and/or social conditioning of individuals, an approach characteristic of certain social scientific methodologies in religious studies. In this view the study of religion is understood as the collection and classification of external facts and opinions about religion. The symbols themselves and the experiences to which they refer are not taken seriously on their own terms as representing that which is ultimately true, good, and beautiful.

The irony of this fact should not be lost on us. Hannah Arendt in *The Human Condition* makes the point that for the ancients the case was exactly reversed. Economic matters were private, administered and conducted behind the walls of the *oikia* or household as the sphere of necessity. The public realm of the *polis* was concerned not with physical needs or wants and their administration but by deliberation on the nature of *eudaimonia* (happiness or the good life) and the discussion and practice of the virtues required for it. This was the sphere of human freedom, characterized by the plurality and creative expression of unique agents and their particular identities in their public speech and action. For the ancients, then, the very term "political economy" would have been oxymoronic, a contradiction of terms and a confusion of categories. Arendt's point is that the reduction of politics to economics in the modern age has brought with it a loss of capacity for dramatic action and speech in the public realm. The public is increasingly taken up with survival and the gratification of material needs, where individuals are related by abstract universal rights in a mass society administered by technical expertise. In such a public – oriented by economic measures of the "common good" rather than by dramatic symbols and memories of the personal actions and interactions of human beings, dramatic events, and their significance – religious symbols and traditions lose their orienting power and ethics becomes a matter of contractual agreement and adherence to technical codes of behaviour.

This study of religious ethical approaches to questions of political economy in North America is not strictly either a history of ideas or a social history. It is rather an analysis of influential twentieth century approaches to Christian social ethics in the attempt to understand what happens to religious ethical discourse when it is related to or translated into the policy parameters of North American political economy. The overall thesis shaping the analysis is that all these approaches in different ways accept the assumptions about nature present within the liberal "productivist paradigm," and this leads to the disordered consequences of an anthropocentric utilitarian ethos and the technological domination of nature. In chapter one I try to elaborate the nature of this problematic. My analysis of specific figures and movements and their approaches to ethics and economics comprises the substance of chapters two through four, and I select a u.s. and Canadian representative for discussion in each chapter. Chapter two focuses on the social gospel movement, discussing the work of the theologian Walter Rauschenbusch and of the Canadian politician James Shaver Woodsworth. The third chapter on Christian realism provides a comparative analysis of Reinhold Niebuhr and of the Canadian Fellowship for a Christian Social Order, the central intellectual figure in which was Gregory Vlastos. Chapter four discusses the recent pastoral letters on the economy by the Canadian and u.s. conferences of Roman Catholic bishops. The concluding chapter then offers my own exploration of an alternative religious approach that addresses the problematic outlined in chapter one. It does so by placing political and economic ethics within the symbolic circumference of religious cosmology, as in the classical understanding of the human sciences. My argument in the conclusion proceeds by way of a comparison between Thomas Hobbes (modern liberal "realism") and the Platonic Christian approach elaborated by Augustine (symbolic religious "realism").

I must say a word here about the morphology of my argument and how my normative agenda is related to the critical analysis of the various other approaches examined in chapters two through four. Those readers who wish to pursue the nature of my philosophical and theological ethical understanding and commitments will find it most clearly stated in chapters one and five. Of course my critical analysis in the intervening chapters is to some extent shaped by and developed in relation to this normative theoretical position. But I trust that those readers who remain in basic disagreement with my own position will nevertheless find my descriptive analysis of other approaches fair and even useful. It is for this reason that I have placed my programmatic proposal for a moral theology of creation at the end and not the beginning of the analysis. I therefore move from a statement of the problematic that orients the discussion to a critical analysis of the representative religious ethical approaches, showing how their theoretical positions fail to adequately address the "spiritual crisis" present in the "paradigm of production" of liberal political economy. Had I followed the advice of certain readers to move my own retrieval of Augustinian realism ahead of the analysis of other approaches, elaborating the direction of my programmatic proposal in advance, this may have allowed the reader to follow the critical analysis with greater understanding. But it would also have had the effect of featuring my own external critique of the approaches much more prominently, thereby giving less weight to the internal critical analysis that I seek to provide. It might be useful to point out that the critical analysis of the other approaches was completed before I worked out my programmatic proposal. That is, my theoretical alternative developed in response to the inadequacies I perceived in the theoretical positions of influential approaches within North American religious ethics. It was not developed in advance and then applied to these positions, or simply illustrated with reference to them.

It should also be noted that critical comparative attention is devoted primarily to the theological and ethical proposals themselves. My aim is not so much to compare the differences between the u.s. and Canada as it is to include the often ignored Canadian approaches in the discussion of North American religious ethics and public life. Therefore while the development of the analysis is chronological and attends to the historical contexts within which the selected proposals were made, this study is not primarily a historical analysis but a philosophical-theological and ethical one. However, in my judgment historical analysis and substantive theological or ethical argument are not incompatible. Indeed they can be mutually enriching, and I have proceeded on that premise in undertaking this project. I also recognise that this leaves me vulnerable to criticisms I might otherwise have avoided, but I am prepared to take that risk in the hope that my interpretive strategy also makes possible certain insights that might otherwise have been missed.

Among the many who have helped me in various ways to complete this book, to all of whom I am grateful, several must be acknowledged and thanked by name. Carl Ridd, Gordon Harland, and Egil Grislis helped to set me on the path of theological and ethical reflection many years ago. I owe a special debt of gratitude to James Gustafson under whose supervision an earlier form of this manuscript was written as a dissertation at the University of Chicago. His discerning criticism forced me to clarify my interpretations and arguments, and his generous support gave me the confidence to pursue my own line of inquiry. Robin Lovin and David Tracy also read that earlier manuscript and made some challenging comments which have helped to form the subsequent reconception and revision of my work. Certain colleagues at McMaster University have been generous in their helpful critical engagement and encouragement of this project. Zdravko Planinc, John Robertson, and Gérard Vallée have read and commented on portions of this book, and my work is the better for it. Finally, my deepest personal gratitude for their sustaining support belongs to my family: my parents, to whom this work is dedicated; my children, Sarah, Miriam, and Peter; and my truest companion in the dialogue of life, Catherine Stewart-Kroeker.

Christian Ethics and Political Economy in North America

1 Introduction

The question of the relationship between religion and economics is currently the site of a raging ideological battle between proponents of democratic capitalism and democratic socialism, liberalism and communitarianism, and neo-conservative and leftist theologies. In attempting to negotiate this battleground of ideas and positions in order to clarify the issues at stake, one is often caught in a confusing crossfire of claims – some of which are religious, others economic or social scientific. Some claims appeal to revelation and tradition; others to empirical economic and social analysis. Sometimes the claims have a normative or prescriptive thrust; at other times they appear to be purely descriptive. How might we reflect on the complex relations between theology and economics so as to achieve conceptual clarity on the issues and an intelligible terrain on which to assess possible courses of action and policy proposals? How do those who wish to contribute to issues of economic policy arrive at and argue for the moral judgments that inform their proposals?

These questions are hardly new, either to social and political theory or to theological ethics. This book will restrict itself mainly to a discussion of certain religious attempts to deal with them in the context of North American political economy, and the analysis will be primarily directed toward theological ethics. But the classic theoretical attempt to clarify these issues remains, in my judgment, the work of Max Weber. In terms of both his historically based theoretical account of religion and the rise of capitalism and his general methodological approach with its strong distinction between facts and values and the attempt to illuminate significant relations by constructing "ideal types," Weber has had a profound influence, not only within the social sciences but also upon the development of theological ethics in North America. Part of Weber's greatness is that he clearly understood and theoretically formulated the shift from traditional politics and political theory, in which religion and religious ethics played a central role, to modern social scientific methodology rooted in "*Wertfrei*" instrumental or technical procedures modelled after the natural sciences. Weber understood the "sublimation of [classical] politics" into the organizational, technical demands of highly rationalized and bureaucratized modern industrial societies.[1] He grasped the profound implications in the substitution of a scientific worldview for religious cosmology, establishing a new foundation not only for social and political order or "legitimation" but also for public rationality and what will count as "true" or "right" or "meaningful."

In the context of this shift, religious and theological claims have lost their public rational authority. Rational discourse and the reality to which it refers are now established by the mathematical and physical sciences. That is, the cosmos is construed as fundamentally material; hence it follows that the orienting socio-political microcosm shifts, in the modern age, from the founding myths and symbols of the spiritual community or polis to the mechanistic processes and technical imperatives of the modern economic order. Weber traced this fateful shift in his now-classic work, *The Protestant Ethic and the Spirit of Capitalism*, and it is necessary to rehearse briefly here once again Weber's well-known thesis, since it sets the context for my interpretation of North American theology, ethics, and political economy.

The question Weber finds most interesting – and most troubling – about the capitalist ethos concerns how and why the process of "rationalization" (the rationality and organization of political economy in terms of capitalistic calculation) has attained such pervasive power and predominance in the modern West. For it is the success of this process of "disenchantment" (*Entzauberung der Welt*) that has led to the impoverishment of politics and public life: "Precisely the ultimate and most sublime values [*letzten und sublimsten Werte*] have retreated from public life [*Oeffentlichkeit*] either into the transcendental realm [*hinterweltliche Reich*] of mystic life or into the brotherliness of direct [*unmittelbarer*] ... human relations."[2] Clearly this process is linked to the rise of the modern sciences – in particular the natural, experimental, and mathematical sciences – and the technical calculations and developments they make possible.[3] But science on its own does not and cannot specify or determine the practical applications, the concrete socio-economic consequences of its knowledge. In order to account for the practical directions of the process, therefore, one must attend to the capitalistic interests and social values that constitute the "spirit" or "ethos" of modern occidental culture. Normative judgments of value cannot be derived, elaborated, or validated scientifically. Weber rejects the Hegelian and Marxist attempts to develop a total philosophy of history, a universal humanity, on scientific or rational grounds. Weber postulates no comprehensive historical dialectic (be it speculative or materialist) that claims to read normative meaning from the immanent "facts" of history and society.[4] Such normative meaning and value judgments require faith and therefore belong to the realm of seers, prophets, and ideologues – to charismatic leaders, not technical experts. Social science can clarify the consequences (intended and unintended) of such normative visions, it can show the means by which they might effectively be pursued or realized within particular social conditions, but it cannot originate or justify them.

This means that Weber operates from a dualistic separation of objective scientific facts and subjective normative values, a dualism that requires the language of "elective affinity" (*Wahlverwandschaft*) and ultimately of "compromise" between facts and values. It also leads to Weber's own sense of the tragic, fateful nihilism of a civilization that systematically excludes all public normative meaning by extending a utilitarian, scientific rationality over all of life, with inevitably irrational moral consequences for political life:[5] "Not summer's bloom lies ahead of us, but rather a polar night of icy darkness and hardness, no matter which group may triumph externally now."[6] Politics without a substantive discussion of the common good is reduced to ideological warfare, the purely external power struggle of interest groups seeking "control" of the instrumental processes and rational organizations that alone provide common purpose in modern society.[7] Those groups that do seek to put forward a normative vision of the good are either condemned to political irrelevance and the private margins of social life or compelled to develop "rational" strategies that finally lose any inner spiritual significance they might have had. Weber was highly sceptical about the future of religious ethics as a public ordering power, and his great fear was that in the increasingly bureaucratized, mechanistic "iron cage" of industrial society, public justice would degenerate into "*Herrschaft ohne Recht*" – a matter of competing ideologies seeking external legitimation and power without concern for moral meaning or justice.

How did we get to this point? Weber gives us his account in *The Protestant Ethic*. He sees the historical development of capitalist society as neither the logical causal product of an idea nor merely the outcome of material economic forces. Rather, one must examine the "elective affinities" between ideas and practical conditions and conduct within which social organizations and changes occur. In the case of the rise of capitalism, argues Weber, Protestant beliefs played an important part in shaping practical conduct, particularly in economic matters. He singles out three doctrinal tenets of ascetic Protestantism that produced highly consequential psychological conditions for practical motivation and action in the everyday world: (1) the idea that all things were created for God's glory and ultimately serve the divine will, (2) the incomprehensibility of the eternal divine will, and (3) the doctrine of the predestination of the elect. The psychological consequences of this dogmatic Calvinism are linked to "salvation anxiety," a "feeling of unprecedented inner loneliness of the single individual"[8] in a world stripped of any sacramental mediation of divine grace. This repudiation of sacramental mediation as "magic" is a decisive step in the disenchantment of the cosmos. Cosmic reality is best understood in utilitarian, materialist terms, as a divinely created mechanistic order.[9]

How then are individuals, plagued by paralyzing "salvation anxiety," to work out their salvation in this non-sacramental, rational world order? The pastoral and ethical strategy of ascetic Protestantism was to glorify God by serving the divine will in one's worldly calling, namely to "labour in the service of impersonal social usefulness."[10] Certainty of election could be gained via intense ascetic activity in one's daily vocation, whereby one becomes a tool of the divine will. Such an ethic, given its doctrinal backing, leads to the ascetic rational organization of all of life in the service of God, whose purposes in the world are ultimately understood in terms of "anthropocentric utilitarianism."[11] One's primary moral and religious duty is therefore to exercise systematic self-control in fulfilling one's vocation in this larger divinely willed rational order. This is the practical social consequence of transforming asceticism from a spiritual act in a sacramental cosmos to rational action within mundane occupations in a disenchanted cosmos.

The unintended socio-economic consequences of these doctrinal ideas provided a religio-moral basis for several key components of modern capitalism. The emphasis on labouring actively and methodically in a calling as fulfilling one's special place in God's larger purposes in the world offered an ethical justification for modern specialization and division of labour.[12] Dogmatic Protestantism's ascetic attitude toward the everyday world, emphasizing the sober utility and rational uniformity of life as ordered by God, greatly aided the capitalist interest in the standardization of production[13] and the formalistic constraints of legal organization and procedural rationality in political society.[14] Finally, these ideas provided a doctrine of stewardship that combines a strong impetus toward the systematic, rational acquisition of profit – understood as taking advantage of divinely given opportunities for service and resulting in the accumulation of productive wealth as a sign of God's blessing – with a stringent limitation on consumption that enjoins frugal productivity and rational reinvestment as a moral duty toward one's divinely entrusted possessions.

These values and practical forms of conduct were institutionalized and routinized in the capitalist economic order. As the religious motivations waned, a "sober economic virtue" and "utilitarian worldliness" took the place of the religious search for the Kingdom of God.[15] Weber describes the bleak consequences of this process of rationalization in a paragraph that is worth citing in full:

The Puritan wanted to work in a calling; we are forced to do so. For when asceticism was carried out of monastic cells into everyday life, and began to dominate worldly morality, it did its part in building the tremendous cosmos of the modern economic order. This order is now bound to the technical and economic conditions of machine production which today determine the lives of all the individuals who are born into this mechanism, not only those directly concerned with economic acquisition, with irresistable force. Perhaps it will so determine them until the last ton of fossilized coal is burnt. In Baxter's view the care for external goods should only lie on the shoulders of the "saint like a light cloak, which can be thrown aside at any moment." But fate decreed that the cloak should become an iron cage.[16]

Weber ends *The Protestant Ethic* with a wistful jeremiad on the irony that the rationalized embodiment of the ascetic Protestant "theoretical attitude toward the world"[17] within the totalizing institutions and autonomous organizational structure of industrial capitalism has resulted in the very exile of religious ethics from the public realm. Such are the unintended consequences of fateful "elective affinities" and inevitable compromises between the "spiritual values" of religious ethics and the objective "world of facts" as presented to us in the modern sciences. Indeed, Weber would seem to agree with Tolstoy and Dostoevsky that the process of disenchantment, linked to the scientific conception of "progress" as technical control over nature and experience, has led to the death of ultimate meaning and

substance in the human spirit.[18] All meaning is reduced to the immanent realm of phenomena, the purely external means of the instrumental expansion of rational control over all of life – "no more than
the means for procuring vegetables."[19]

While mainstream North American religious social ethicists have
generally accepted Weber's account of the triumph of modern scientific rationality and its socio-political and economic implications, they
have not generally shared his fatalistic despair over it. Indeed, for
the most part they have displayed the optimistic conviction that
prophetic religion (concerned about the spiritual fate of the community) and rational public policy can be effectively reconciled, if not
harmonized. "Compromises" between political economic facts and
religious values are necessary, perhaps, but they need be neither
irrelevant nor nihilistic. I am referring here not only to such defenders
of modern capitalism as, among others, Robert Benne[20] or Max Stackhouse.[21] Rather, all the approaches analyzed in the following chapters
understand themselves to be in some sense *critics* of liberal capitalism. And all of them develop their critical positions on religious
ethical grounds. However, all these approaches believe that they can
elaborate a "mediating" position in which Christian ethics can provide public moral norms by which to orient modern political economic policy in North America.

In my judgment, we are dealing here with a phenomenon not
unlike the process Weber described in *The Protestant Ethic*, although
I also include a chapter on Catholicism and am examining a rather
different "spirit" from the one described by Weber: the ethos of
North American "liberalism." I shall argue that in each case, the
acceptance of the modern liberal "rationality" of technology and its
liberating promise, linked to the pervasive social power of a scientistic vision of the world, results in the unintended consequence
that religious ethics end up providing support for the expansion of
the iron cage of industrial capitalism and thereby contributing to
the modern crisis of the spirit – even as they attempt religiously
and ethically to resolve it as a social or economic crisis. However,
this thesis cannot be understood or argued on Weberian grounds,
since I will attend – as Weber, whose very method prohibited him
from doing so, did not – to "the world of judgments of value and
of faith."[22] I do not, moreover, accept his neo-Kantian theoretical
separation between facts and values, which forced him to represent
"value-ideas" (*Wertideen*) as subjective human constructs by which
human beings "confer meaning and significance" upon "the mean-
ingless infinity of the world process."[23] Such a historicist view of
meaning combined with a modern scientific orientation in the world

is indeed a manifestation of the spiritual crisis itself, and remains (as Weber recognised) fatefully trapped within the "ironic cage" of technological progress.

SPIRITUAL CRISIS AND POLITICAL ECONOMY

It is necessary now to elaborate more precisely the nature of this spiritual crisis and how it is related to the political economy of liberal capitalist societies. In his chapter on the nature of modernity in *The New Science of Politics*, Eric Voegelin states tersely: "The death of the spirit is the price of progress."[24] By this he means that the spiritual source of human and social order – the human orientation toward the divine ground of existence – has been lost in the disordered, purely immanent quest for scientific and technological control over nature. The gain of such control through the instrumental objectification of nature has led, ironically, to the loss of meaningful participation in an ordered cosmos precisely because all purposes have become identified with immanent human needs and desires. Having lost sight of the inner meaning of human and non-human nature as related to God and God's purposes, reality is reduced to an outer set of material processes and resources to be functionally subordinated to the purposes and interests of human subjects, whose immanent purposes are themselves instrumentally fulfilled through the production and consumption of external commodities and artifacts.[25]

These assumptions, and indeed the whole productivist paradigm of liberal political economy, are rooted in powerful modern habits of thought. The Cartesian "detached observer" model of human subjects who investigate the objective world and utilize it for their own purposes has been vastly influential in the modern natural and social sciences – with impressive results in terms of both technological development and socio-political legitimation. The progressive expansion of human freedom and fulfilment is then understood in terms of the progressive domination of nature through technological control. It is the ability of this paradigm – with its anthropological, natural, and socio-historical assumptions – to define reality, ideologically and institutionally, that Voegelin and others call into question.[26]

How did we get to this point? Weber attributes the feeling of cosmic loneliness and "salvation anxiety" in a desacralized universe to certain doctrinal beliefs in ascetic Protestantism. However, it would seem more accurate to understand these doctrinal developments themselves as part of the larger, radical shift in modern cosmology – a shift from a spiritual creation that declares the glory of God and furnishes the stage for the drama of salvation and the revelation of God's eternal purposes to a homogeneous material universe ordered by mechanistic processes and impersonal laws of physics. Whereas John Calvin could still affirm a religious cosmos with whose inner logos the reverent heart could feel a living attunement,[27] Pascal, a century later, could only sense the terror of a silent, indifferent universe in whose infinite physical immensity the individual exists as a lost, contingent stranger.[28] Between Calvin and Pascal, of course, lived the prodigious figures Galileo and Descartes, and the Copernican revolution took firm root – with important consequences. Scientific hypotheses, such as Galileo's theory of motion, not only fly in the face of traditional meaning but also betray the testimony of the senses, and therefore call into question the reliability of experience concerning the nature and meaning of the universe. Indeed, in the modern scientific age, experiment replaces experience as the method of the discovery and verification of knowledge, the results of which are made available in mathematical formulas, not religious or philosophical propositions. Traditionally, in Aristotle and Thomas Aquinas, for example, theories of motion focused on *why* things move as they do, and this was described in terms of the actualization of a thing's proper essence in relation to the inner meaning of the cosmic whole. With the loss of such a cosmology of creation, science focuses on the *how* of motion via the empirical measurement of bodies. In contrast to traditional cosmology that attends to the normative meaning of actions, purposes and ends, modern science reduces everything to the observable motion of material processes formulated in mathematical laws.

This loss of cosmological orientation cannot be replaced in lived experience, as Weber also recognised, by the abstractions of mathematical and scientific formulas: "The intellectual constructions of science constitute an unreal realm of artificial abstractions, which with their bony hands seek to grasp the blood-and-the-sap of true life without ever catching up with it."[29] Therefore, while the cosmos is emptied of inner moral or spiritual meaning, of divine purpose and personality, moderns compensate for this existentially by emphasizing the active, intra-worldly purposes of human subjects. Human beings increasingly become the active constructors of meaning and values in a disenchanted world that furnishes the resources for their particular purposes and self-fulfilment. While nature has become an object devoid of will, the actions and motives of human agents cannot be so understood. In fact, for Enlightenment thinkers, human beings alone have will, and the world comes to be seen as the object of human will. The world may no longer declare the glory of God, but human beings still can do so through their reason, and the materials of nature are ready to hand for human experimentation and use.

This "Copernican revolution" in philosophy was proclaimed by Kant as a turn to the rational human subject. Meaningful experience of the world, including religious and moral meaning, is grounded in the structures of human consciousness and is in some sense a creation of our own minds. Descartes, the father of modern philosophy, had earlier represented this as the division of reality into thinking subjects (*res cogitans*) and inanimate material objects (*res extensa*). Freedom and intellectual authority are located in the individual rational intellect, the thinking subject, who by the proper use of reason gains power and control over external nature. Human consciousness and subjectivity are now detached and divided from nature, constricted within the skulls of particular individuals. It could be said that, banished from nature, moral and spiritual meaning reappear in the human psyche as "values" – regulative ideas postulated by the rational will that enable us freely to realize our purposes in an indifferent external reality.

Hans Jonas argues that the anthropocentrism present in certain strands of western understandings of nature is radically intensified in Cartesianism.[30] In Stoicism, nature exists for the benefit of humankind as the sole possessor of reason; in Christianity, as the sole possessor of the *imago Dei* in creation. Cartesian dualism goes further to make human beings the sole possessors of inwardness or "soul" of *any* kind, and therefore the only creatures of whom "end" can be meaningfully predicated. All other life, as the product of physical necessity, can be considered means. This entails a change in the meaning of "soul": from the spiritual principle of life and action present throughout the cosmos, it becomes the principle of purely individual subjectivity. The semantic history of the word "subjective," as we know from the *Oxford English Dictionary*,[31] reveals some interesting unintended consequences of this change in meaning. The lexical meaning of seventeenth century usage is still influenced by traditional cosmological meanings: "Pertaining to the essence or reality of a thing; real; essential." In the first half of the eighteenth century we find the meaning has changed to "having its source in the mind," and in the second half of that century to "pertaining to or peculiar to an individual subject or his mental operations." These meanings are clearly influenced by Cartesianism. By the second half of the nineteenth century, we find a complete reversal of the lexical meaning of "subjective": "Existing in the mind only, without anything real to correspond with it; illusory, fanciful."[32] The world we share in common is increasingly external, the realm of extension, in which the Baconian vision of scientific knowledge as power – over nature, over society, over other nations – comes to prevail. The life of the spirit and of the good is increasingly seen as the product of individual human imaginations, and eventually, in modern liberalism, as mere value preferences that gain public legitimacy only as social conventions that serve functional needs in a society collectively devoted to scientific "progress."

Hannah Arendt observes in the same vein that Cartesian doubt, which grows out of a loss of confidence in "truth," in the reliability of humanity's relationship with the world, leads to a preoccupation with processes and the experimental development of knowledge rather than the attempt to discern the truth about life in the world.[33] This signals a shift in the human relationship to nature and history, and technology emerges as the meeting ground of the natural and historical sciences, with its promise of delivering human control in both natural and socio-historical processes. The successful direction of these immanent processes into the human artifice (the unending, all-comprehending process of production and consumption) constitutes the very meaning of "development" and "progress" in modern liberalism. Hence "meaning" (including religious and moral meaning) is no longer something revealed or given in the common structure of reality, but is rather socially constructed and legitimated by its results, that is, does it contribute to human "progress"?

In technologically advanced liberal industrial societies, then, "means" have become "ends," and human fulfilment and justice are reduced to purely external questions of access to the process of production and consumption.[34] The ends are present within the means as commodified goods, and public policy discourse accordingly instrumentalizes "values" in the service of these material ends.[35] As Albert Borgmann puts it, in a liberal democratic social order, "technology comes into play as the indispensable and unequaled procurement of the means that allow us to realize our preferred values."[36] This consumer culture vision of the "good life," specified by technology as the control over nature, leads rather to Nietzsche's "last men" – bourgeois citizens disengaged from skilled and bodily commerce with reality in the mindless production and consumption of commodities. Borgmann calls this the "irony of technology": the increase in the production of consumer goods has led also to the degradation of work and the pollution of nature; the high mobility and bureaucratization of modern social life undermine kinship ties, community stability and meaningful citizenship participation; the abundance of commodities represents a superficial variety but underneath is characterised by a narrow and rigid pattern in which people take up with the world, leading to the overall atrophy of our human capacities; and the technical constraints of policy discourse preclude any substantive public consideration of "the good."

The irony to be pondered is that this progressive expansionism has created an increasingly mechanistic, spirit-less "iron cage" reality, in which human beings are isolated from each other, from meaningful human community, and also from nature. As this narrow vision of reality is lived out in our institutions and practices (even as we think that we are objectively perceiving it as detached observers of "factual reality"), we discover not that we are more free but that our choices are ever more narrowly constricted within short-term utility calculations and collective slavery to material processes and commodities, and that our collective actions and purposes have harmful consequences.

The domination of public life by the political economy of liberal capitalism has led to a principle of social legitimation that focuses narrowly on economic growth, on permanently rising consumption for the satisfaction of material needs. Both politics and economic institutions in modern societies are single-mindedly dedicated to the pursuit of affluence and raising the "standard of living" as the very meaning of human fulfilment. Not only does this create false expectations and high social costs but it entails a utilitarian consumption ethic that fails to provide a coherent interpretation of human needs and their satisfaction.[37] Oriented by the ideal of unlimited technological expansion, our "civilization of productivity"[38] lacks normative principles of judgment by which to discern needs and obligations, freedoms and responsibilities within the larger society. Human choices are primarily shaped by the confusing symbol system – or rather, system of commodified signs – of the marketplace, and the quest for consumer abundance is restrained chiefly by external regulations and technical procedures that become increasingly difficult to enforce in an acquisitive society, especially during times of slow growth.[39]

The spiritual crisis therefore concerns the centrality of the paradigm of production – the technical rationality, institutions, and ends of liberal political economy – in modern social life. The problem here is not primarily the dominance of capital and self-interested profit maximization over most other needs and goods, nor is it the absence of economic democracy or the full participation of all in the economy. It is, more fundamentally, the entrenchment of an anthropocentric utilitarian ethic that fails to look beyond narrowly defined human needs and desires to the divine ordering of life, in which we are always already participants. It is a problem of orientation and self-understanding that constricts our vision of reality within a very myopic framework of interpretation and action – and thereby clouds our judgment, our ability to discern and to respond to meanings that are not humanly created but are part of the divinely ordered whole of reality.

A THEOLOGICAL ETHICAL HYPOTHESIS

The critical issue to which this study must attend, therefore, is what Kenneth Burke calls "placement" or "selection of circumference."[40] Is justice (in the case of this study, economic justice) ultimately to be related dramatistically to God's purposive design in creation, or is it to be related mechanistically to the temporal processes of nature and finally to the "forces of production" that are humanly constructed to manipulate those processes for *our* immanent purposes? It will not do to apply prematurely a rationalistic "Occam's Razor" here, for we are dealing with fundamentally different visions of reality – one rooted in creation theology and a theocentric piety or spirituality, the other rooted in the scientific representations of impersonal natural processes. They lead to different rationalities of action and motivation.

In creation theology, the ultimate ground or circumference to which all meaning and reality is related is the divine "act of creation" as the substantial ordering of all things according to God's good purposes, an act that can only be represented "dramatistically" or symbolically. In scientific naturalism, the circumference of interpretation is an impersonal field of relative forces ordered by efficient causality, abstractly described and calculated in the differential equations of physics. The placement of reality within the latter circumference gives us a great deal of instrumental power over phenomenal nature, but if taken literally as the only true knowledge of reality, it blinds us to certain basic problems and substantive realities of human nature and its relation to the cosmos that can only be discerned within the circumference of divine creation, that is, that are not a matter of efficient laws of objective causality. Indeed, ultimately to treat nature and society, both human and non-human existence, simply in terms of utilitarian rationality is a form of idolatrous magic that leads to the oblivion of spiritual values and to a distorted understanding of the meaning of life.[41] Utilitarian rationality leads to a falsely externalized orientation that assumes we can solve our problems and realize our purposes by implementing the correct methods by which to control natural and social processes, methods that are based on experimental knowledge and the exact classification of data.

These assumptions are institutionalized in modern industrial society,[42] leading to the growing irrelevance of creation theology and the moral wisdom it cultivates. Acquisition of technical knowledge rather than the formation of character and judgment becomes the focus of public policy and the institutional processes of education.[43] The social pressures of these developments and their tremendous power cause the spiritual circumference and orientation to divine creation to appear increasingly abstract and otherworldly, an unnecessary hypothesis. Within such a context, the temptation is strong for theological ethicists to seek "relevance" by rendering their theological symbols and ethical principles "more concrete" in the language of public policy. Too often such attempts commit the "fallacy of misplaced concreteness" (A.N. Whitehead) by reducing concrete religious symbols that relate the meaning of reality to God and God's purposes to instrumental policy discourse oriented toward the purely immanent quest for technological control over nature so as to meet material needs. This is not to say that material needs are not concrete or religiously important, but that these needs are themselves interpreted differently when viewed from within the paradigm of production than when viewed from within a theological vision of creation and divine justice. The problem is that a circumference with a wide and complex symbolic scope (divine creation) is reduced to a narrow literal one (human production) that causes us to misconstrue the nature of reality itself as an outer set of material and social processes to be functionally subordinated to human purposes, purposes instrumentally fulfilled through the production and consumption of external commodities.[44] When policy discourse, backed by the powerful instruments of production it helps rationalize, becomes the lowest common denominator that "mediates" between the plurality of private values and motives, the hard currency into which all communicative acts can be translated and "cashed out," then theological ethical discourse is emptied of public meaning or relevance. In the process, the deeper moral complexities and diversity of goods in creation are sacrificed to the abstract rationality of policy monism – the bottom line of technological production and consumption "opportunities." We will not find in liberal policy discourse a substitute for (or an adequate mediation of) concrete religious and moral discourse. So long as such reductions are attempted, *theological* ethics will remain politically irrelevant, to the impoverishment of public discourse concerning economic justice.

Of course, none of the theological ethical approaches examined in these pages are so crassly reductionistic as the preceding paragraph suggests. However, I shall argue that each of their mediating positions concedes too much to the modern liberal paradigm, albeit in different degrees and forms. In each case the contraction of religious vision and the circumference of creation results in a false understanding of the proper relations of things in reality. It is a matter of narrowing the scope of considerations by which moral judgments are made, particularly with reference to nature and the human relation to the natural world mediated in modern industrial societies. Each of these approaches accepts the instrumental objectification of nature as a commodity to be technologically mastered in the service of economic productivity. The point is not to locate the problem in technology *per se*, just as the problem in *any* idolatry is not merely a false external image or process or rationality. The problem is a wrong relation to truth and goodness, the larger meaning of reality that results in a disordered and unfitting response to the world. The defect is not a lack of knowledge but a lack of wisdom, rooted in the failure to recognise the Creator and to be instructed by the revelation of God's purposes in creation.[45]

An idol is a false object of human trust that falsely represents the divine and our true relation to the divine in and through the creation. It results in faulty vision and disorder, even chaos and violence. Idolatry often begins with the identification of some experienced form of the divine presence with the presence itself, with the ultimate meaning of reality. It entails a false objectification of God in some thing or object that can be possessed or controlled, and emphasis is placed on the human end of the relationship – frequently the gratification of immediate needs. Relation to the living God is lost and objectified images are mistaken for the ultimate source itself, leading to disorientation.

Such a wrong relation to and false objectification of divine creation is equally destructive of truth and justice both in the reifications of technological scientism and in the reified abstractions of religious dogmatism. However, while all the theological ethical approaches I consider reject dogmatic and moral reifications and seek to represent religious symbols in accounts that are more faithful to lived human experience, they all remain to some extent in the thrall of the liberal promise of technology and to scientistic images of nature and society taken to be "literally true" representations of the "real world." All these approaches accept the assumptions concerning the technological mastery of nature in the service of economic productivity within the liberal ethos. They take for granted the subject-object dualism and anthropocentric utilitarianism embodied in the vision of nature espoused and institutionalized in North American political economy. This contraction of vision is a product of passive perception, the inertia of habit,[46] that fails to consider the wider context of our thought and action, accepting the "tissue of faded metaphors"[47] that constitute the dominant literalisms of our society and its institutions as objectively given.

The political economic practices and institutions of modern North American societies do constitute the objective context and conventional constraints to which economic policy proposals must address themselves if they are to be of immediate relevance. However, the predominant focus of this study, and of all the approaches examined in it, is a critical analysis of the broad institutional and moral parameters within which economic policy matters are considered and the general standards by which they are judged. I will be especially attentive to how the various theological perspectives accept, establish, or seek to transform those parameters, and how they interact with particular social and political theories in doing so. Therefore this study is not concerned primarily with the economic "viability" of particular policy positions as these concern existing structures (such as, for example, business corporations or government agencies or various industrial sectors and their interrelations). While empirical studies of such phenomena will be referred to at certain points in the analysis, no attempt will be made to treat the vast literature on these complex matters in a systematic way. The purpose of this study is not to develop policy proposals by which to address specific issues of political economy in North America. The aim rather is to investigate some important twentieth century attempts to do so, with primary attention to the political "ethos" and theological issues.

Perhaps the best answer for now to those who insistently raise the question in economic ethics, "What about policy?" is to cite Dr Rieux's response to the policy directives given by the Oranese officials in the face of plague symptoms: "Des ordres! Et il faudrait de l'imagination."[48] In theological ethics, policy must be related to one's construal of reality – which comes first, especially if the distortions of short-sighted anthropocentric ethics are to be avoided. Within a theocentric theology of creation, moreover, *being* precedes *doing*, so that ethics cannot ultimately focus simply on "doing the right thing" within existing conventional parameters.

In brief, my intention is to show, through an analysis of influential representatives of contemporary Christian social ethics, what happens to religio-ethical discourse when it is translated and "cashed out" in the economic policy discourses of North American liberalism.

The salience of the "productivist paradigm" of North American capitalism, which orients society toward the creation of continual economic growth and expansion via technological development, leads to two critical problems:

1 The hegemony of narrowly construed material and economic interests in public life, which threatens to undermine and even destroy a participatory, democratic public life by displacing practical moral discourse about the common good and justice with technical discourse on how to manage economic growth in order to maximize the satisfaction of private needs and wants.
2 The mastery and domination of nature via instrumental technologies for the satisfaction of commodified human needs, which reduces nature to a mechanistic object and dangerously misconstrues the meaning of human and non-human nature as related to God and God's purposes in creation, leading to destructive socioeconomic practices and priorities.

I will argue that while all the approaches recognize and address (with varying success) the first of these problems, they do not adequately perceive or address the second – in my judgment more important – problem. This has to do with their theological assumptions.

The larger argument that shapes the analysis in the following chapters is a theological critique of liberalism from the perspective of a theocentric theology of creation. I will develop this theological perspective more explicitly in the concluding chapter in the form of a constructive proposal. Just as a religious concern for social justice results in a critique of the humanly destructive consequences of the predominance of narrow economic interests in public life, so also will a theocentric theology of creation disclose the disordered consequences of the anthropocentric utilitarian approach to nature present in modern economic practices and policies. The call for the development of a more participatory democratic society and ethos, in which deliberation upon and pursuit of collective goods and needs take priority over short-term individual wants, is not enough. More important is an expanded vision of the real meaning of participation in nature and society. Such a vision would situate the imperatives of economic productivity and technical expansion in the context of the larger created order of which human beings are a part and to which they bear certain moral responsibilities.

2 The Cooperative Commonwealth and the Kingdom of God: The Social Gospel Quest for a Public Morality

The social gospel movement in North America was born in the populist struggles against business power that emerged during the economic recession of the late nineteenth century.[1] Growing reaction against monopolistic corporations and industries by farmers and urban workers – through militant strikes and grassroots political alliances – contributed to widespread social conflict and the rise of class-based, reformist "social movements," in which the social gospel was an important factor. The social gospel movement articulated a critical interpretation of and response to the "social crisis" in the form of a social ethic informed both by a religious vision of the kingdom of God ideal and by the insights of modern social science.

It is clear, at least in the representative approaches of the two figures I will examine in this chapter, Walter Rauschenbusch and J.S. Woodsworth, that social gospellers understood this crisis to be the result of a conflict between two opposing visions of society. These men saw democracy, backed by the kingdom of God ideal and characterized by freedom, equality, and solidarity, being challenged and undermined by the competitive individualism and the priority of profit over the common good fostered by the capitalist economic system. Capitalism, they argued, was tearing apart the moral fabric of democratic society and will ultimately destroy its progressive spirit, its normative ethos.[2] Only the extension of democratic principles – rooted in the "ethical monotheism" of prophetic religion[3] – into the economic realm (the last bastion of autocratic power) will make possible the continued evolutionary embodiment of the kingdom of

God ideal in the public practices and institutions of modern society. It is not farfetched to understand the program of the social gospel as a religious version of the rallying cry of the left Hegelians: "the realization of religion."[4] The social gospel has bequeathed to North American social ethics an influential model of religious social theory, one that attempts to religiously reorient the progressivist assumptions and objectives of modern liberal society by relating them to an interpretation of biblical Christianity.

At the same time, the social gospel also contributed significantly to the growth and development of the social sciences in North America, linking them to the quest for a more just social order. Claus Offe has recently observed that liberal social science has forgotten that "all great social and political theorizing in the nineteenth and early twentieth centuries received its problematic and inspiration from social movements and contested social conditions,"[5] and in this oblivion has cut itself off from a source of critical analytical strength. One might also say that, in its eagerness to be accepted as a genuine academic science, social science has forgotten its practical moral roots and thereby deluded itself into thinking that its theoretical findings are "value neutral."[6] As T.B. Bottomore has pointed out, there is a significant reciprocity and interaction among social change, critical social theories, and movements of socio-political protest and reform.[7] Social movements generate new ideas and proposals concerning practical social problems, while critical theorists seek to interpret the nature and meaning of the social conflicts and processes in which the movements are involved. Social movements have often served to link social theories and practical political policies and action. This was the case with the social gospel movement. The elective affinity between the social gospel's theology and critical social theories and movements of the day thus provides an interesting focus for study. Walter Rauschenbusch was clearly the foremost theologian and interpreter of the social gospel, and J.S. Woodsworth one of the preeminent politicians to emerge from the movement, so this essay will focus on these two representative figures.

Before turning to these two social gospel leaders, however, it is necessary to say a few words about an important historical point. The United States and Canada have not always understood themselves to be secular societies. In the late nineteenth and early twentieth centuries the social gospel movement elaborated a public ethic rooted in the general consensus that these were Christian societies espousing Christian morals. In a recent study of religious social criticism in nineteenth and twentieth century Canada, Ramsey Cook argues the popular historical thesis that the social gospel, far from bringing about a religiously inspired social reform, actually contributed to the secularization of Canadian society and the growing irrelevance of the Christian church to the public order.[8] Cook claims that the theology of immanence and accommodation to culture propounded by the social gospel led to the replacement of religious social morality by secular social science. He suggests that the challenges to orthodox Christian theology by Darwinian science and historical criticism led to an intellectual religious crisis. The social gospel responded to this crisis by transforming the traditional message of Christianity into a new social message which obliterated the distinction between sacred and secular realms. This loss of sacred transcendence destroyed the religious legitimation for social morality and paved the way for a purely secular view of human beings and society.

The problem with this thesis is that it ignores the substantive content of the social gospel message and thus fails to take seriously its religious claims. Indeed it functionalizes religion as a "belief system." In that case, religion serves either to legitimate traditional social morality and orthodox doctrine (which Cook identifies with the "sacred") or it serves the purely immanent objectives of secular social science (as a strategy for saving the social relevance of Christianity). Such an approach cannot do justice to a significant premise of the social gospel vision – that intellectual and spiritual crises cannot be divorced from social and political crises. To do so is to render religion and morality politically irrelevant from the outset, and this has fateful theoretical and practical social consequences. To argue, as Cook does, that J.S. Woodsworth's social criticism was the *result* of his religious unorthodoxy[9] is completely to ignore (or ideologically obscure) the way in which his religious and social vision of the cooperative commonwealth grew in response to the social and spiritual conditions of his day. It neglects the important religious grounds underlying the social gospel vision, which cannot simply be reduced to a secular social science outlook. That is, my problem with Cook's thesis is that he represents the social gospel agenda as a strategy for saving the relevance of Christianity in the face of an intellectual crisis of belief; he does not see the movement as growing out of a substantive religious vision of reality. The social gospel theology and social theory may be flawed, but to reduce the one to the other does not clarify the substance of the problem: the relationship between religion and politics in modern liberal societies.

To return to my earlier comparison of the social gospel program with the rallying cry of the left Hegelians, the question then becomes: what is the religion to be "realized" and how and where will it be fulfilled? To what extent does the social gospel buy into the Hegelian account of the immanent historical realization of universal spirit, which substitutes temporal progress for the divine will, historical rationality for religious transcendence? The question can be stated even more graphically by using the imagery employed by Albert Camus in an essay on "the artist and his time": "History's amphitheater has always contained the martyr and the lion. The former relied on eternal consolations and the latter on raw historical meat. But until now the artist was on the sidelines ... But now the artist is in the amphitheater."[10] The social gospellers argued that, like Camus's artist, contemporary theologians no longer have the luxury of remaining on the sidelines – they are in the historical arena.[11] The question then is, Will their theology be conscripted to issue-oriented sloganism and ideological activism, which "consumes" theology and religion as but another functional means toward a purely immanent end? Does the social gospel contribute to the transformation of religion into "raw historical meat" to be devoured by the ideological lions? Or does it rather mediate the eternal truths of religion within the welter of worldly history in a way that faithfully relates the whole of reality to the divine will?

Cook's charge that the social gospel's mission was an ironic failure must be seriously considered. I will argue that it failed, not by leaving the sidelines of dogmatic orthodoxy to enter the socio-historical amphitheatre, but by accepting too many of the assumptions of the modern ideology of liberal progress. The irony to which the social gospel succumbs is not simply the secularization of the sacred. It is the belief that the kingdom of God is gradually being realized through the instruments of human control over nature and history, and that all that remains to be done is to democratize the instruments of production, since their morally disordered organization lies at the heart of the social crisis. Such an approach cannot discern the spiritual crisis that lies behind the hopeful anthropocentric vision of liberal progressivism.

THE THEOLOGY OF THE SOCIAL GOSPEL: WALTER RAUSCHENBUSCH

Walter Rauschenbusch is generally recognised as the theological leader of the social gospel movement; his books contain the classic expression of the movement's vision, purposes, and contributions to theology and social ethics. This discussion begins, therefore, with an interpretation of his theological ethics. Later in the chapter I will correlate this model with Rauschenbusch's analysis of the capitalist economy of his day in order to draw some conclusions about the relationship between theological ethics and social theory in his thought.

Based on his reading of Scripture and the history of Christianity – that is, his theology of history – Rauschenbusch asserts that "the essential purpose of Christianity [is] to transform human society into the kingdom of God by regenerating all human relations and reconstituting them in accordance with the will of God."[12] This statement points toward the organizing perspective of Rauschenbusch's theological ethic, the concept of the kingdom of God. This is the interpretive idea by which he exegetes history and it functions as *the* discriminating principle for what Rauschenbusch considers truly progressive in humanity, society, and the church.

What does this mean theologically? As "the sum of all good, the essential aim of God himself," the kingdom of God is to Rauschenbusch virtually interchangeable with God: "It is the energy of God realizing itself in human life."[13] There is for Rauschenbusch no merit in speculating on the nature of God in transcendent abstraction from the mediation of God's presence and purposes in history. Conceptions of God are social products.[14] A theology which relegates God to an otherworldly realm of autocratic transcendence tends to legitimate autocratic social conditions, whereas belief in an immanent God concerned with justice and fraternity in all human relations legitimates a democratic social order.[15] Rauschenbusch contends that not only is the latter conception more faithful to the highest expressions of the Christian religion, but it is also in concert with the most progressive trends of modern western culture. As he puts it, "The social gospel tries to see the progress of the Kingdom of God in the flow of history" since "the Kingdom of God is history seen in a religious and teleological way."[16]

God is therefore primarily viewed as immanent – the earth is God's place of habitation and theatre of action.[17] This religious orientation originated, in Rauschenbusch's view, with the Old Testament prophets' interpretation of God at work in the world. Their study of contemporary social and political life enlarged their conception of God and God's purposes, resulting in a universal ethical religion.[18] Such a comprehensive religious social vision demands a public morality backing a reconstituted social order of economic justice. It establishes an "organic union between religion and morality, between theology and ethics,"[19] which Rauschenbusch asserts is central to the Christian religion.

This prophetic union between religion and ethics reaches its perfect expression, according to Rauschenbusch, in the life and teachings of

Jesus, the initiator of the kingdom in whom the kingdom got its first "foothold" in humanity. Jesus took the prophetic idea of the kingdom, purified it of nationalistic, monarchial, and apocalyptic elements, and elevated it into a new religious synthesis, a historical force through which God is redeeming humanity. Jesus broke through the nationalistic particularity of the concept to establish the ideal of the universal solidarity of all people under God. In fact, says Rauschenbusch, Jesus "saved God" by democratizing our conception of God.[20] He "democratized" the concept by speaking of God as "our Father," thus conceiving the kingdom more in terms of a cooperative commonwealth of God and humanity rather than the arbitrary rule of a transcendent God. Finally, Jesus exhibited an original scientific insight into the law of evolutionary development in nature and history, employing organic metaphors for the coming reign of God rather than the catastrophic images of apocalypticism.

Although these Christological motifs reveal more about nineteenth century ideas and values than they do about the Jesus of the Gospels, for the social gospel Jesus' conception of the new commonwealth of God on earth initiated a process whereby human society would be gradually transformed toward ever higher levels of God-consciousness and its attending values of justice (which Rauschenbusch largely equates with equality), freedom, and fraternity.[21] But the fundamental virtue of Jesus' ethical religion, of the kingdom of God, is love. Love is not only the "social instinct" of the human race; it expresses the basic character of God which grounds all social unity.[22] All human relations are ultimately based on the equalizing and society-building force of love, and Rauschenbusch calls for a "new avatar of love"[23] that will become engaged in social reconstruction. He calls for the recognition of God's presence in the modern "social movement" which opposes exploitation and supports a democratic distribution of power and property.

Thus, while Rauschenbusch carefully attaches an "eschatological proviso" – "The kingdom of God is always but coming"[24] – there is an overwhelming emphasis on the solidarity of God with humanity which grounds and fulfils the progressive realization of the kingdom of God in history. This is the key to Jesus' revelation of God: that in the kingdom of God, God and humanity are so reconciled that the will of God and the human good are one and the same.[25] Rauschenbusch states this explicitly in *The Social Principles of Jesus* – "But the will of God is identical with the good of mankind"[26] – and it enables him to establish a convergence between the purposes of God and the "true spirit" or "essential values" of modern western civilization.

In view of the intimate correlation between God's will and the common human good in Rauschenbusch's concept of the kingdom of God and his immanent view of divine agency, it is hardly a surprise to discover Rauschenbusch's emphasis on the close relation between religion and practical social experience and human needs. If it is to be vital and effective, religion must be linked to modern social life, its problems and possibilities. The essential test for religion is therefore its social value in interpreting the social situation, elevating social aims and attitudes, creating solidarity, and invigorating the human will to work for a just social order.[27] Rauschenbusch is convinced that only the Christian concept of the kingdom of God can pass this test, can create a public morality and social vision adequate to the needs and possibilities of modern society. For the kingdom of God is the goal and driving power of human history. As such it both judges the distortions and failures of socio-cultural history and transforms that history, impelling it toward its fulfilment.

The social gospel movement has often been stereotyped as "cultural Christianity," baptizing the dominant values and ideas of its time – especially the myth of "progress" – in the naïvely optimistic belief that the kingdom of God is right around the corner. While there is some resemblance between Rauschenbusch's theology of history and this popular portrait of the social gospel, this caricature entirely overlooks certain important features of his thought.

According to Rauschenbusch, Jesus' social convictions are not alien to the common human social instincts but rather heighten and purify them, pointing them toward their true end.[28] Recognition of the sacred value of human life and the feeling of human solidarity, especially with the poor, are generic social principles which are given a religious intensity, a universal scope, and a breadth of application by Jesus' concept of the kingdom of God. It is important to note that Rauschenbusch grounds this claim not primarily in the doctrine of the *imago Dei* and the infinite destiny of the human soul, as, for example, in Christian natural law models. Rather this is a historical claim that the religion Jesus founded is the normative basis for the organic, evolutionary unfolding of western civilization and its generic values. In Rauschenbusch's reading of history, this original social vision of Jesus was inevitably routinized, institutionalized and spiritualized by the church, with the result that "official" Christianity pursued no effective, direct program of social reconstruction, accepting as "given" whatever social system happened to be in place and preaching an otherworldly, individualistic gospel.[29] However, the idea of the kingdom of God as a social ideal was reawakened with the advent of modern democracy following the Enlightenment and the Reformation.[30] The spirit of modern society, characterized by an enthusiasm for democracy, the movement toward a universal human culture, the spread of evolutionary ideas, and the scientific comprehension of socio-historical development (as opposed to a natural or immutable "given"), is moving in the direction initiated and mediated by Jesus' concept of the kingdom of God.

If the spirit of Christianity can be thus identified with the spirit of modern civilization, can Rauschenbusch not clearly be placed into H. Richard Niebuhr's "Christ of culture" type?[31] Important elements in Rauschenbusch's writings resist such unequivocal type-casting. He speaks of the "great reversal" of values involved in Jesus' conception of the kingdom which requires that people be converted to the life orientation of a "new humanity" and that the social order be reconstituted according to these new values.[32] While his theology certainly has its "healthy-minded" emphases,[33] there is also a profound recognition of pervasive personal and social evil, of the conflictual nature of reality.[34] Solidarity, by far the most frequently cited ethical principle in Rauschenbusch's work, involves not only love but also opposition to evil forces. Hence the cross is a fundamental social principle by which to understand and interpret human existence, representing the struggle against radical evil.[35] These assertions more readily belong to Niebuhr's "Christ transforming culture" type.[36]

One way to bring together these somewhat paradoxical claims is to realize that in Rauschenbusch's view, Jesus set in motion a great "reversal in values" in a direction developed in the history of western Christian civilization, especially in post-Enlightenment liberal democracy. In this sense Christianity is the founding religious and moral force of western civilization, providing its fundamental direction and ideal. This evolutionary historical trend is leading to the increasing "Christianization" of society as the realization of the deepest and greatest human instincts. But Rauschenbusch does not envision an undialectical, linear evolution toward the full realization of the kingdom, the inexorable unfolding of some utopian blueprint. The coming of the kingdom in history is subject to "terrible reversals" and but fragmentary realizations in the struggle to transform human society in its fundamental relations according to the will of God.[37] Indeed, Rauschenbusch maintains that modern western society is experiencing a critical crisis, a crucial conflict between Christian and "unchristian" forces, over which ethico-political vision of humanity and society will prevail and shape the social order.[38] Western society is torn between the "mammonistic" principles of capitalism and the cooperative, democratic aims of the social movement. The outcome of this battle has decisive implications for the "Christianization" of society.

It is important to emphasize that for Rauschenbusch this is above all a matter of religious morality. Even though the current crisis exists in the realm of economics, of large social and material processes, the solution lies not in the direction of scientific socialism with its deterministic interpretation of inevitable social forces. What is required is a religiously grounded ethical solution, a public morality, which will bring about personal regeneration and a sense of social responsibility and solidarity.

Before turning to the relationship between Rauschenbusch's theological ethic and social theory, it is necessary to say something further about his interpretation of the relationship between divine and human agency. The kingdom of God is not a particular social theory or political program, but the supreme *task* in which God and human beings cooperate. However, this task requires the insightful interpretation of circumstances and intelligent, responsible action on the part of human agents, a combination of religion, social science, and ethical action.[39] Rauschenbusch's view of human agency recognizes both the human capacities for making rational moral choices and the larger forces which shape, limit, and order human action. "The forces working together in the mass of human life are so numerous, so intricate, so mysterious, that it baffles us to explain historical events after they are all over; and foretelling them is slightly more difficult. But I do believe that it is not beyond the moral intelligence of man to get a fairly correct conception of the direction in which we ought to move, so that we may guide our practical decisions by our larger outlook."[40] Rauschenbusch recognizes that human beings are not only interdependent, their actions constituted in complex webs of social relations, but that their interests and orientations are powerfully shaped by the interests present in social systems and the organization of material forces. Thus the powers of moral agency can be inhibited or misdirected by such systemic distortions in society as are present in a capitalist economy, where the self-interests of the owners of capital structurally dominate the working classes.[41] Rauschenbusch speaks of "super-personal forces," institutional or collective social forces which contradict the values of the kingdom of God and thwart the good intentions of individuals (including capitalists) operating within their bounds.[42] These forces can be discovered and illuminated by the social sciences, but to transform them requires a moral vision.

This restriction and misdirection of human agency is particularly evident in modern economic relations, which are undemocratic and unequal. Hence the class struggle between labour and capital points to the "overshadowing moral problem of our age."[43] The labour movement does not only represent the demand for a more just share of economic profits, but even more fundamentally the demand for a fuller and freer humanity, free and responsible human agency.[44] The movement represents the demand for a truly democratic society. Hence, to increase the scope of their power for action and the development of their human capacities, individuals will need to change the economic organization of industrial society. Personal regeneration and heroic virtue, while important and necessary, are not in themselves sufficient to bring about a social order in which the full capacities of human agency can be exercised. This can only be done through collective action – in cooperation with the processes of socio-historical change illumined by the social sciences and in solidarity with social movements whose interests represent the larger human good.

There is evidently a circle in Rauschenbusch's model of agency, as is perhaps the case in any non-reductionist understanding of social change. The concept of the kingdom of God and its values is necessary as a socio-religious vision to which people are converted and toward which they direct the processes of social change. The realization of God's kingdom would mean the fulfilment of human history and the human good according to their divinely created ends. As an alternative ideal conception of society and human nature, the kingdom of God inspires and directs human action. But human agency is itself conditioned by the very social order it seeks to change so that, due to social structural constraints, people cannot do the good they would wish to accomplish. In other words, for human action effectively to transform the social order, the conditions it seeks to bring about must already exist.[45] In Rauschenbusch's thought, however, this is not a vicious circle, but rather an evolutionary dialectic in which regenerated persons acting together – according to a public morality inspired by the kingdom ideal and informed by scientific insights – cooperate with the larger forces of social change to bring about such transformations as are possible in the current situation.[46] Since the actions of God are cooperating with human efforts behind all social change, Rauschenbusch has faith that progress toward the kingdom of God will be the result. In the social gospel's theology of history, divine agency and human agency cooperate to bring about the reign of God in the world.

Social Theory, the Economy, and Public Morality

In this section on Rauschenbusch's thought, as in the preceding one, it is important to attend to the social gospel's call for a public morality. The tremendous historical human possibilities in the industrial revolution, the modern sciences, political democracy, and the reconstructive social dynamic of the Christian ideal of the kingdom of God are dangerously threatened by the absence of an adequate public morality.[47] Only if the religious and ethical values of Christianity are combined with modern social forces in formulating practical ethical principles and public policy proposals will the possibilities for social transformation toward the larger human good in both be realized. Such a public morality is especially exigent in economics, where the competitive individualism and the priority of profit over the common good fostered by the capitalist system are creating unjust, unfree, and unfraternal social relations, relations which are increasingly undemocratic and devoid of love. A Christian ethic for public life would translate the moral values of the kingdom of God into social principles in accord with the findings of the social sciences, in order to guide human decisions and judgments in the current social crisis.[48] Within the current historical context, Rauschenbusch specifies this: "The most comprehensive and intensive act of love in which we could share would be a collective action of the community to change the present organization of the economic life into a new order that would rest on the Christian principles of equal rights, democratic distribution of economic power, the supremacy of the common good, the law of mutual dependence and service, and the uninterrupted flow of good will throughout the human family."[49]

While Rauschenbusch does not appropriate in an extensive or consistent way any particular social theory, he draws on a variety of sources – progressive, liberal, and socialist – to elaborate his interpretation of capitalism and proposals for social action. He is quite candid, however, in his preference for some form of socialist analysis and political program: "The modern socialist movement is really the first intelligent, concerted, and continuous effort to reshape society in accordance with the laws of social development."[50] Rauschenbusch views capitalism as a ruthlessly selfish, competitive system that exploits workers, creates economic disparities, and undermines community life and the common good through privatization and class division. One of the chief tasks of social analysis is to "see through the fictions of capitalism" to show how "these misleading theories are the complacent self-deception of those who profit by present conditions."[51] The dominance of the principle of private profit rather than democratic cooperation in capitalist social relations has led not only to economic parasitism through unearned market increments, the inefficiency and unjust inflation of monopolization, and the loss of economic power and rights by workers. It has contributed also to the loss of those higher human values which foster the common good of all, values of liberty (of workers), equality and democratic justice, through its concentration on the unlimited accumulation of private capital. Capitalism has lost sight of the human end of economics and, by detaching private ownership from service and accountability to the community, it results in the legalized disinheriting of the community.[52] The life of the many is sacrificed to the profits of a few. As long as such economic inequalities exist, supported by law, political equality means relatively little, since at bottom politics is dominated by economic interests. Political democracy and rights without economic democracy is impotent and illusory. Rauschenbusch was well aware of what Marx called the "juridical illusion":[53] "We have allowed a great and growing class of our people to be submerged in economic unfreedom so deep that 'liberty of contract' has become an instrument of enslavement for them ... Economic freedom is an essential part of human freedom. Without economic independence political and religious liberty become hollow and fragile."[54] Capitalism perpetuates injustices in legalized institutions propped up by ideological theories and results in the loss of the commonwealth.

This situation gives rise to the class struggle between labour and capital. Labour, represented by the labour movement and socialism, espouses the principle of industrial democracy and the goal of the cooperative commonwealth, whereas capital represents the principle of economic autocracy, the rule of private monopoly profit. Social progress and public, community interests, in Rauschenbusch's view, are clearly linked with labour – with socialism as its theoretical and practical basis, and with the working class as its agency.[55] Because socialism is "the most thorough and consistent economic elaboration of the Christian social ideal" and "far and away the most powerful force for justice, democracy, and organized fraternity in the modern world,"[56] the Christian church must align itself with the working class and with socialism, both for its own self-interest as a social institution and in order to be true to the ideal of the kingdom of God. This alliance must not be only idealistic, but a "working alliance" which participates in the conflictual class struggle on the side of the working class – not because workers are morally superior to capitalists, but because their *interests* represent a higher moral ideal.[57]

Thus Rauschenbusch recognizes the powerful role of economic interests and class conflict in social change, which the church cannot escape if it is to become involved in these issues, as it must. This acceptance of a critical social theory bears affinities with Marxism.[58] However, he is also careful to distinguish himself clearly from any form of "dogmatic" or "scientific" socialism, calling rather for the religious purification or "Christianization" of socialism.[59] Scientific socialism, with its strict materialist philosophy of history, rejects all immediate social reforms as ineffectual and indeed as simply post-poning the revolutionary catastrophe that must inevitably be brought about by capitalist economic conditions. For Rauschenbusch such a view is too economistic. It ignores the religious and ethical dimensions of history and social change and the importance of public consensus, the democratic process, and moral values in bringing about social transformation. Christianity, with its appeal to the religious and ethical values of the kingdom of God, its vision of human fulfilment toward which gradual progress can be made through practical social reform, must purify socialism.

The social sciences, while important, are not sufficient to understand and to bring about social change. Some larger vision of fulfilment is required which confronts human beings with an "ought," with a moral imperative that discloses possibilities and evokes a response. Social analysis cannot be substituted for religion; the two must cooperate.[60] While socialist theory, with its penetrating analysis of socio-historical processes and ideologies, is one of the most important forces making possible the current historical *kairos* (critical moment of opportunity), the true end and meaning of this kairos can be clarified only with reference to the symbol of the kingdom of God. For Rauschenbusch socio-historical forces are not inexorable, nor can they simply be discerned and directed scientifically. The vision of a just, cooperative, and fraternal society is above all a religious and moral vision and can only be realized through the actions of regenerated persons who set justice above profits and serve the interests of the common good above their own. Therefore it is important that the Christian church contribute its moral force to socio-economic forces in order to create a cooperative commonwealth. The church's role is valuable as a mediator between the classes, calling the elites of society to commit themselves to the vision and implementation of economic democracy,[61] thus facilitating a process of gradual social change and preventing a revolutionary class struggle.

A number of critical questions could be posed at this juncture, but I will raise only two. First, was Rauschenbusch's close identification of Jesus' concept of the kingdom of God with the "values" of modern liberal culture appropriate, and could it really ground an adequate public morality? Obviously it is impossible today to speak convincingly of the "Christianization" of North American society, given the reality of cultural and religious pluralism. And this fact makes it impossible to assume that the spirit of Jesus and his particular historical ideal grounds the generic values and meanings of western civilization. For example, that modern western societies strive to be citizen republics is not simply the result of Christianity. Indeed, our conceptions of justice, democracy, and the good are greatly influenced by the tradition of civic humanism, and this is more a Greek heritage than a Christian one.

Rauschenbusch's second and larger claim is that the biblical vision of the kingdom of God backs certain moral aims and virtues that fulfil human instincts and orient socio-historical forces toward their true meaning and end. The ideal, in other words, is not alien to human experience: God is immanent and "at work" in history through various normative mediations that can be discerned and acted upon. Indeed, this is the point in Rauschenbusch's theology of history. In making overdetermined claims about Jesus' scientific insight and democratic tendencies, he is proposing that these modern directions and insights (insofar as they represent the human good) are in accord with the will of God as revealed in Christ. The insights of social science into social processes thus enable us better to understand the will and purposes of God, but they must be guided and "purified" by the normative values of the kingdom of God. And this vision must in turn be made relevant to current issues through the mediating axioms of a public morality that contributes to public policy and social reform.

There is, therefore, an important reciprocity between theology and social theory in Rauschenbusch's social ethic, and this becomes a central feature of subsequent theological social ethics in North America. This more formal point about the methodological approach of the social gospel, however, must be related to the substantive theological and theoretical claims Rauschenbusch makes. Is there perhaps an unresolved tension between his optimistic view of the divinely willed destiny of history to realize the human good and his recognition of the reality of social conflict, the limiting constraints of human sin, and "super-personal forces" which prevent the realization of the moral aims of individuals and groups? It is interesting to note that while Rauschenbusch's social theory shows evidence of influence by Marx and Weber,[62] he prefers to cite such thinkers as Richard Ely, Henry George, and John Stuart Mill, all of whom are more optimistic about the rational and moral capacities of individuals to bring about the human good in nature and society in a gradual and harmonious way through the agency of growing scientific control. This is in keeping with his confident view of the cooperation between divine and human agency to realize the kingdom of God ideal. The question is, to what extent do one's religious and theological convictions shape the appropriation of social theoretical perspectives, and reciprocally, in what ways do social analyses delimit the range of possibilities for religious social ethics and theological beliefs themselves? What social and historical counterevidence could be adduced which would render Rauschenbusch's theological ethical claims incredible?

I have suggested that despite the problems with Rauschenbusch's historical reading – attributing modern insights to Jesus, the restrictive notion that Jesus' kingdom ideal grounds the generic values of western civilization, which is therefore gradually being "Christianized" – his basic theological ethic is still very much in line with much of current Christian ethics. But what if the forces of social change do not bring about the human good? What if workers do not want the responsibility of participation in an open society but only want consumer affluence; what if their image of human fulfilment and the good life is the consumer society? What if the sciences contribute to the increasing rationalization of a technocratic society in which persons are but cogs in a huge bureaucratic machine devoted to the material production and consumption of commodities? Would this conception of human fulfilment qualify as a "good society" even if it represented the wishes of a democratic majority and ensured equal access and distribution of consumer goods and services to all? At what point would such developments render implausible Rauschenbusch's concept of an immanent God guiding the processes of social and historical change in cooperation with the efforts of rational, liberal human beings toward the kingdom of God as the fulfilment of the human good? These questions are important, for they concern the possibility of discovering rational grounds in experience for ultimate moral norms and the true meaning of the "common good," without which the elaboration of a public morality becomes most difficult.

In my view, (a) the evolutionary optimism entailed in the theological vision of an immanent, progressively incarnate God who wills the human good, and (b) the positivistic progressivism entailed in the technocratic vision of scientific control of history and nature[63] stand and fall together in Rauschenbusch's approach. The social gospel shares what Jackson Lears identifies as a central tenet of modern liberal culture in America, namely "faith in the beneficence of material progress."[64] This is a positivist faith that a modern scientific society led by enlightened managers in the service of cooperative community can overcome natural and social alienation. In order to bring about this social gospel ideal of a productive, middle-class society providing freedom, equality, and security for all,[65] it is necessary to meet two crucial strategic requirements. First, the civilized and educated elites must be guided by the Christian ethic to a model of leadership as service,[66] in business as in the other professions, using their scientific expertise and productive power for the common good rather than to build private empires. This is the necessary "spirit of democracy" infused by Jesus' vision of the kingdom of God. And second, there must be a reform of the instruments of economic distribution so as to harness and develop the tremendous capacities of human mastery over nature and history for all members of the community. That is, in keeping with the evolutionary growth of industrial interdependence, the socialization of knowledge, and the unity of the human race, distribution must be democratized. Economic expertise and its benefits must become accountable to the community, rather than remain a means for unjust privilege and monopolistic tyranny.

However, this hopeful anthropocentric vision of using the cooperative unity between God and humanity, technology and ethics to bring about the human good, contains some questionable assumptions. For example, the unabashed language of social Darwinism in Rauschenbusch's evolutionary views: "The intellectual standard of humanity can be raised only by the propagation of the capable. Our social system causes an unnatural selection of the weak for breeding, and the result is the survival of the unfittest."[67] One can discern also the ethnocentric Protestant biases of both Rauschenbusch and J.S. Woodsworth, expressed in their negative judgments on alien immigrants who are "tainting" the nation and threatening its progress toward an egalitarian, liberal Christian (white middle-class) ideal.[68] The "positive laws" of natural and social development strongly favour the inevitable normative superiority of a particular culture and its religious vision, which alone represent the human good and therefore the will of God. The ideal is legitimated both religiously and scientifically with reference to the particular views of "progressive" North American Protestant culture – a culture into which all others must be gradually educated in order to experience human fulfilment.

The implication is that when people are educated into this ideal vision, they will consent to enlightened leadership and cooperate to realize its goals. And these goals include, it would seem, the creation of a technocratic welfare state in which enlightened social science, technical development, the socialization of industrial production, and the ethic of service compensate for "natural" inequalities. We will return to the question of the relation between the theological substance and policy positions of the social gospel. But first we turn our attention to the Canadian social gospel politician, James Shaver Woodsworth, with whom the policy agenda of the social gospel finds concrete political expression.

THE PUBLIC POLICY OF THE SOCIAL GOSPEL: J.S. WOODSWORTH

Walter Rauschenbusch, while interested in public policy and social reform, was more concerned as a theologian and seminary professor with the role of the church in providing ethical guidance and religious depth to the social movement. J.S. Woodsworth was much less sanguine about the agency of the church in social change, and, resigning from the Canadian Methodist ministry in 1918, he devoted his life to direct political action as the way to bring about the cooperative commonwealth. While Rauschenbusch talked about the need for an indigenous North American socialism, Woodsworth contributed directly to its formulation and organization as founder and leader of the Cooperative Commonwealth Federation (CCF), forerunner of the New Democratic Party in Canada. Whereas Rauschenbusch's audience or "public" was primarily the church, Woodsworth's was primarily society. And where Rauschenbusch as a theologian kept a circumspect distance from any partisan commitment to socialism, Woodsworth was a socialist politician who tried to make policy proposals and decisions in accordance with his religiously rooted moral vision of the cooperative commonwealth.

Theological Ethics

Insofar as it is possible to extrapolate a theological social ethic from Woodsworth's occasional, non-systematic writings, his appears in many respects to be quite similar to Rauschenbusch's model. But the fact that Woodsworth's vocation and context was political rather than academic and ecclesial makes a difference to the way he understood and employed the ethical model of the social gospel. In particular, Woodsworth provides an example of how the social gospel was translated into public policy proposals and a political reform movement.

Woodsworth was an eminently practical thinker. Neither a theologian nor a social theorist, his life of intense social and political action brought him face to face with a wide range of issues and problems, upon which he was constantly reflecting. As his early books demonstrate,[69] Woodsworth brought a wide variety of resources to bear on his reflections, from detailed empirical and statistical social studies to newspaper articles to historical, religious, and philosophical treatises. He states in his preface to My Neighbor that his purpose is not so much to "write a book" or to provide a "dispassionate study of the social phenomena of urban life" as it is to "present a situation" as an involved participant.[70] By presenting a situation through empirical description and evaluative interpretation, by posing a set of searching questions, he elaborates a moral and religious *response* to the problems and issues presented. Woodsworth, moreso than Rauschenbusch, fits Richard Allen's description of the social gospel as not primarily a theological movement but a religious and moral response to concrete human needs, a social passion which links social reform and religious convictions and ideals.[71]

The organizing theme of Woodsworth's theological ethic is similar to Rauschenbusch's, but the difference in focus is revealing. The central question posed in *My Neighbor* is, as one might guess from the title, the question posed by the parable of the Good Samaritan, "Who is my neighbor?" – a question that has become exceedingly complex in the contemporary situation of growing human interdependence combined with the loss of personal immediacy in social relationships. In such a situation, human responsibility can no longer be construed in individualistic terms but rather must be understood in terms of social solidarity. People must awaken to a sense of this enlarged scope of responsibility and be willing to sacrifice their personal interests for the public welfare of society.[72] A new public language of morality must be elaborated which is adequate to the modern context of social relations and needs, where neighbours, though strangers, are radically interdependent. In contrast to Rauschenbusch's more explicitly theological centre in the concept of the kingdom of God, Woodsworth's organizing paradigm is best identified as the cooperative commonwealth. While Woodsworth appealed to the "teachings and spirit of Jesus of Nazareth"[73] throughout his life, this spirit was for him even more diffuse than it was for Rauschenbusch.

The idea of God, for Woodsworth as for Rauschenbusch, is related to the socio-historical conditions of human experience and is therefore constantly changing. However, Woodsworth's concept of God is, if anything, even more immanentist than Rauschenbusch's. He identifies God with the growing self-conscious understanding and control by humankind of its own destiny. Religion is not supernatural or other worldly but "like all ideas and institutions, is closely related to the everyday experience of mankind."[74] It is therefore above all social and ethical, a response to the infinite in terms of ever greater resolve to attain a community of justice on earth. Woodsworth characterizes the "religion of the future" as a *progressive*, dynamic movement which is *scientific* in its spirit and methods, *practically* concerned with present conditions, *social* in character – involving fraternity and democracy – and *universal* in scope.[75] As does Rauschenbusch, Woodsworth identifies the divine will and the human good: "We regard man's cause as God's cause always and everywhere."[76]

However, from the beginning, even as a minister, Woodsworth downplayed the agency of the institutional church: "Should we mourn that the church is losing ground or rejoice that her life is now pulsating in a hundred new organizations?"[77] For Woodsworth the church's mission must be identified with the social mission, and when it became clear to him that the church was dominated by the vested interests of the conservative wealthy classes and that its narrow sphere of action could not address the problems facing Canadian workers, he left the church to become involved more directly in wider social and political movements.[78] This transition is related, in my view, to the understanding of human experience as fundamentally socially and historically constituted – response to the divine is to a purely historical "spirit." Hence also the centrality of the sociopolitical ideal of the cooperative commonwealth for his thought and action, rather than the more theological ideal of the kingdom of God to which Rauschenbusch was devoted. While these two ideals are strongly linked for both social gospellers, the difference in priority and emphasis is revealing. Both Woodsworth and Rauschenbusch espouse the key principle of solidarity, but for Woodsworth this is not so much focused upon the virtue of love as it is upon the concept of responsibility. The coming of the kingdom of God, the establishment of the cooperative commonwealth, requires not so much a public morality derived from the law of love as it does the commitment of citizens to feel and to exercise the responsibilities of citizenship in a common social order and to realize the opportunities provided for attaining a more just and fraternal society.[79] For Woodsworth the greatest sin is what he called "the sin of indifference,"[80] of being culpably irresponsible with regard to social needs, problems, and obligations.

The imperative of responsibility is thus given primarily a sociopolitical meaning by Woodsworth. But it is related to the moral ends of the cooperative commonwealth, which requires the exercise of commensurate and adequate means – education and democratic consent founded on justice and good will – to realize this goal in Canadian society.[81] Thus Woodsworth helped to formulate a Canadian version of British gradualist socialism which was informed both by his religious social ethic and by his understanding of Canadian society, its problems, and its possibilities and resources for social reconstruction.

Social Theory and Politics

Woodsworth, as already mentioned, was not primarily a theorist, and he made no attempt to formulate a systematic social or political theory. But he was a most important social critic who became the catalyst for establishing the Cooperative Commonwealth Federation as an influential social movement and political party which not only had a coherent alternative conception of Canadian society but also generated important systematic social study in Canada.[82] Woodsworth too rejected the dogmatic socialism of the radical Canadian Marxists of his day in favour of the social democracy of British socialism, which was revolutionary in its aims but constitutional and reformist in its methods.[83]

Woodsworth's basic principle throughout his political career was "human needs before profits or property rights," and he favoured any reforms and transformations that would enable the community as a whole to become more "just."[84] Although he kept in sight the ideal of the cooperative commonwealth and its principles of cooperation, equality, and industrial democracy, he had no absolute program or grand theory for how this ideal was to be realized or even what it would finally look like. In this way Woodsworth was able to draw upon a variety of sources to build a populist movement founded both on the moral and social values present in the culture and on a uniquely Canadian social analysis, rather than on an abstract or doctrinaire theory.

Woodsworth's aim was to forge a distinctively Canadian socialism:

Perhaps it is because I am a Canadian of several generations, and have inherited the individualism common to all born on the American continent; yet with political and social ideals profoundly influenced by British traditions and so-called Christian idealism; further with a rather wide and intimate knowledge of the various sections of the Canadian people – in any case, I am convinced that we may develop in Canada a distinctive type of Socialism. I refuse to follow slavishly the British model or the American model or the Russian model. We in Canada will solve our problems along our own lines.[85]

To this end, he brought together various Canadian movements of social protest against monopoly capital – agrarian radicalism, the labour movement, and several varieties of socialism – in a practical movement which sought to replace the competitive capitalist system with a publicly planned, democratic economic system. The CCF proposed to do this not by establishing a highly centralized state bureaucracy but through the decentralized public ownership of cooperative institutions and the participation of workers and farmers in regional economic planning. Woodsworth recognized that the Canadian class structure was not like that of industrialized European countries. Rather it was comprised of farmers, labourers, and small business people who had a common interest in fighting monopoly capital represented by the "Triple Alliance" of banking institutions, the railway and transportation system, and large manufacturing industries, an alliance supported and aided by the two mainline Canadian political parties. He realized that only if these groups were organized into a pragmatic coalition could they effectively combat the interests of monopoly capitalism through political and industrial action.[86]

While the situation Woodsworth and the CCF addressed was uniquely Canadian and led to the creation of a Canadian socialism, British Fabian socialism greatly influenced the methods and vision of this movement.[87] This means that class interests, while important, were related to a body of social and economic ideas and ideals that emphasize the model of education and rational persuasion rather than revolutionary struggle. Woodsworth and the CCF combined political ethics and social analysis to ground their critique of the existing economic order. One of Woodsworth's primary concerns was that the values of participation, cooperation, and the development of human capacities (both individual and social) endemic to political democracy be extended to the economic realm. He was concerned that public responsibility and the service of human needs and ends characterize the economic order, rather than the exploitation of many persons for the sake of the private property of a few. Since capitalism undermines these aims, leads to the loss of public responsibility, and thus fails to serve the human good, he concluded, it must be abolished and replaced by the cooperative commonwealth, with socio-economic institutions adapted to the fulfilment of human nature and its capacities. Woodsworth was convinced that when people became conscious of these social realities and their moral and human implications, they would join the movement of social reform represented by his party. Social science, therefore, as in the case of Rauschenbusch, is in the service of moral ends, here defined in terms of the realization of the cooperative commonwealth.

The democracy the social gospel movement advocated can be clearly identified with what has been called "developmental democracy,"[88] a moral model of democratic culture that focuses on the development of human powers and capacities in cooperative community. While the realm of capitalist economy in modern liberal societies is dominated by narrow self-interest, the political realm is characterised by cooperative, progressive rationality in the service of the common good. According to the developmental model, it is necessary only to translate the democratic principles of the latter into the domain of the former in order to overcome the social crisis.

Two problematic assumptions in the social gospel version of this model are especially worthy of mention, since they drastically undermined the political realism of the movement. The postulation of a positive political rationality and Christian moral ideals as inherent within modern "democratic culture" failed to take into account the complex plurality and conflict present also within the political realm. The social gospel attempt to formulate a normative cultural consensus and public ethos based on a historical Christian ideal scientifically applied to modern social problems proved untenable. Second, the implicit economism of the social gospellers' appeal to the working class as the agent of reform even while attempting to build a broader base of political, electoral support, caused them (in order to gain political power) to appeal to the very immediate economic interests they were concerned to overcome.[89] In effect, the CCF and the reformism of the social gospel's policy proposals in general called more for the transformation of relations in production (its distributional arrangements and the monopolistic, private control of its products) than for a critical examination of the liberal productivist paradigm, with its anthropological, natural, and socio-historical assumptions. This paradigm is rooted in the Enlightenment conception of scientific rationality and reality, in which the progressive expansion of human freedom and fulfilment is understood in terms of the progressive control of nature through scientific investigation and technological development. The social gospel movement stands within this paradigm; indeed, Rauschenbusch credits it for having "saved humanity" from religious superstitions and for making a scientific modern theology possible.[90] This chapter concludes with some reflections on the implications of this progressivist liberal theology.

CONCLUSION

The social gospel clearly stands in the liberal Protestant tradition of Schleiermacher, Ritschl, and Troeltsch, where the theological task becomes one of mediating between the Christian tradition – its essential meaning or *Wesen* – and the modern world.[91] This mediation is thoroughly historical, rooted in an analysis of the human experience or consciousness of God as the immanent "spirit of the whole" of reality. As Ernst Troeltsch argued, the mediation is also fundamentally an ethical task, a practical moral task carried on in relation to Christian social formations and their interaction with social and cultural forces. It entails "taking a stand" by formulating the meaning of the Christian "idea," rooted in its normative symbols, and realizing it in critical correlation with the modern historical situation – its

possibilities and problems.[92] This means, of course, that these traditional Christian symbols must be translated into terms compatible
with the canons of modern historical, natural and social sciences,
but that provide a religious teleology and moral orientation for
modern life which the scientific study of objective, external facts
cannot provide.

While it is true that the North American proponents of the social
gospel fell considerably short of their Continental liberal Protestant
counterparts in terms of theological erudition and intellectual sophis-
tication, they far exceeded them in developing a practical religious
morality, a public social ethic. They attempted to appropriate Jesus'
vision of the kingdom of God within the modern context as a critical
principle of interpretation by which to evaluate those socio-historical
developments in harmony with, and those opposed to, the divine
entelechy and good of life. Less interested than their European counterparts in the theoretical coherence and rational justification of
Christianity in the modern world, the North American social gospel
sought the practical realization of Christianity through social and
political action. The American pragmatist tradition was influential
here – historical development and progress are the active result of
the "fruits for life" of religious experience, not the result of theoretically validated ideas. This influence is evident also in the language
of evolutionary adaptation and gradual progress via the practical
process of meeting functional human needs, and in the analysis of
religious ideas and their consequences in terms of "social products."

In this regard, the social gospel has contributed significantly to the
shape and direction of religious social ethics and the quest for a
public morality in North American society. It articulated a religious
ethic and a political vision that critically addressed the socio-
economic situation, calling society and individuals to live up to their
own religious traditions and democratic institutions. It pointed to the
moral context of economic practices and interests to which people
are often blind and which must be related to the common good, the
meanings and institutions of the larger social community. It convincingly argued that the descriptive and the normative, the social scientific and the religio-ethical, the sacred and the secular are inextricably
joined: there is no religion unrelated to socio-historical conditions and
there is no morally neutral human science.

On this point, I disagree with the thesis that the social gospel
confused the sacred and secular realms, resulting in the growing
irrelevance of the church and of religion to the public order. The social
gospel movement represents a religious response to the social problems of capitalist society and an attempt to make theology relevant

to the social order by elaborating a public ethic. Rauschenbusch and Woodsworth sought to relate the sacred to the secular, religion to society, in a more concrete and responsible way. They provided a distinctively North American theological social ethic and social theory, rejecting both the dogmatic reifications of orthodox religious "belief systems" and the foreign ideological categories of European scientific socialism.

The social gospel argued and struggled for the articulation of a democratic political *culture* as a spiritual and moral order, not just a formal procedural process, lest our public discourse and institutions be reduced to instrumental means for the realization of private economic interests. It therefore opposed the totalization of capitalist economics as the public paradigm by which to interpret social needs and relationships, the criteria by which to formulate public policies. Only the democratic accountability of economic decisions in which the needs of the community as a whole are considered will lead to a public ethic of responsible service for the common good, a reorientation of motivation and judgment from narrow self-interest, and the calculation of short-term material benefits to a concern for the community and its larger purposes. The social gospel, in contrast to more secular and positivistic forms of liberalism, did not believe that the methods of the modern social sciences, modeled after the natural sciences, could substitute for spiritual order and its theological or religious symbols in providing such moral orientation.

The failure of the social gospel, however, is to be found precisely here, in its interpretation and mediation of the spiritual order represented in Christian symbolism as a humanly constructed social ideal to be realized historically. In postulating a "new humanity" – historically achieved in the God-consciousness of Jesus who thereby revealed the "absolute unity of human and divine life,"[93] an idealistic faith progressively incarnated in modern society as the Kingdom of God on earth, the "transfiguration" of the social order and the whole of human life[94] – the social gospel claimed the spiritual meaning of Christian symbols as a human possession and construct, an object of socio-historical knowledge and realization. The ideal was rooted in the modern liberal confidence about the human ability to overcome limits to the realization of human fulfilment and the human good in history. There are two related issues here. First, how is the human good defined, and second, can it be realized historically in the manner envisioned by the social gospel's religious social theory?

The first issue concerns the social gospellers' acceptance of what Charles Taylor calls the modern liberal identity and its contradictory conceptions of the good.[95] In this view, human fulfilment is conceived as the rational discernment and actualization of humanly chosen and defined purposes. It is important therefore that individuals autonomously discern and control their purposes and are given equal rights to realize them. This will lead to the common good – the fulfilment of human life – and its chief sign is the productive and instrumental transformation of outer nature in the service of those purposes. The resulting tension between instrumental scientific reason or technical mastery of nature and history on the one hand and expressivist human aspirations for self-realization and social fulfilment on the other is embedded in the practices and institutions of modern liberal society.[96]

The social gospel movement recognized this tension, but it failed to question the very possibility of a harmonious, rational integration of individual human fulfilment and the common good within the paradigm of liberal progressivism. Rauschenbusch and Woodsworth chose instead to interpret the social crisis as the result of a market system unfairly biased toward the interests of monopoly capitalists. Thus they attacked the economic structure of capitalism as the last barrier to the democratic culture in which individuals would finally attain fulfilment in accord with the will of God who wills the human good.[97] If only the instruments of production are socialized and brought under the scientific control of public servants concerned with the mastery of nature and history for the benefit of all, the tension can be overcome. Rauschenbusch asserts:

The salvation of the super-personal beings is by coming under the law of Christ. The fundamental step of repentance and conversion for professions and organizations is to give up monopoly power and the incomes derived from legalized extortion, and to come under the law of service ... The corresponding step in the case of governments and political oligarchies ... is to submit to real democracy. Therewith they step out of the Kingdom of Evil into the Kingdom of God.[98]

Here we arrive at the second issue, which concerns the historical realization of the human good, of the religious ideal, through the cooperation of divine and human action. How are politics and economics related to the religious ideal? The social gospel historicized the kingdom of God ideal in a way that produces Promethean aspirations to the complete mastery of nature and history by human agents in a harmonious social order free from alienation, conflict, and exploitation. The social gospel finally falls into the Hegelian trap: the substitution of historicity for a lost spirituality, the attempt to resolve the spiritual tension of human existence temporally, through political action. It translates religious symbols into historically created, humanly realizable social projects. The immanent and dialectical process of history leads to the progressive realization of *Sittlichkeit*, a public morality in which the material needs of all are equally met and individual wills find their harmonious expression in a universal *volonté générale*, sustained by human control of the processes of nature and history. The divine will is identified with historical progress and in the process reality is decisively transformed. Human action politically mediates this Parousia.

I have tried to argue that insofar as the social gospel movement falls into this trap, it does so for substantive theological reasons (its interpretation of Christian symbols in a theology of history), not purely formal methodological ones. In my view, the primary problem here is the link between material (scientific, technological) and moral progress established by the social gospel assumption that God is becoming present in the evolutionary development of western civilization, which is bringing about – through democratization, technological growth, and the modern sciences – the realization of the human good. It is the anthropocentric immanence of their theological ideal that allows the social gospellers to universalize a particular religio-cultural and social vision and to ignore or fail to see the ambiguities implicit in modern liberal culture – ambiguities present not only in the instruments of economic distribution but also in the technocratic control of nature, scientific positivism, and ethnocentric religious elitism. The social gospel mediation of theology cannot discern – indeed, it gives expression to – the spiritual crisis that continues to plague modern societies: the denial of transcendence and the consequent estrangement from nature and its spiritual order disclosed in the symbol of creation.

The New Testament understanding of the kingdom of God is neither a practical political ideal nor a doctrinal or moral system. It is a religious symbol representing the truth about human nature and the world in relation to the purposes of the transcendent God in the created order. The true good of the cosmos is understood not as a historical construct or a social product that can be applied to reality by human beings in order to master it for their own fulfilment. When the transcendent spiritual reality tensively revealed in symbolic truth is reduced to a spiritual possession of human beings, a historical ideal that promises to "transfigure" all of reality, it becomes an idol. That idol misrepresents the divine and the relation of human beings to the divine in and through the created order – a participatory relation that can be historically mediated but never possessed, that can measure political life but can never fully be realized or fulfilled within it.

3 Christian Realism: Reinhold Niebuhr and the Fellowship for a Christian Social Order

"Christian realism" was an offspring of the social gospel movement, and as is often the case, the most devastating and incisive critiques of a movement come "from within," by family members sensitive to their progenitor's weaknesses. Reinhold Niebuhr's criticisms of the social gospel are widely known and frequently adduced,[1] but the family resemblances should also be recognized, for the prophetic power of Niebuhr's work is heavily indebted to his social gospel background. His insistence that religion and theology must be related to and validated by human experience is, as we saw in chapter two, an important social gospel emphasis. And significantly, this theological attention to human experience constitutes an important source for Niebuhr's rejection of the social gospel's optimistic theology of history. The idea that God is immanent in the socio-historical processes of western civilization, guiding them toward the progressive fulfilment of the human good in the kingdom of God, simply could not be sustained in the face of world wars, economic depressions, and political tyrannies. Liberal optimism about the rational and moral capacities of individuals to bring about a cooperative commonwealth of justice, freedom, and solidarity is simply not warranted by the realities of historical experience. A more adequate view of God, human nature, and the possibilities and limits of history is therefore required to make sense of our experience and to address the complex problems that trouble modern societies.

A second major family resemblance between Niebuhr and the social gospel is the prophetic tension between the ideal and the real, which generates a powerful normative critique of society. For Niebuhr, as for the social gospellers, the religious ideal illuminates the true nature and fulfilment of human life, thus exposing the distortion present within current ideologies and practices and reorienting human agents toward their true nature and ends. But again there is an important difference. Whereas Rauschenbusch argues that the ideal is to be found and realized within history – that is, the ideal is immanent in western civilization and its generic values – Niebuhr denies both claims. The ideal can neither be derived from history nor realized in it. Rather the ideal is transcendent, revealed only in religious myth and fulfilled only beyond nature and history. This means, of course, that the ideal itself is conceived differently. Consequently, Niebuhr elaborates a very different understanding of the relationship between theological ethics and social theory from that of the social gospel, and this difference has important implications for the way he addresses matters of economic policy.

The Fellowship for a Christian Social Order (FCSO), active in Canada from 1934 to 1945, is in some ways a more loyal progeny of the social gospel movement. While its leaders eschewed a progressivist theology of history and concentrated, like Reinhold Niebuhr, on theological anthropology, they – like their social gospel forerunners – emphasized the immanent presence of God in socio-historical and natural processes. Their "natural" theology identifies the primary religious norm (unlike Niebuhr and the social gospel, they avoid language of the "ideal") as mutuality, the combination of love and justice established in the reality of human community. Indeed the FCSO was critical of Niebuhr's religious supernaturalism and individualism, arguing that his realism does not focus adequately on the social nature of the human self – that the self (including the religious self) is constituted by its participation in political and socio-historical relationships.

The occasional exchanges between Reinhold Niebuhr and the FCSO (especially one of its foremost leaders, Gregory Vlastos) published in religious periodical literature of the thirties and forties point to an interesting and illuminating dialogue between two different theological ethical descendants of the social gospel movement. Both men seek to preserve the prophetic social critique of that movement while at the same time correcting the theological and social theoretical inadequacies they perceive in it. Both develop critiques of the economic and political consequences of modern capitalism, particularly as they were experienced in the Depression era. However, Vlastos and Niebuhr's theological and ethical analyses employ different interpretations of God and God's relation to the world, of human nature and experience, and of the root causes of the crises and distortions of economic life. Hence they also develop different social theoretical models and provide different proposals for addressing economic issues, which prove illuminating for our project.

The religious social theories of these two representatives of "Christian realism" overcome some of the major inadequacies of the social gospel approach. Their more sophisticated theological and philosophical interpretation of human nature and society enables these theories to develop more complex notions of justice, social change, and conceptions of democracy that are more pluralistic (they break the myth of organic, homogeneous, rational harmony in the social gospel's progressivist liberal ideal) and less idealistic and anthropocentric. The greater distinction the Christian realists draw between the purposes of God and the modern liberal understanding of the human good enables them to recognise that human action, social identity, and scientific achievements will always be ambiguous and limited, that any premature closure or totalization in the social order must be resisted through the ongoing exploration of the limits, possibilities, and problems of social life in every society.

However, I will also argue in this chapter that the theological ethics of Reinhold Niebuhr and the FCSO are themselves ultimately rooted in a modern liberal view of reality, albeit in different ways. I will argue that Niebuhr's transcendent ideal of love cannot ground an adequate social theory – it could neither illuminate the socioeconomic crisis of the 1930s nor provide effective strategies for avoiding future crises. The problem here lies in Niebuhr's dualistic understanding of revelation (the idealization of love) and reason (as instrumental). Not only practical partisan politics but political reason and social theory as such are thus, for Niebuhr, inevitably rooted in the irrational play of ideological forces. I believe that this is due to an inadequate theology of creation.

The FCSO grounded its social theory in the immanent priority of membership in a historical, covenant community, sustained in its complex interdependencies by the sovereign God.[2] The centrality of "covenant" language of interaction employed by FCSO writers illuminates the complexity of the social and historical context of human agency and identity in a way that Niebuhr's dualistic model cannot. But it also causes the FCSO to focus exclusively on human history and community, thereby losing sight of the realm of nature and natural interdependencies within the created order. The FCSO's orientation develops an understanding of revelation and reason in history in a way that enlarges their moral perspective on the social crisis of the 1930s and on economic practices in general, but it fails to call into question the basic subject-object dualism in the anthropocentric utilitarian vision of nature implicit in the productivist paradigm of modern political economy (whether socialist or capitalist).

REINHOLD NIEBUHR

One could as easily begin with social theory as with theological ethics in examining Niebuhr's work, since in his view both are raised and validated in human experience. Any social analysis that seeks to do justice to the realities of our experience comes up against the underlying religious problem of the *meaning* of human life – the need for a comprehensive principle of interpretation that illumines the sources of social conflict and the paradoxes of history and human nature.[3] Any religious or theological perspective, on the other hand, will need to provide precisely such a comprehensive and complex framework of meaning, one that can coherently disclose the heights and depths of experience, and must therefore be adequate to the concrete conditions of social life. But clearly Niebuhr always pushes toward the religious question in his work, the question of the ultimate meaning of life apprehended only by faith, not through rational social or historical analysis. It is the revealed myths of Christianity that provide the foundation for realistic social interpretation and action, not social scientific or historical analysis and models. And it is their *religious* inadequacy that renders contemporary social theories delusive and dangerous. We begin, then, with an examination of Niebuhr's theological ethic before considering his social theoretical assumptions and his critique of capitalism.

Theology and Ethics

For Niebuhr, vital religion must be related to human experience. Hence, as with the social gospel, there can be no radical disjunction between theology and ethics. Like Rauschenbusch, Niebuhr has no interest in speculating on the divine nature in itself, but rather on God's relations to the world and the consequent implications for ethical insight and action. However, contrary to Rauschenbusch, religious conceptions of God are not for Niebuhr social products but are grounded in the self-transcendent consciousness of the human self who seeks the meaning of life beyond nature and history, in an unconditioned ground of existence.[4] Religion is for Niebuhr above all a vertical relationship between human beings and God, which entails a permanent structure of human existence. Niebuhr thus elaborates his theology in terms of theological anthropology, and he begins *The*

Nature and Destiny of Man with the statement: "Man has always been his own most vexing problem."[5]

Part of the problem is that human experience is not intelligible in and of itself. Human nature in its paradoxical location at the juncture of finite nature and self-transcendent spirit cannot be understood through any finite system of rational or natural coherence. Such reductionist models obscure the essential freedom of the human subject to transcend the constraints of any given forms of life or thought. The meaning of human experience can therefore only be found in the infinite and transcendent ground of existence, in God. This means that only religious faith can provide the coherence, the principle of interpretation by which to understand the essence of human nature as the capacity for free self-determination. But the problem runs deeper than this, since this capacity is itself tainted insofar as human beings deny their finitude and make themselves the centre of meaning. Human beings contradict themselves by elevating the capacity to the source, and thus once again substitute a finite meaning for an infinite one, with destructive consequences.

The enduring problem, therefore, is sin located in the human self which prevents the self both from apprehending its transcendent ground and from acknowledging the constraints of nature and society on human freedom and creativity. The problem is fundamentally religious and moral. The failure to acknowledge oneself as created by God and thus the refusal to obey the law of one's essentially free nature: "Love, a harmonious relation of life to life in obedience to the divine center and source of … life."[6] The consequences of this are distorted forms of life that either inhibit the creative freedom of individuals in history by denying the depth of the human spirit or destroy the organic cohesions of life in nature and society by viewing individual freedom as self-sufficient rational autonomy. In order to avoid the consequences of a false – because finite – heteronomy (a tyrannical harmony) or a radically relativistic autonomy (an irreducible conflict of individual interests), Niebuhr argues that we need a trans-historical Archimedean point that can comprehensively ground the meaning of life and provide a universal moral ideal. This transcendent norm must be revealed by God, apprehended through faith, and dialectically applied to human experience.

To state the problem of the Archimedean point another way, one could speak as Hannah Arendt and Richard Bernstein do of "Cartesian doubt" or "Cartesian anxiety,"[7] the quest of the finite and contingent self for absolute certainty. Following Kierkegaard, whom Arendt identifies as providing the "deepest interpretation" of Cartesian doubt, Niebuhr views anxiety as the "inevitable concomitant" of human freedom and the "internal precondition" of sin.[8] The self's quest for an essential foundation for meaning is ultimately for Niebuhr a religious and moral quest – the anxiety can only properly be resolved by faith in God and willing obedience to God's universal will. This is because the essential self, the free, self-transcendent self which "stands outside all relations"[9] is constituted by its vertical relation to God.

But the self in contemplation recognizes that the self in action lacks faith, choosing to resolve its anxiety through some form of self-asserting will to power. There is an element of self-love rather than love of God and neighbour in all action. Hence the recognition of sin as the fundamental problem: "We cannot, therefore, escape the ultimate paradox that the final exercise of freedom in the transcendent human spirit is its recognition of the false use of that freedom in action. Man is most free in the discovery that he is not free."[10] Human experience confirms that this paradoxical tension between the essential self and the existential self is a permanent dialectic which is never overcome in history. The law of love as the norm of freedom can therefore never be realized in historical experience. It is not a simple possibility. But its claim always discloses possibilities that transcend relative norms and historical achievements. Moral life is a perpetual struggle, the endless quest for impossible perfection. Religious revelation discloses both the possibilities and the permanent dangers and limitations in this struggle.

To clarify Niebuhr's view of the relation between religion and morality, we can distinguish his view from those of Immanuel Kant and Karl Barth, who also affirm the essential freedom of human nature, but do so from different perspectives. Niebuhr agrees with the Kantian insight that experience is shaped by the structure of human consciousness, not mere conformity to the structures of phenomenal reality; that is, human beings have the essential capacity for self-determination.[11] Like Kant, Niebuhr therefore makes a rigorous distinction between is and ought – morality cannot be grounded on phenomenal experience given the fact of radical human freedom; nor, given the reality of human finitude and particularity, can it be subjectively founded on the empirical or existential self. But whereas Kant links freedom to morality through the formal capacity for rational agency and the formulation of universal laws, Niebuhr links freedom to morality through revealed religion.[12] For Kant morality means rational and uncoerced conformity to universal laws – an act is moral if the human agent wills it voluntarily according to the dictates of reason, regardless of the consequences. For Niebuhr reason cannot perform this universalizing function since it too is caught up in the paradox of evil arising out of freedom – the rational will is as partial and sinful as are natural inclinations. Human freedom is rooted in something more eternal and infinite than finite reason – divine transcendence, whose reality is apprehended by faith and confirmed in experience as the only incomprehensible principle for the comprehension of the whole meaning of life.[13] And this principle discloses the problem, the solution, and the norm of human moral experience. "The issue of Biblical religion is not primarily the problem of how finite man can know God but how sinful man is to be reconciled to God and how history is to overcome the tragic consequences of its 'false eternals', its proud and premature efforts to escape finiteness."[14]

In contrast to Kant's formal rational principle for ethical justification, then, Niebuhr's ethics appeals to a religious revelation of the transcendent regulative ideal or norm that grounds, judges, and discloses meaningful human experience and moral action. The full stature of human freedom and the "essentially human" is found in the revelation of Christ as the incarnation in history of the perfect love which transcends history. Like Karl Barth, Niebuhr relates human freedom to divine revelation: "The will of God is the norm, the life of Christ is the revelation of that will, and the individual faces the awful responsibility of seeking to do God's will amidst all the complexities of human existence with no other authoritative norm but that ultimate one."[15] For Niebuhr as for Barth the Archimedean point that reveals both the essential human nature (in Barth's terms, the "real man") and the gracious will of God toward human beings, is Jesus Christ.[16] But in contrast to Barth's emphasis on the radical discontinuity and contradiction between revelation and experience, where ethics becomes obedience in faith to the personal command of God,[17] Niebuhr argues that revelation, while not deduced from experience, illuminates and is validated by human experience.[18] The created structures of human nature and history, while finite and distorted by corruptions of meaning due to premature human solutions, nevertheless point toward and are fulfilled by the truths of faith. Revelation discloses the depth dimension of human experience and thus provides the principle of comprehensive coherence necessary to recognize the true meaning and end of these natural and historical realities, while at the same time disclosing their limitations and sinful distortions. In Niebuhr's view, Barth correctly rejects all natural law theories, which rely too much on rational guidance and rigid finite principles. But in contrast to Barth, Niebuhr argues that the revelation of God in Christ does provide an ideal norm of life which must be related dialectically to the contingent and relative calculations of practical ethical reason. Revelation provides not only inner religious resources (such as forgiveness, humility and hope) for facing the ambiguities and contradictions of historical experience, but also discloses the objective "law of life" which can be elaborated into a basis for social ethics and can inform relative moral judgments.

The dialectical, tensive relationship between this transcendent law of love revealed in the cross of Christ, and the prudent, calculating judgments required by a realistic social ethic constitutes the structure of Niebuhr's theological ethics.[19] In order to understand this structure properly, it is important to be clear about Niebuhr's understanding of the God-world relationship and what this implies about human agency. God's purposes and will are not immanent in historical processes and therefore cannot be discerned through a socio-historical interpretation of human existence. The kingdom of God ideal espoused by the social gospel is not a simple possibility in history, nor can it be made the basis for a comprehensive social ethic that realistically guides human action. Rather, God is related to the world as the transcendent ground of the essential self, and God's will – clarified in the religious myths of Christianity which disclose the reality of the human situation – is given with the very constitution of the self as its "impossible possibility" or transcendent "ought." It is this vertical, self-transcendent relationship to God, not natural or socio-historical commitments and contexts, that constitutes human being in the world. What is revealed in the Christian ideal of love is not a model community but rather the permanent structure of human nature, which is the basis of human history.[20]

Memory is the "fulcrum of freedom" in history[21] – not insofar as it recalls the narrative structure of a common identity but insofar as it reveals the permanent symbolic structures of meaning that disclose the comprehensive character of history, grounded in the human self. For Niebuhr prophetic religion is not, as it was for the social gospel, the interpretation of God at work in the world through the study of social life and historical processes, where Jesus becomes but the initiator of the kingdom of God in history. Prophetic religion rather preserves the vertical dialectic between the transcendent ideal and the historical reality. The drama of divine-human engagement can be apprehended only through the mythical paradoxes of faith.[22] And the central myth of the Christian faith is found in the doctrine of the Atonement.[23]

Niebuhr's view of the way in which God is related to the world therefore entails a very different Christology from that of the social gospel. Already in his early work he argues that the "ethic of Jesus" is a "love absolutism," an "unprudential rigorism" that emulates the divine model of self-sacrificing love and therefore cannot be justified in social ethical or historical terms. It is an utterly transcendent ethic and thus cannot provide specific guidance in adjudicating relative moral claims.[24] The law of love is the basis for social ethics insofar as it transforms the moral possibilities in every situation by enlarging the scope of human responsibility and furnishing inner religious resources to individual moral agents so that they can act on those possibilities. But since love is primarily an impulse or attitude it cannot specify a hierarchy of goods or make judgments between alternative political choices. It is not concerned with the calculation of consequences of various social strategies, and is therefore finally neither politically expedient nor socially efficacious. The religious ideal must be supplemented by a political or pragmatic ethic which, in the quest for social justice, takes into account the conflicts of interest and power struggles that characterize a sinful social order. Hence Niebuhr calls for a "frank dualism in morals," a recognition of the distinction between what is possible for self-transcendent individuals and the more limited moral capacities and resources of collective action.[25]

Human ethical agency is understood, therefore, in terms of the permanent vertical dialectic between the ideal and the real which discloses the illusions, limits, and possibilities of experience. Religious myths provide individuals with an understanding of the total human situation so that they can (1) avoid the illusions of liberal optimism, which reduces the ideal to a prudential ethic and leads to unrealistic social strategies, but also (2) critique otherworldly dualisms that separate the ideal from human experience and thus fail to appropriate religious resources for social change. Niebuhr's "frank dualism" in morals does not allow for separation between religious and socio-political realms, but rather calls for realistic recognition of the possibilities and limits of social action so that the resources for change can be more effectively chosen and pragmatically employed.

Clearly for Niebuhr the fundamental distinction between individuals and collectivities is the individual's capacity for self-transcendence. This means that only individuals, not collectivities, can apprehend and mediate the ideal law of love.[26] The best that can be attained in collective life are contingent balances of power, relative systems of "rough justice" that restrain the egoistic quest for dominance by particular interest groups. These balances of power cannot be founded upon or sustained by rational social consensus since reason is always tied to particular interests that, as noted above, are anxiously directed toward self-preservation. All relative systems of justice, the constant (re)adjustment of power to power, interest to interest, depend rather upon the law of love – the transcendent harmony of life with life – which grounds the provisional and imperfect harmonies of historical experience. It is therefore the sensitive consciences of self-transcendent individuals that mediate the necessary resources for bringing about higher levels of social justice.[27] Such individuals, without confusing pragmatic political strategies with perfectionist religious ends, are able in a self-critical and forgiving spirit to make policy judgments that best channel social powers and interests to serve the general good.

But how can an individual, transcendent ideal sustain the general social good without being mediated through some common vision of the good society? To answer this question we must examine more carefully Niebuhr's understanding of the Atonement and the relations between love and justice that flow from this focal point of meaning. In *The Nature and Destiny of Man* Niebuhr develops his Christology beyond his earlier emphasis on the absolute ethic of Jesus to a focus on the disclosure in Christ of the comprehensive meaning of history, the divine sovereignty that governs and fulfils historical existence. In the suffering love of Jesus on the cross, divine sovereignty is displayed not as power over evil but as divine love and mercy toward evil doers. This truth must be appropriated inwardly by faith since the sinful contradictions of human nature and history are overcome "in principle but not in fact."[28] Human life is therefore not fulfilled within history; God's grace is not a possession; the limits and contradictions of experience remain. Indeed it is precisely the depth and pervasiveness of human sin and historical conflict that are revealed in the Christ event. The doctrine of justification by faith does not mitigate the tragic realities of history but enables people to face them responsibly, without pretension or illusion and yet with the knowledge that the evil in responsible action is resolved ultimately in divine mercy.[29]

But the cross of Christ also discloses the norm of human nature, the perfection of self-sacrificial love, or *agape*.[30] Again, this norm cannot be justified within history since it transcends historical possibilities – it faces evil by suffering its consequences, not by changing the structures of history through the exercise of finite power. "The Cross symbolizes the perfection of *agape* which transcends all particular norms of justice and mutuality in history. It rises above history and seeks conformity to the Divine love rather than harmony with other human interests and vitalities."[31] Here, as in the relationship between the essential and the existential self, Niebuhr again emphasizes the paradoxical relation of supra-history to history. Sacrificial love cannot be justified in history, but it is the Archimedean point that supports all historical ethics. The lesser historical possibilities of mutual love and justice (lesser because there is always an admixture of other-love and self-love in the calculation of consequences) are possible only because the transcendent lure of the ideal makes other-regard a factor in the calculus of alternative actions. Niebuhr asserts: "Mutuality is not a possible achievement if it is made the intention and goal of any action."[32] Without the ideal, mutual relations would degenerate into the calculating conflict of self-interested, anxious individuals. The survival impulse, the egoistic will-to-power, rather than an impulse to community and harmony, would then become the ethical norm.

On the other hand – paradoxically – the ideal of *agape* must not be made the external norm for action, since it would lead to socially irresponsible action. How can one act in a self-sacrificial way toward many persons and groups whose interests or conceptions of the good may be in conflict? The ideal of love illuminates the inevitable self-interest of human beings, but it does not elaborate the basis on which to sort out competing social claims, nor does it offer guidance for effective social strategies. For this we need the rational calculations and relative norms of justice.[33] Of course, the rules and structures of justice are not grounded in universal natural law discerned by common human reason. As we have repeatedly observed, there are in Niebuhr's view no fixed natural or historical structures – only the permanent paradoxic structure of human existence characterized by freedom and finitude. Justice is therefore the relative historical formulation and embodiment of the love obligation within the complexities and vitalities of social life.

While all standards of justice are but contingent approximations of the ideal of love, it is nonetheless possible and necessary to make relative ethical judgments between greater and lesser achievements of justice. This is done by examining the objective historical consequences of sinful actions.[34] All persons and groups are equally sinful, but those with greater power are guilty of greater pride and injustice than those who lack power and position: "Wherever the fortunes of nature, the accidents of history or even the virtues of the possessors of power, endow an individual or a group with power, social prestige, intellectual eminence or moral approval above their fellows, there an ego is allowed to expand."[35] The fundamental problem of social justice is therefore the problem of sinful will-to-power in all of its many possible masks, rationalizations, and distorting configurations. These can only be exposed from the transcendent perspective of the ideal, but they can be dealt with only through the pragmatic deployment of countervailing powers which restrain their sinful consequences and establish a modicum of balance and harmony. It is at this point that a realistic social theory and a pragmatic social ethic become crucial. An adequate social theory will disclose where the "accidents of history" have provided the occasion for egregious abuses of power that result in unjust forms of domination and self-interested exploitation.[36] And an adequate social ethic will then develop effective strategies which "use, beguile, harness and deflect" power and self-interest in order to bring about a more just and inclusive community.[37]

What then is Niebuhr's answer to the question of how a self-transcendent, trans-historical ideal of love can sustain the common good without a vision of the good society? Niebuhr would argue that any vision of the good society is finite and therefore a premature, pretentious completion of meaning likely to have destructive consequences. There can be no general definition of the good society, only pragmatic judgments about better or worse societies in view of the possibilities the ideal discloses. This is so because the real source of the social problem in the first place is neither social structures and relations nor a false vision of society. The social problem is rooted in the human will-to-power which destroys social harmony through domination. The real problem is sinful human nature.

The fundamental problem is closely correlated with the fundamental meaning and law of life, which too is not socially constituted but is found in the vertical relationship of the self to God. Even the most adequate social institutions are "only a bare base upon which the higher experiences of love must be built."[38] These higher experiences are found in individual religious experience and interpersonal relations of self-transcendent intimacy. The true meaning and nature of communal life is not to be found in social patterns, structures, and processes, but rather in the interpersonal encounters between human selves and their interests.[39] To do justice to the self-transcendent character of human selves demands more than reliance upon finite rules and structures of justice in one's actions. It demands a *spirit* of justice informed by the contemplative awareness of individuals who in conscious relation to God understand the limits and ambiguities of all finite principles, structures and actions, and seek for such higher approximations of love as are possible within particular social institutions and practices without identifying such possibilities with the religious ideal.

A number of critical questions could be raised concerning Reinhold Niebuhr's theological ethics. One could, with Paul Tillich and Henry Nelson Wieman,[40] challenge Niebuhr's doctrine of knowledge as too sharply separating faith and reason, so that reason becomes merely technical or pragmatic, unable to adjudicate the questions of meaning or truth that properly belong to the religious realm of faith and myth. While they do so from different theological perspectives, both Tillich

and Wieman criticise Niebuhr's view of revelation as too supernaturalistic, fostering too great a discontinuity between God and the
world. Consequently Niebuhr's religious ethical Archimedean point
is too unrelated to the structures and forms of life to inform coherently practical moral discourse and action.

Or one could pursue a similar criticism by examining the meaning
of love in Niebuhr's thought, as do Daniel Day Williams and Gene
Outka. Williams argues that Niebuhr's impoverished view of reason
leads to a technically calculating or utilitarian understanding of the
liberal definition of love as mutuality.[41] Reason, Niebuhr insists,
"mechanizes human relations."[42] Only the sacrificial love apprehended by faith can overcome the self-interested calculation which
destroys the organic harmony of life with life. In Williams' view,
however, if God is conceived as more intimately related to concrete
history, and if God's purpose in history is understood as the community of life, then the meaning of love must include the demands of
mutual love and justice in a more integral way. The question for
Williams is love's intention – trans-historical fulfilment or the historical community of good. For Williams it is the latter, and on this
theological perspective, as Paul Ramsey correctly notes, the ideal is
essentially mutuality in community to which the individual is subordinate.[43] The community provides religious and ethical resources
to the individual which he or she could not have alone, so that the
norm of self-sacrifice takes on quite a different status and meaning
than it has for Niebuhr. Self-sacrificial action *can* be justified historically, although not strictly in terms of a utilitarian calculus. Moral
reasoning cannot be reduced to the pragmatic calculation of consequences even in public and social life. Gene Outka points out that
Niebuhr's understanding of mutuality as "frictionless harmony" in
contrast to interpersonal or social conflict misses the point that proponents of mutuality have in mind: the quality of relations *between*
persons and/or groups.[44] "Those actions are loving which create and
sustain community,"[45] not some ideal of frictionless harmony. The
aim of social morality and justice here is not merely to balance
conflicting interests, but to orient individuals and groups within a
common order that establishes meaningful cooperation in the service
of a larger good.

The second part of this chapter will consider these questions more
carefully, since the FCSO challenges Niebuhr precisely on these issues.
But it will also be helpful to keep them in mind while investigating
Niebuhr's social theory and economic analysis, for I shall argue
that Niebuhr's social theory, while critical of liberal individualism
from a religious point of view, implicitly accepts its model of democ-

racy and rationality as the inevitable "reality" in social and economic life.[46] Where one locates the Archimedean point – the normative ideal or the good – by which to evaluate existing social relations is crucial for understanding the source of one's critical leverage in social theory. And the adequacy of the content of the ideal is crucial if it is to elaborate the enabling conditions and possibilities for better social practices.

Social Theory and the Economy

Given the above interpretation of Niebuhr's thought, it should come as no surprise that his social theory is full of paradoxes, dialectical relations, regulative principles held in tension, and provocative analyses. And here, as in his theological ethics, one must be attuned to the subtle and not so subtle changes of perspective and opinion in Niebuhr's social and economic thought over time. From his early stated preference for communist over capitalist oligarchy,[47] through his gradual acceptance of the New Deal economic remedy,[48] to his later praise for the plutocracy of American democratic capitalism[49] (not to mention his growing appreciation for the British conservative Edmund Burke), it would appear that Niebuhr's social theory underwent dramatic transmutations. Many commentators describe this as a shift from a form of Marxist socialism in the early Niebuhr to the pragmatic liberal "realism" of his later work.[50]

I will argue for a somewhat different interpretation. In my view Niebuhr never at any point elaborates a systematic social, political, or economic theory. His social analyses are desultory and frequently illustrate general principles drawn from his religious conceptions of human nature and experience. This follows from the fact that socio-historical analyses do not constitute the "total schemes of meaning" which inform social and historical interpretation. Social analyses can refute extravagant ideological claims regarding the causal relations of particular social conditions, but they cannot resolve the "irreducible ideological preferences" espoused by the various interest groups and classes in a society.[51] Throughout his career Niebuhr excoriated all forms of naturalism and rationalism which derive the causes of good and evil or the meaning and obligations of life from the "obvious unities and affinities of historic existence."[52] Such theories tend to exaggerate the capacities and historical possibilities of human reason and obscure the spiritual roots and organic vitalities of human nature. They submerge the individual in a mechanistic society, unable to account for the creative and destructive freedom of the self-transcendent structure of human personality. Niebuhr constantly attacks Marxism and liberal individualism, the two predominant social theories in the modern western world. For him, only a religious understanding of the meaning of life can furnish an adequate perspective on the problems, possibilities, and limitations of social life.[53]

Again it is interesting to note how different this religious understanding is from the more immanent, socio-historical theology of the social gospel, in which social analysis and theory play a more constitutive role. Niebuhr is critical of the consensual model of society the social gospel assumes, a model which places too much confidence in tentative social harmonies and human possibilities in history.[54] Such a view fails to understand the fundamental moral dynamics of human nature and thus fails to comprehend the true source of social conflict in the human will-to-power. Conflict cannot be overcome in history since it is rooted in the very structure of the self and is one of the consequences of the creative power of human freedom. The basic social problem is how to balance the competing interests of individuals and groups that occupy different functional roles in society. Such a balance will always be provisional and will depend to some extent on the coercive hegemony of certain interests and functional powers over others.[55] The perduring problem of justice is to establish the best possible harmony by restraining disproportionate powers that threaten social stability and by establishing an acceptable pragmatic compromise between freedom and equality. Niebuhr's social theory throughout his writings may thus be characterized as a functional analytics of the various forms of power and their relations.

For example, in his early work Niebuhr argued that economic interests and power are preeminent over political power in modern capitalist democracies and that economic reconstruction must therefore take priority in the struggle for justice.[56] But even in these early writings his analysis of power relations and of the social problem is primarily functional. His reflections lack a substantive political economic analysis, even though the social crisis is understood to be economic. The real problem will not be disclosed through a concrete systematic analysis of the development of modern political economy, since the economic factor of private ownership of the means of production is but the occasion, not the cause, of the crisis. The cause of the crisis is that sinful owners of capital have exploited the privilege of their functional power to create social inequalities which can no longer sustain the political order. Hence the capitalist social order has become dysfunctional; it has degenerated into a vicious class struggle. The crisis is fundamentally "moral" and its solution calls for a new political order that can reestablish a functional balance of power.

In the early period Niebuhr was convinced that this would require the socialization of property and the transition to a more socialist political order. Only such an order, he believed, would be able to maintain democratic principles of justice through a relative equilibrium of social forces. However, when the capitalist economy was able to recover from the crisis through New Deal welfare programs and Keynesian regulation policies as well as the general economic expansion spurred by a variety of factors including World War II, Niebuhr revised his apocalyptic scenario. Capitalist democracy could provide a functional socio-economic equilibrium much more effectively than a socialist state.[57]

A more detailed consideration of Niebuhr's economic views appears below. Here I simply want to point out the centrality of power and the functional socio-political analysis that characterized Niebuhr's social theory from the beginning. The reason for this lies in his view of human nature and the relations between love and justice. We begin, therefore, by (a) looking at the relationship between the individual and society in Niebuhr's thought, in order to delineate the basic assumptions of his social analysis. Then we will (b) consider his concepts of justice, power, and democracy, which will provide the context for (c) understanding his changing views on the capitalist political economy.

The Individual and the Community. While Niebuhr rejected the progressive evolutionary model of social change advocated by many social gospel thinkers, he nonetheless employed an organic, evolutionary model of society.[58] Individual freedom and creativity are sustained only in organic communities which nourish the pre-rational vitalities, sentiments, and loyalties imparted by nature and cultural tradition.[59] Hence Niebuhr opposes both the atomistic individualism of bourgeois liberalism, with its doctrine of the autonomous individual, and the collectivism and materialistic determinism of Marxist social theory. Both these ideologies foster mechanical and impersonal, rationalistic forms of culture that undermine the organic relations, resources and depth of meaningful social life. Both destroy the basis for creative individuality and the vital dynamism of human existence: "Life requires a more organic and mutual form than bourgeois democratic theory provides for it; but the social substance of life is richer and more various, and has greater depths and tensions, than are envisaged in the Marxist dream of social harmony."[60] Only a "religious individualism" can provide a satisfactory understanding of the relationship between the individual and the community.

In contrast to atomist conceptions of self-sufficient human beings for whom society is purely instrumental in the service of individual maximization and fulfilment, Niebuhr is not opposed to a social understanding of the self. The social contract theory of society as created by fiat of the human will obscures the primordial character of human community, the rootedness of individual consciousness and choice within socio-historical bounds. While the human essence is defined as the capacity for self-transcendent freedom, this cannot be reduced to the formal freedom to choose one's mode of life. Rather it implies a certain conception of the good as well, namely the harmony of life with life. On this basis one can make moral judgments between different modes of life. Individual freedom of choice, while important, is not the foundational right. Rather the capacity for self-transcendent freedom entails as its correlative the human capacity for love as a potential which ought to be developed, a capacity which could not be developed or fulfilled outside society.

One could go even further to say that this capacity requires for its development a certain kind of society; that freedom and love – or at least particular understandings of them – are socially embodied in the practices, institutions, and discourses of historical communities. But this is to go further than Reinhold Niebuhr is willing to go. In Niebuhr's view it would be to ascribe too much to a particular social identity. It would fail to recognize the a priori givenness of these capacities in the *religious* transcendence of the individual consciousness over every actual community and every historical process. Religious individualism protects this "pinnacle of individuality" from being undermined by the community.

Once again we become enmeshed in Niebuhrian paradox, this time articulated in terms of individual freedom and community order.[61] There is no preestablished natural harmony here, nor can an ideal harmony be established in history. The forms of social order are historically created in contests of power between various vital impulses and creative (and destructive) forces. Order is necessary to restrain unlimited human vitalities, but freedom to express the creative possibilities of human life is necessary for the development of individuality. Principles of justice are elaborated in every society to guide this process of adjusting interests and vitalities to one another in an acceptable, though tentative, balance between freedom and order. However, these principles must be ultimately rooted in religious conceptions of the meaning of life discerned by the sensitive individual and not derived from the ambiguous hegemonic cohesions of actual social life.

Hence individual and community, freedom and order, self-transcendence and organic relatedness are constantly held in tension, but Niebuhr does not clearly specify or even carefully attend to the relations between them. The character of the relations between individual and community remains vague, I suggest, because Niebuhr does not investigate them socio-historically and interpret them in a coherent theoretical framework. Niebuhr must specify more concretely what kind of community enables us to be the kinds of persons we ought to be since this is not given by nature. More is required than simply proposing the avoidance of tyranny and anarchy and the need for a balance of power. The nature of the constraints to which individuals are subject and of the capacities they develop are related to certain common social conditions and political understandings. These are not given a priori and cannot be attained on our own.

This raises questions about the social conditions of freedom and love, about the socio-political matrix – the common public practices, institutions, and meanings – that makes possible and sustains these "essential values." It also raises questions about the social conditions of human agency, which need to be elaborated if there is no context-free human nature or essence. While Niebuhr does acknowledge that human individuality is subject to historical development, he rejects the notion that it is historically constituted.[62] Rather it is an "original endowment," religiously constituted in the vertical relation of the individual to God. Hence society and history are not constitutive conditions of and limits to human freedom and love, the essential human capacities. Human identity is essentially religious and transcendent. The ideal harmony of life with life is not a social possibility nor can it be historically realized. This is why Niebuhr spends relatively little time on concrete social analysis. The timeless truth of human life is found in religious myths, which can be applied to all social conditions and processes in a paradoxical way through individual conscience.

Yet Niebuhr does want to argue for the validity of certain principles of justice and the democratic form of social organization as most suited to human nature. We turn now to this argument.

Justice, Power, and Democracy. Reinhold Niebuhr does not have a theory of justice such as John Rawls,[63] for example, has developed. Nor does he give priority to the category of justice in his social thought. Niebuhr's view of human nature precludes such rational, Procrustean theories of the well-ordered, just society. "Rules of justice do not follow in a 'necessary manner' from some basic proposition of justice. They are the fruit of a rational survey of the whole field of human interests, of the structure of human life, and of the causal sequences in human relations."[64] Definitions of justice are therefore historically and socially contingent and they are subordinate to (judged and fulfilled by) the ideal of love or harmony revealed in the essential structure of human life. Indeed the most profound principles of justice "actually transcend reason and lie rooted in religious conceptions of the meaning of existence."[65] Hence it is misleading to suggest, as Robert Benne does, that Rawls' theory "fleshes out" Niebuhr's skeletal conception of justice.[66]

The Archimedean point from which Niebuhr assesses the basic social structure is not found in a heuristic, procedural "original position" in which individuals freely choose principles of justice under conditions of abstract equality and fairness.[67] Rather, the Archimedean point is found in the "essential self" revealed in the ideal of love. Principles and specific rules and structures of justice only approximate this ideal. Due to the greater purity and transcendence of thought or contemplation over action, the principles of justice – liberty and equality – have a more general and permanent validity than do their historical embodiment in particular social systems and structures. But even these principles do not have an unconditioned status. They must be related to the higher harmony of love. The principles of justice must be related to a thicker conception of the "good" rooted in theological anthropology than can be found in Rawls' deontological liberalism. In this regard Niebuhr would agree with Michael Sandel's recent critique of the priority of justice in Rawlsian liberalism. Sandel argues: "The universe of the deontological ethic is a place devoid of inherent meaning, a world 'disenchanted' in Max Weber's phrase, a world without an objective moral order ... Only a world ungoverned by a purposive order leaves principles of justice open to human construction and conceptions of good to individual choice."[68] The deontological liberal self lacks moral depth and hence meaningful agency. The autonomous individual is reduced to exercising instrumental reason in order to realize his or her inner, given desires in a mechanistic world.[69] There is not enough recognition that as individuals we are constrained by our social and historical attachments, allegiances, and convictions which shape our self-understandings and our personal identity in community. Such a deontological view cannot sustain even Rawls' theory of justice itself – the theory cannot justify itself as an Archimedean point.[70]

With this critique Niebuhr would perhaps generally concur. But he could not concur with Sandel's alternative: that our basic human identity and conceptions of the good (or goods) are constituted historically in community. Niebuhr preserves a trans-historical Archimedean point which raises the individual beyond all historical and natural relations to "a final pinnacle of freedom where he is able to ask questions about the meaning of life which call into question the meaning of the historical process itself."[71] Niebuhr adheres to a religious individualism in which the ideal, the transcendent good, is represented not as a social possibility but as a religiously motivated and discerned self-sacrificial love. The religious meaning of life is not mediated through a public rational understanding of the good. No such common purpose or meaning guides social life. In collective social relations, therefore, instrumental justice does become primary in order to restrain the conflict among competing individual needs and interests. Niebuhr's religious individualism is tied to a fundamentally liberal conception of society where the overriding moral and political consideration is order within conditions of freedom, the best possible adjustment of interest to interest.

Justice, in Niebuhr's view, entails the setting of limits not according to a shared understanding of the nature and meaning of social goods, but according to an ideal religious conception of persons and existing relations of power. The boundary lines of justice are compromises between the transcendent ideal and the real possibilities of the social situation. Human communities are governed not by normative ethical or rational meanings, but by power: "These two elements of communal life – the central organizing principle and power, and the equilibrium of power – are essential and perennial aspects of community organization."[72] The two quasi-transcendent principles of justice are related to these two forms of social power – equality to the functional balance of power, liberty to the organizing unity or cohesive power of society.[73]

Niebuhr recognizes of course that the primacy of these two principles of justice is rooted historically in the development of democracy as a normative conception of social life. But he wants to say more than this: "Ideally, democracy is a *permanently valid* form of social and political organization which does justice to two dimensions of human existence: to man's spiritual stature and his social character, to the uniqueness and variety of individual life and to the common necessities of all men."[74] Given Niebuhr's stated antipathy toward any form of political idealism and his general caveat against making normative any particular historical form of social life, this quotation forwards a rather surprising claim. What does he mean to say? What does Niebuhr understand the ideal of democracy to be? In Niebuhr's judgment, the twin principles of democratic justice best guard against the twin perils of socio-political life, tyranny and anarchy. These principles are thus able to produce a harmony within conditions of freedom and plurality, recognizing that these conditions are codetermined by egoistic self-interest as well as the creative quest for individual fulfilment in terms of the general good. Democratic justice recognizes the need for an order, a form of government that maintains an equilibrium of social powers in order to prevent the domination of any particular power, even while ensuring that this political power is itself held under moral and constitutional checks in order to prevent tyranny. Hence justice holds the two principles in tension as it seeks proximate solutions to the inevitable problems of power in modern society.

In my judgment, Niebuhr's view of democratic justice fits well with certain assumptions of what C.B. Macpherson calls the "equilibrium pluralist" model of democracy.[75] While Niebuhr rejects the narrow market rationality of "economic man" and seeks to preserve the moral content of democratic theory, he tends to see democracy primarily as a procedure which maintains social stability through the balance of conflicting interests and powers. Given the realities of human nature, the priority of the individual, and the inevitable inequalities of social function, an equilibrium of power – especially between economic and political power in modern democratic capitalist societies – is the most workable model of social justice, the best protection against tyranny.[76]

This model of state-regulated capitalism certainly functioned to moderate the class conflict that caused Niebuhr such concern in the 1930s. But it could only do so, as Niebuhr himself realized, within an ever expanding capitalist economy, which Niebuhr called "a gift of providence."[77] This gift has been a mixed blessing, as subsequent economic crises attest.[78] For that reason alone the equilibrium model of justice is in question – it lacks historical perspective. While it allows for a dynamism of social function, it does not consider the substantive historical and political sources of class struggles and economic crises, nor does it consider their possible consequences in future crises. In practice, historically, there can be no stable equilibrium in a system fundamentally dominated by the capitalist need for material expansion and accumulation. Niebuhr, along with other "realist" theorists of the equilibrium model, failed to perceive the extent to which politics is implicated in and determined by an instrumental system of extractive and increasingly pervasive economic power. This failure is rooted in an inadequate analysis of the underlying assumptions and dynamics of liberal industrial societies.

I will return to this critique below, but it is necessary now to give more careful consideration to Niebuhr's view of political economy.

Political Economy. As I pointed out at the beginning of this section, Niebuhr's economic views underwent considerable change, from his

early pessimism about the survival of capitalism to his gradual acceptance and eventual support for democratic capitalism. From the
beginning, however, his analysis of economic issues focused on the
moral problem of the inordinate power and privilege assumed by
particular social functions, resulting in inordinate social inequalities.[79] Note his early explanation of economic crisis (which he erro-
neously assumed to be Marxist): "The oligarchs of capitalism, who
own the productive processes upon which the weal and woe of all
people depend, take too much for themselves out of this process,
depriving the general public, and particularly the worker, of the
consumption power by which the markets for goods are kept open.
Thus capitalism suffers from increasingly serious crises of overpro-
duction, unemployment, and depression."[80] The fundamental economic problem is moral – the excessive greed of self-interested
capitalists – and functional, in that the excessive privileges of ownership result in a maldistribution of wealth which cannot sustain the
necessary consumption capacity of the social masses. In the life cycle
of social organisms, capitalism has outlived its usefulness. It has
become dysfunctional and moribund, and it must be replaced by a
more functional balance of power.[81]

As late as 1939 or 1940 Niebuhr held that this replacement of
capitalism would require the transition to a more socialist political
order, but when it became clear to him that Keynesian policies of
economic regulation and demand management within an expanding
American economy (particularly after World War II) provided the
kind of consumption capacity necessary to mitigate class conflict and
to establish what appeared to be an acceptable equilibrium, Niebuhr
revised his view. Democratic capitalism, he decided, can provide a
functional political equilibrium. Hence the Keynesian compromise
between capital and labour through a politically controlled crisis
management struck him as a pragmatically sound solution.[82] Indeed,
Niebuhr's understanding of the economic crisis from the beginning
as a problem of underconsumption is more compatible with Keynes
than it is with Marx. Of course Niebuhr could not have fully foreseen
that Keynesian policies would contribute largely to subsequent economic and political crises and would foster a culture of consumption
and the flourishing of interest-group liberalism.[83] Nor did he approve
of an economistic vision of "man as consumer" and the "culture of
abundance" created by continual economic expansion.[84] If anyone
did, Niebuhr had a strong sense of the limits of finite human existence
and the dangers of seeking security or fulfilment through material
accumulation alone. He did not see economic expansion and abundance as the ultimate solution to the problems of economic justice:

The original expansion of the economy through an advancing frontier and the subsequent expansion through ever new achievements of technical efficiency have created the illusion of life's unlimited possibilities. Actually human existence is definitely limited, despite its apparently unlimited possibilities. The serenity of man and the sanity of his life with others finally depend upon a wisdom which knows how to come to terms with these limits. This wisdom of humility and charity must be derived from a faith which measures the ends of life in a larger context than that which the immediate desires of man supply.[85]

Niebuhr did not, however, apply to the realm of economic policy this relativization of the quest for economic security by recognizing that there are limits to human domination and control of nature. Although Niebuhr's theological anthropology "thickens" the concept of human agency and social change by attending to the religious dimensions of the human situation – particularly the affective, dispositional, and motivational powers of religious myths – and thereby avoids the dangers of economic reductionism in his own analysis, he universalizes these dimensions in a way that abstracts from their concrete socio-political implications.[86] The rules of the dialectical process of history are dictated in advance as a permanent tension in human nature between the transcendent ideal of harmony and the finite reality of ideological conflict. With such a dualistic anthropology, as I have argued, the only possible ("realistic") politics is one of functional compromise between given competing powers and ideologies. What is missing from Niebuhr's anthropology, as I shall argue in the conclusion to this chapter, is an adequate account of practical reason that can relate the "law of love" in a principled, non-mechanistic way to the concrete order of socio-political existence. What is missing, and what the FCSO sought more consistently to develop, is a social or political theory adequate to orient practical discussions and policy debates on the economy.

THE FELLOWSHIP FOR A CHRISTIAN SOCIAL ORDER

The Fellowship for a Christian Social Order (FCSO), as the name indicates, identified itself more closely than did Niebuhr with the social gospel movement. The FCSO was officially formed in 1934 as a Christian socialist organization which had its roots in the earlier Movement for a Christian Social Order and the Christian Socialist Movement.[87] It was also closely affiliated with the League for Social Reconstruction (LSR), the socialist think-tank which carried out much of the socio-economic research that informed the policy positions of the democratic socialist party in Canada, the Cooperative Commonwealth Federation (ccf). Indeed, several important figures in the fcso – R.B.Y. Scott, Gregory Vlastos, Eugene Forsey, J. King Gordon, and Eric Havelock – were also founding members of the lsr. Eugene Forsey's chapters on economics in the major fcso publication, *Towards the Christian Revolution*,[88] relied heavily on the analysis (to which he also contributed) of the Research Committee for the lsr, published in a volume called *Social Planning for Canada*.[89]

As a Christian socialist movement, the fcso quite explicitly linked itself with the ccf for theological as well as strategic reasons, and it carried on an explicit theoretical dialogue with Marxism. This raised the hackles of a number of American Christian "realists,"[90] among them Reinhold Niebuhr. In his review of *Towards the Christian Revolution*[91] Niebuhr confessed, "The book leaves me deeply troubled." He accused the fcso "radicals" of collapsing proximate political goals into the absolute demands of the gospel: "If these unconditioned demands are merely reduced to a demand for increasing mutuality ... the result is not only a corruption of the historical meaning of the gospel but also an evasion of the actual human situation." For Niebuhr, as we have seen, the religious ideal cannot be found in mutuality or social justice since the fundamental human problem is not found in faulty social organization but in the contradictions of the human self. No social reorganization can address this spiritual problem. The fcso Marxist Christians "falsify the ultimate problem of human spirituality, however correctly they may analyse the mechanics of justice." In linking the quest for political and economic justice with the overcoming of human alienation, they eviscerate the human spirit: "For the mark of man's humanity is the tension in his soul between the eternal and the historical, a tension from which all human creativity comes and which also makes the emergence of evil on every level of social existence inevitable."[92]

In what follows I will contrast the fcso's conception of theological ethics with Reinhold Niebuhr's in order to show why it could enter into a critical dialogue with Marxist theory not only as a (utopian and shallow) form of religion, as Niebuhr interpreted it, but also as a critical analysis of capitalist political economy. Their social understanding of human agency as constituted by the structures, practices, and discourses of particular historical communities leads to a fundamentally different construal of the relationship between religion and social theory than is present in Niebuhr. It is a construal that demands a much more concrete and critical understanding of material socio-historical relations, since these have a religious importance

– they are integral to human self-understanding and rational agency. The approach of the FCSO more closely links revelation and faith to reason and to the theoretical and practical matters of economic policy.

However, I shall also ask whether or to what extent the problems in the social gospel approach – a naïve faith in progress and the possibility of a harmonious integration of individual human fulfilment and the common good in a classless society – recur in the FCSO model. While the FCSO'ers claimed to have recognized and surpassed these flaws in a more realistic religious and social vision,[93] Reinhold Niebuhr attributes to them precisely those illusions as characterized the older social gospel.

Theology and Ethics

Like Niebuhr, the FCSO writers sought to elaborate a religious realism that could overcome evangelical orthodoxy's separation of religion from the social nexus, as well as liberal Christianity's reduction of religion to the realm of piety (Schleiermacher), an autonomous a priori of human consciousness (Troeltsch, Otto), or a social utopia (social gospel). At least they sought to overcome the weaknesses evident in their caricatures of these positions. The former was too dualistic and individualistic, while liberal Protestantism was overly optimistic and romantic regarding human possibilities, espousing an excessively anthropocentric theology.[94] John Line writes: "We need a theology that is more realistic about human possibilities as dependent upon and accountable to the objective constraints and demands of the divine will and order."[95] What is required, argues Line, is an objective theism which discerns the purposes of God in the concrete processes of the actual world, such as Whitehead's conception of God as the "Principle of Concretion" or Henry Nelson Wieman's naturalistic conception of God.

However, we need not turn to Whitehead or to Wieman (or to John Macmurray, whose work greatly influenced the FCSO) in order to amplify the FCSO's conception of God. Such amplification can be found in the writings of the most profound writer in the FCSO itself, Gregory Vlastos. His chapter, "The Ethical Foundations," in *Towards the Christian Revolution* develops a religious ethics which "conceives its Object in moral terms, and is also supremely concerned with the living reality of that Object."[96] Such an objective theological ethics moves beyond the Niebuhrian gap between an ideal "ought" and the existing state of affairs in a way that unites material and spiritual goods, consciousness and activity. It does so by enjoining an absolute loyalty to the purposes of God discerned in the concrete processes of the actual world:

God is not the sum of men's moral ideals. He is the patterned ground of value in the world itself. He is the structure of reality which men must discover and express in their ideas, in order to conform to it in their actions. Moral idealism is the last refuge of anthropomorphism. God is not the Ideal. The Ideal is a partial, fleeting glimpse of God that needs correction, supplementation, revision. It may need to be discarded completely after its work is done for a more authentic, contemporary vision. The first principle of true religion is God's holiness, God's otherness, God's distance from man's ideas and ideals, God's refusal to be comprised within the circle of human consciousness. God's objectivity is his reality in the world of fact. His transcendence of morality is his immanence in history. He manifests his reality by breaking in upon our world of consciousness, resisting our wishes, reversing our judgments.[97]

This lengthy quotation expresses Vlastos' and the FCSO's conception of God as the foundation for a radical religious realism. God makes demands through the particular, concrete structures of the world. Religion is a commitment to something objective, not to inner experience or a supernatural (or transcendental) ideal. The realistic morality of the Gospels is not a timeless ideal or love perfectionism but rather an ethic of love and justice in which actions are recommended by "an historical fitness." Indeed, claims Vlastos, Jesus' ethic of love is more "Marxist" than it is "Hegelian" in that it is historical and seeks to *change* existing beliefs and practices through "fit" praxis rather than merely interpret the world as it is from the standpoint of an eternal ideal.[98] More pertinent, perhaps, given Vlastos' later fame as a Plato scholar, is his contrast between Plato's *Republic* and the Gospels. Whereas Plato's social vision, in Vlastos' view, is "utopian" and his ethic "visionary" rather than "revolutionary," the Gospels emphasize an active ethic of practical love that prepares for the "imminent Kingdom." Whereas Plato's political idealism is rooted in a social and intellectual elitism, Jesus' concern for the common people and his active identification with social outcasts leads to the active pursuit of social egalitarianism.[99]

Here we come upon an initial problem, one suggested by Niebuhr's form of realism. If one seeks to derive a religious ethic from interpretations of historical and natural structures of value and meaning, how can one arrive at a principle by which to criticize existing states of affairs? How does one justify a particular moral action or social program or "religious revolution" as historically fit? We are confronted with the problem of the Archimedean point: How is a realistic religious ethic grounded? Vlastos addresses this problem very differently than Reinhold Niebuhr does, and he criticizes Niebuhr's approach for a residual idealism and individualism that renders it unrealistic. In many respects, Vlastos elaborates his alternative theological anthropology in explicit contradistinction to Niebuhr's model, so it will be helpful to consider Vlastos's critical reviews of Niebuhr's work.

Conceding Niebuhr's stature as an "expert diagnostician of sin," who provides a "terrifyingly true analysis of the spiritual condition of the isolated self,"[100] Vlastos is less impressed by Niebuhr's normative paradoxical model of the human self where anxiety, as the permanent concomitant of freedom, becomes the basis of all human creativity as well as sin. Such an individualist model of human nature, focusing on the inordinate quest for security and the inevitable self-assertion of anxious individuals, is descriptively accurate of contemporary capitalist society, but it cannot be justified as normative. Furthermore, Niebuhr's perfectionist conception of the ideal of love as self-sacrifice is not sufficiently immanent or social to reorient social practices in a way that overcomes distorted forms of community life. A quotation from Schlomo Avineri, commenting on the socialist critique of the individualist model of human existence, helps to elucidate the problem Vlastos raises:

The main difficulty encountered by such an [individualist] hypothesis is that the only possible contacts between individuals behaving according to this model are antagonistic. No human action aimed at solidarity can ultimately be immanently derived from it ... The only way to overcome this lack of solidarity which is the natural consequence of the application of the individualistic model is to add to it a regulatory element. But ... such an element must be external and heteronomous. It will only accentuate the inner contradictions of the initial model.[101]

Reinhold Niebuhr's theological anthropology does not escape the realm of the paradoxical – the normative law of the essential human self remains an "impossible possibility."[102] Actual human nature is defined and evaluated in terms of what it cannot be or do in history. There is no relief from anxiety and its inevitably sinful consequences.

Vlastos singles out two related defects in Niebuhr's anthropology – an isolationist conception of freedom and a perfectionist understanding of love. Vlastos disagrees with the notion that anxiety is a permanent concomitant of freedom and the basis of human creativity. Such a view derives from the classical liberal understanding of freedom as a purely individual possession, a theory of freedom that views all forms of social organization as a sacrifice of liberty. Freedom for classical liberals (and Niebuhr) is the domain of individual sovereignty.[103] The anxiety that inevitably attends this conception of freedom is not a source of creativity but rather a symptom of "the contradiction in which man is involved when denied a basic requirement of his very humanity: community."[104] Far from liberating, anxiety stifles human action and creativity, constricting it into the alienating pursuit of one's own security.

In contrast, a social understanding of human being does not perceive society and the individual as two abstract, contrasting entities that need to be constantly adjusted in a tentative compromise. Freedom and love, no less than justice, are social realities, defined and realized within social relations. When individuals are understood as social beings there can be no radical hiatus between individual self-consciousness (which for Niebuhr is a permanent "given" that lifts persons beyond their communities as a "pinnacle of freedom") and the society to which it relates. Such a hiatus leads inevitably to instrumental social relations and abstract calculi of justice which distort the concrete forms of reciprocity and interdependence that constitute human communities.[105] The problem of freedom requires the establishment of social relations in which persons are treated as members of a community wherein they can best develop their creative capacities together – this is what justice means, and it relates to a common social understanding of the good.

Anxiety is not produced as the result of human spiritual transcendence over material realities, but is the product of the lack of cooperative community. It is not merely a state of consciousness but is related to a material state of affairs. The fundamental problem of contemporary society is a sense of individualistic isolation and the need for community. The human essence is not found in transcendent spiritual freedom but in the freedom and reciprocity of covenant community. When the FCSO'ers speak of prophetic religion they do not speak of a vertical dialectic between transcendent ideal and historical reality but rather – more like the earlier social gospel movement – in terms of covenant community.[106] Prophetic biblical religion, argues R.B.Y. Scott, is a social, ethical, and historical religion "pertaining to men and women as persons rather than as economic units and relating them to one another in a way that also relates them to God."[107] Prophetic biblical religion resists the sharp dichotomy between spiritual and material goods, between individual and society, by focusing on the quality of human relationships, structures, and obligations of common life as defined by social covenant under the sovereignty of God. Freedom understood as individual sovereignty denies the sovereignty of God expressed in the interdependence of all of life. It leads to a moral egocentricity which in turn results in social oppression and the loss of common freedom. Prophetic religion, by contrast, links freedom to justice in such a way that the latter is not understood as an equilibrium of competing egocentric powers, but as fidelity to the shared meanings and obligations of covenant community. Sin in this view is understood as the breakdown of mutuality in community.

A realistic religious ethics, therefore, is grounded not in a transcendent (or transcendental) Archimedean point, but in the quality of human relationships in a historical community. Hence the primary moral norm is mutuality or solidarity, not as a counsel of perfection, but as a necessity for survival in an increasingly interdependent world.[108] The practical moral task is one of reflecting upon and illuminating what is at stake for a community and not just for individuals. As William Connolly puts it: "When civitas is firmly entrenched, one does not have to be a hero to do one's part. It is enough to be a citizen."[109] Vlastos' second criticism of Niebuhr's theological anthropology is that it converts the common need for social solidarity and the mutual reciprocity of community into a perfectionist ideal of love, again conceived in individualistic terms as self-sacrifice. Vlastos does not begin with an abstract human essence inherent in the self-transcendent consciousness of each individual, which cannot be socially or historically modified. Nor therefore does he seek a transcendent ideal which does not and cannot exist in material historical reality and concrete action. Such an impossible ideal, as Niebuhr himself concedes, cannot provide specific guidance in the complex problems of social life. Indeed, such a perfectionist, individualistic ideal can only produce anxiety.

Vlastos proposes an alternative starting point: "Let us look at reality itself and discern its own structure, its own historic direction, its possibilities, its opportunities, its commands."[110] It is to historical, material reality that we must look if we are to perceive the character and purposes of God.[111] And it is in the concrete, interdependent structure of human life in the world that love as mutuality is found as a necessary practical requirement. Love must be rooted in material relations and it can exist only in material activity. It is not an ideal revealed to human consciousness from beyond history. The truth about life is found as well as validated in practical human experience.

This is a very different view of what constitutes realistic faith than we find in Niebuhr. Faith is not linked to an ideal, nor does it transcend history. Faith rather is loyalty to the "living whole" of reality – to its sovereign power, order, and goodness. Vlastos defines faith as follows: "It is the impact of reality upon one's whole being, and the wholeness of one's response. It is the affirmation of reality and willing self-subordination to it … Reality alone is of any account. I must seek to understand it, approach it humbly, reverently, inquiringly, always ready to be transformed and renewed by it."[112] But this view of faith as loyal consent to reality is not a status quo realism which simply accepts things as they are, as naturally given. Vlastos develops a more complex and interactive view of social change and human agency than this, and he does so by elaborating his conception of love as mutuality in community.

In a 1935 article, "What is Love?"[113] Vlastos rejects three alternative definitions of love – as emotion, altruism, and self-interest – in order to specify what he means by love as mutuality. Love as an ethical imperative cannot be reduced to an emotion, since ethics inquires into the objective conditions of the good or the right, and the habits and situations which realize it. For love to be a moral attitude, it must aim at objective ends. Otherwise it is mere sentimental fancy, pathetically detached from reality.

However, this attitude cannot simply be characterized as the opposite of self-interest, as self-sacrifice or altruism. In an obvious though not explicit reference to Reinhold Niebuhr, Vlastos states: "If one approaches love with the idea of self-transcendence, I see nothing to save him from complete cynicism about human nature."[114] Not only is such a view frequently oriented ultimately toward self-realization, but it also fails to specify the nature of the good that one selflessly seeks for the other, or rather others, in one's community. Here the problematic relation between love and justice arises, but finds no satisfactory explanation. Without such an explanation, which an individualistic view of love can never provide, altruism cannot be an adequate ethical attitude.

Love as self-interest seems at first oxymoronic, especially in light of the view of love as self-sacrifice which is so widespread in Christian ethics. But it is the respectable view of many modern utilitarians – enlightened self-interest is the best way to express one's love for the whole community; seeking one's own good contributes to the general good. The problem with this view, as with the preceding one, argues Vlastos, is its conception of the self as always prior to and independent of any constitutive attachments, loyalties, or influences within its social context. Vlastos argues that the self is fundamentally social, constituted within its changing relations. He opposes the understanding of individual persons as complete and autonomous entities who enter into social relations to pursue their (chosen) interests but who are not formed by those relations. Vlastos' understanding of human nature as socially constituted does not preclude deliberation and calculation with regard to relations, but such relations do not only satisfy self-interests. They also entail a process of self-discovery and a changing and, it is hoped, enlarged, identity. It is neither a matter of clinging to an abstract, fixed self nor of completely abandoning the self and its interests. Such narrow conceptions of the self cannot do justice to the rich social concreteness of human experience and the interactive meaning of love as mutuality: "Altruism sacrifices the self; egoism annexes the other. Both do violence to the *relation*, which is essential to love. When A and B come together in mutuality, a new entity is created, which demands the participation of both, yet is more than either alone. New values emerge, which could not possibly exist for A and B in isolation from each other."[115]

Mutuality, in Vlastos' terms, includes cooperative activity in a *community* of interest in the true meaning of interest, the "being between" of human beings. Therefore it entails justice, not negatively understood in terms of mere restraint or the procedural balance of interests, but as the positive rights and duties that mutual relations confer upon their participants. It is not, as Niebuhr has it, that justice must be leavened with love, but that legalism must be tempered with mutuality, sentimentalism with justice. Faith and love are not paradoxically related to reason and justice; these goods are integrally related in the context of real community. Rational calculations of justice cannot *create* a community of interest, but they can help us understand the direction in which our interests and needs converge or expose barriers to such a community. Mutuality, as Vlastos understands it, requires "the justice which makes love possible, and charity unnecessary."[116] Love thus understood is not sentimental nor is it a call either to self-sacrifice or to self-interest. It is a pattern of social relatedness which therefore focuses primarily on objective human relations and the social structures of common life. There can be no hiatus between the ethic of love and the struggle for justice when both are centred on the reality of human community.

The religious realism of the FCSO, then, defines justice and love as "the pattern of human relations that grow out of conscious atoneness with the creative pattern of reality," the divine law of life discerned · in the "intelligible order" of reality.[117] This is "mature religion," a prophetic religion which abjures the egocentric and illusionary "magic religion" of supernaturalistic or otherworldly faith that exempts itself from the ordinary checks of responsible thought and conduct. A mature faith faces the limits of life without fear or the need for consolation, it looks to concrete social and historical processes to discern

God's purposes, and it acts responsibly to choose political strategies that meet the demands of reality. Faith thus defined entails a process of practical moral reason in which reasonable evidence is given for one's purposes, which are pragmatically tested "by their fruits."[118]

Such a religious faith is a "revolutionary" (as opposed to a cynical or status quo) realism insofar as the structure of reality is dynamic, not static, and requires choices on the part of free and responsible moral agents. Human beings are not simply fated by natural or historical processes; they help to shape these processes in an interactive and creative common destiny. Therefore "unreal thinking can have terrible existential reality" when human agency is employed destructively and irresponsibly.[119] Free human actions and decisions have critical and sometimes irrevocable consequences. It is important, then, to be clear here about what is meant by "revolution" and by revolutionary principles for discerning responsible action. Given the concrete social anthropology of the FCSO, the demand for social change must come from an interpretation of socio-historical realities. But in contrast to Marxism, this demand, though mediated in historical crises, is not understood in terms of an epistemological commitment to the economic mode of production (and therefore to a particular economic class). Nor is the revolution anthropocentrically conceived as the quest for Promethean human freedom, the creative mastery of history and nature through a transformed mode of production. Rather the revolution is God-made, "the relentless pressure of a structured order,"[120] and it must be religiously discerned and responded to. Loyalty here is not to a socio-political revolutionary movement or to the proletariat but to the "divine order of value": "Faith means detachment from any segment of reality through attachment to the living whole."[121] Neither class partisanship nor the egocentric pursuit of particular human interests, but love for the good, a supreme and relativising loyalty to the purposes of the sovereign God, makes finite commitments for social change possible and sustainable.[122] A religious loyalty to the one God clears the way for moral consideration of concrete problems that are historically and materially mediated in the contradictions and crises of particular human societies.

Social Theory and Political Economy

The social crisis of the 1930s, argued the FCSO, arose from the structural conditions of class conflict understood both as an economic and as a moral distortion: the objective contradictions between the demands of capitalist development and the requirements of a democratic polity.

Capitalism is directly responsible for the class struggle which has made genuine community impossible and has resulted in a crisis in democracy.[123] Vlastos avers, "The problem is not unconverted capitalists, but ... capitalism. It is the existence of a social structure which breaks from our common life two groups, mutually dependent, yet mutually antagonistic."[124] While the material realities of modern economic practices involve complex relationships of social interdependence and cooperation, the structures of capitalism are oriented toward the protection and growth of private profits according to a market rationality based on maximizing individual interests. The historical crisis grows out of the contradiction between private, autocratic economic decisions of self-interested capitalists (which have a profound public impact), and a democratic polity which recognizes and promotes the right of all citizens to participate in decisions about the allocation and use of public resources. The crisis is therefore not simply a question of inadequate economic demand or "underconsumption" but rather of the collision between capitalist and democratic social relationships and values, a question of the consensual criteria by which to evaluate and justify socio-political and economic choices.

In order to compare and contrast more clearly the the FCSO's social theory with that of Reinhold Niebuhr, the following analysis will follow the same rubrics used in the discussion of Niebuhr's social theory.

Individual and Community. The FCSO theorists held to a social conception of human nature, one in which society and the individual are not two discrete entities that need constantly to be adjusted to one another in an acceptable compromise. Rather than contrast individual and community in abstract terms, the FCSO tried to define community by focusing on the concrete socio-historical relations and identities that define the obligations of persons in community. It is necessary therefore to attend to the complexity of human life in society and to specify its multiple claims, goods, and needs. John Line argues that there is no fixed or given moral pattern of human nature. Human beings are creatures of "mixed tendencies and possibilities" that become determinate or actualized within complex interactive relationships in society.[125] The practical character and institutional forms of these interactive relationships must be analysed and understood if one is to elaborate an adequate anthropology and social theory.

To think of a human being only as an individual requires an act of abstraction from the relationships that give concrete shape to his or her identity, and to think of "society" in structural terms apart from human agents is equally an abstraction. An individual who is not a member of mutual social relationships, argues Vlastos, becomes an abstract object, vulnerable to treatment as a "living instrument," (Aristotle's description of the slave) – a commodity or piece of property to be exchanged in the marketplace, without a truly human identity and therefore without freedom and responsibility. The problem of personality, therefore, is a social problem "of developing the kind of social relations within which men can be persons."[126] Human freedom requires a community that sustains it in appropriate relations of mutual association. Outside community, not obligation but power and violence rule.[127] Indeed, outside community there is neither difference nor individuality, for without a social and historical texture of identity and meaning we confront one another as abstract universals – with equal rights, perhaps, but with no particular needs, claims, and obligations.

Equally important is the fact that not every kind of political society facilitates the development and expression of free persons. Fascist totalitarianism, for example, subordinates persons to an abstract, spiritualized corporate identity based on emotional states of consciousness. Its projection of an ideal, mystical personality and equality based on racial, ethnic, or patriotic solidarity ignores material inequalities and political dominations which prevent the achievement of genuine personality.[128] As Hannah Arendt points out, totalitarian movements are characterised by the organization of masses who lack common interests and specific political or social goals, who lack particular political representation, participation and responsibility. Such movements arose in this century in situations of apathy and even hostility toward public life, produced, as Vlastos also indicates, by the personal isolation and self-sufficient individualism of a competitive and acquisitive society.[129] Destruction of public life leads to isolation and ripens the conditions for ideological distortions of reality, because of the loss of common orientation. In contrast, then, to the individualist subordination of human community to the abstract individual and the totalitarian subordination of human persons to the abstract society, religious realism seeks a "real personality based on material facts of cooperative community."[130]

The religious model of political community appropriated by the FCSO to clarify the relationship of individual and community is that of covenant community.[131] Biblical religion, argue R.B.Y. Scott and Gregory Vlastos, is not otherworldly or magical but an intelligible, reasonable system of human relationships patterned after the moral principles of the common life in covenant community. The concept of covenant is central to the prophetic tradition, in which Jesus stands, and it refers to an agreement upon the conditions of common life that confers dignity, responsibility, and justice to all participants in the community. Each member is a covenanter with God to exercise freely his or her powers of moral and historic agency in a way that contributes to the well being of the community and its destiny. Human dignity entails the capacity for ethical self-determination guided by insight into the meaning and requirements of community relationships and destiny. But to expect responsible discernment and action from community members presupposes certain *conditions* of dignity and freedom in society, presupposes justice. And these conditions of justice are not understood in terms of abstract universal principles, but in terms of the sovereignty of the covenant community through the agreement of its members to fulfil their particular obligations to one another in relationships of mutuality.

In this rich idea of covenant community, Vlastos argues, it is possible to discern the religious foundations of the meaning of democracy as a normative social system.[132] It remains to spell out the implications of this idea for modern social theory and ethics as the FCSO understood them.

Democracy and Justice. In his *Journal of Religion* articles on "The Religious Foundations of Democracy," it is clear that in Vlastos' view, fraternity is foundational for both liberty and equality in a democratic society. A non-fraternal conception of human freedom leads to the liberal individual notion of atomistic individual autonomy and a formal, contractarian view of social relationships.[133] Such a "negative" view of freedom in terms of "non-interference"[134] is generally linked in the classical liberal political theorists to a strong doctrine of private property as the asylum of freedom from external – that is, state – interference and control. Liberty here becomes identified with the economic liberty of a "free market" capitalist society, a freedom, Vlastos argues, fundamentally at odds with democratic values and practices.

A fraternal conception of political liberty, in contrast, requires a "positive" view of freedom in which the powers of human agency and self-determination are sustained by a certain kind of political community, one that entails "self-government." Democratic freedom, in this view, does not affirm the claim to individual sovereignty, which leads to the isolation and moral egocentricity of individuals and ultimately to social oppression and injustice since it denies the interdependence of all life. Rather, democratic freedom, if it is to preserve social justice as the obligations of persons to one another in the fraternal structures of interdependence in the community, must incorporate in some form the idea of popular sovereignty. The practical meaning of democratic freedom is not the egocentric pursuit and maximization of individual interests and utilities but the fraternal pursuit and development of the corporate destiny of one's community. Vlastos puts it this way: "This is personal freedom grounded in solidarity. Negatively, it is man's freedom from self, from personal vanity, fear, and self-pity, because of a concern infinitely larger than self concern ... Positively this is freedom through participation in a community whose values exist only that they may be shared."[135] Political liberty, thus understood, is not the possession of abstract individuals in isolation from all attachments and loyalties, but the freedom and responsibility of persons as members of the community who share its common life and participate in its meaning and destiny.

The logic of "fraternal freedom" in this conception of democratic justice, argues Vlastos, has been deflected by the power of private property in a capitalist political economy. If freedom is related to the practical quality of our relations of social interdependence, to our participation as members of the community in contributing to the common destiny, then a purely "negative" understanding of freedom, defined primarily in terms of private ownership, will be untenable and indeed dangerous. The latter defines human agency in abstraction from the network of social relationships and concentrates instead on formal contracts between autonomous individuals. It understands the principles and duties of citizenship and authority in purely procedural terms rather than inquiring into the substantive, material requirements of the common life. Justice is then a matter of rights rather than a question of the goods to be preserved or realized together. Hence property comes to be seen as a claim to independence from the community and its claims, rather than the medium through which we are related to others in complex networks of interdependence. This violates the reality of reciprocity in human society. In the participatory model of democracy the FCSO elaborated, justice must be understood in terms of the claims of community membership upon socio-economic arrangements. Otherwise social meanings and obligations will always be imposed by those with the most power rather than mutually recognized and affirmed by a community of responsible (and therefore free) citizens who together discern and decide upon the needs of the common life. Freedom therefore requires a language of the goods that may be chosen, a language that expresses common needs and obligations.

This leads to the second principle of democratic justice, which too must be grounded in fraternity: equality.[136] Equality must be linked with human dignity, but for Vlastos this cannot be understood solely in terms of a spiritual possession, as otherworldly religion understands it in order to console those who suffer the indignities of gross inequality in this life.[137] Nor can it be understood in terms of natural endowment. It is only with reference to responsible moral agents in the context of concrete social relationships, needs, and obligations, as members of particular communities, that the claims of equality and human dignity can be meaningfully specified. This signals an important difference between charity, which responds to social needs out of its own largesse, and justice, which addresses human needs out of an obligation to the moral structures that sustain the community. And this is not merely an attitudinal difference but a practical matter concerning those claims which are included and excluded from attention in the structures (institutions and practices) of social justice. The very meaning of democracy is undermined when attention is not paid to material relationships of interdependence that deny or exclude in practical terms the membership of certain persons or groups in the community. Yet this is precisely what occurs in modern capitalist political economy, and it is this contradiction that lies at the heart of the social crisis.

However, before turning to a more explicit discussion of the FCSO's views on political economy, I wish to suggest that in contrast to Reinhold Niebuhr, the FCSO conception of democracy can best be described in terms of the model of "participatory democracy."[138] In this view, democracy is not primarily a set of procedures presided over by an "umpire" state that regulates the actions of self-interested individuals and groups in an acceptable balance of powers, a tolerable compromise between freedom and equality. Such a formal, contractarian conception of democracy is not compatible with the notion of "covenant community" that grounds the FCSO's view. Covenant entails the act of *promising*, not simply to obey rules in exchange for protection or security, but to assume voluntarily the obligations of citizenship within a community that is judged to enable its members to contribute creatively and responsibly to the commonwealth. An instrumental, vertical relationship of formally free and equal individuals to the regulative state does not characterize democratic citizenship, rather the development of capacities for political judgment of the needs and possibilities of the particular society in which one lives is its base. Therefore, as J. King Gordon and Eric Havelock argued, one of the primary requirements in the creation of a new democratic society is education in the responsibilities of citizenship.[139]

The participation model of democracy, as Carole Pateman and others have shown, demands a broader definition of the "political."[140]

It must attend to the claims made by community membership upon all public social arrangements, in recognition of mutual interdependence and the conditions of democratic "belonging." Participatory democracy focuses on democratic culture or society understood as a complex set of intersubjective relationships sustained by shared meanings and common goods and purposes – not merely a system of government. The responsibilities of citizenship are understood not only as "vertical" but as "horizontal," mediated within the whole network of social relationships and associations, not merely by a neutral governing state. Responsible social and political action therefore depends on the whole range of public social institutions within which people act. In order to make responsible collective decisions, participatory institutions involve and thereby educate their members in decision-making and in the need to take into account a variety of factors and considerations that go beyond the mere calculation of individual interests and desires. Human capacities, in this view, are not pre-given but are developed socially and historically through participation in particular human societies.

And it is in the economic realm, most participatory theorists argue, that one finds the greatest barrier to social democracy in liberal capitalist societies. Like Marx, the FCSO seeks to expose the political interests at stake in economic practices, thus undermining the liberal separation of politics and economics, and (here perhaps unlike Marx) attempting to extend democracy into the economic domain. The authoritarian prerogatives of property ownership are called into question when economic transactions are placed into the context of covenant justice. Property relations must be understood as materially mediated relations between persons, not merely the exchange of reified commodities.[141] Property ownership of the means of production is therefore a form of political power which in a capitalist economy involves the authoritarian control over those who lack access to productive property except through the sale of their labour power. People are treated as commodities rather than as moral agents, which is a violation of their dignity as members of the community. This results in a class struggle which undermines communal solidarity as people – in accordance with the possessive individualist logic of capitalist economic practices – seek their own material interests by manipulating public rules, procedures, and institutions for private purposes.

Exploitation is inherently and intolerably immoral, because it is a denial of the primary imperative of the community. It transforms the worker's very fulfilment of that imperative, his giving, into its frustration by denying him the conditions of the most creative giving: that is, giving to the whole community rather than to a private master; giving freely rather than under compulsion; and giving with fullest development of his creative capacities rather than with a stunted, impoverished, terrorized personality. Thus it sins against the worker because it sins against the holy interdependence of life. It builds upon interdependence in order to destroy interdependence.[142]

Political Economy. Like the Reinhold Niebuhr of the 1930s, the FCSO locates the primary symptom of the modern social crisis in class struggle. But in contrast to Niebuhr's functionalist analysis, which focuses on the permanent problem of social *stability* and counsels an equilibrium of competing powers, the FCSO attends more to the material and institutional practices of capitalism, which are viewed as constitutive causes – not mere occasions – of the crisis. The fundamental problem, according to the FCSO, is not the excessive greed of capitalists but the capitalist mode of production which commodifies human labour in a non-reciprocal relationship of domination in the economic sphere and therefore undermines the mutual reciprocity of covenant community. Capitalism violates the very meaning of justice in a democratic society, namely the free (voluntary) and equal interaction of persons in cooperative, publically accountable social relationships.

Eugene Forsey, in his chapter in *Towards the Christian Revolution* titled "The Economic Problem," argues that we must begin by understanding the nature of the capitalist economic system. The first thing to note is that "capitalist industry does not exist to supply needs; it exists to make profits."[143] This is endemic to the logic of capitalism, and it results in a certain kind of economic agency – the maximization of profits by increasingly monopolistic corporations. The problem here, suggests Forsey, is not concentration of control, which is inevitable in modern industrial society, but the lack of public accountability in private ownership. An ever-smaller number of capitalists engage in economic planning for the whole society in such a way that their interests are served – for example, through planned scarcity – at the expense of social needs, such as jobs and goods. The resultant growing inequalities of wealth and income generate class conflict and socio-economic crisis.

Both Forsey and J. King Gordon point out that it is at this point – in post-laissez-faire, monopolistic capitalism – that the role of the state in economic life becomes crucial. Gordon states: "As the crisis deepens it becomes more and more apparent that the state stands torn between the demands of private industry, the very existence of which depends upon the making of a margin of profits, and the claims of the great mass of the people who expect from the state the guarantee of at least a minimum of social security."[144] This signals a crisis in democracy, and the FCSO presents the dilemma in terms of a choice between capitalism and socialism, arguing that only the latter can preserve democracy in the true sense. We may recall here that Reinhold Niebuhr in his early work offered a similar view of the social crisis, but revised it when the "Keynesian revolution" appeared to provide a compromise between capital and labour in an expanding welfare state. It is impossible to provide a fair comparison between Niebuhr and the FCSO on their responses to Keynesianism, since the FCSO writings are pre-Keynesian. But a few relevant observations can be made. Clearly state provision of economic security for all citizens was an important concern for the FCSO and a central reason for moving toward socialized economic planning.[145] They also sought to elaborate reformist rather than "revolutionary" (in the political sense) strategies for social change through the channels of parliamentary democracy. In this sense the FCSO resembled the earlier social gospel movement, and perhaps helped pave the way for the "Keynesian compromise" in an industrial welfare state.

However, it is also important to notice the stated reasons for Forsey's rejection of the "controlled capitalism" represented by U.S. New Deal policies on the one hand and state-capitalist public ownership on the other. Simply to call for the intervention of government in economic life, or even the "nationalization" of existing corporate monopolies so that they become state regulated, is a dangerous form of idealism that can easily play into the hands of fascism. "The idealist is so enchanted by the phrase 'state control' that it never occurs to him to inquire into the material nature of the control or the material ends which it actually serves."[146] Forsey insists that under the constraints of capitalism, the strongest interests remain capitalist interests, since they control the means of production and thus preserve themselves as the dominant class. Social democratic reform cannot mean reform of capitalism, the material dynamics of which will inevitably generate new crises. The state, in a capitalist society, will simply enforce the reproduction of the class structure and class relations, perpetuating an ambiguous and incomplete form of democracy.[147] Nor, in Forsey's view, does the "cooperative movement" offer a third way between capitalism and socialism, since cooperatives can neither fight the superior power and resources of monopoly capital in market competition nor compete in the management of heavy industries and public utilities in a capitalist society.[148] The cooperative movement does not effectively address the class structure and conflict in capitalist society and can therefore be too easily coopted by capitalist institutions. No, "This generation seeketh after a sign, and there shall be no sign given it but the sign of the prophet Marx."[149]

Although the FCSO disagreed with Marx's revolutionary strategy for social change and his epistemological totalization of the economic paradigm for social theory, it was generally convinced that the Marxist critique of political economy is correct and that only a socialist society could overcome the material contradictions of capitalist society. The Depression period had its radicalizing effects, and socialism had not yet been tarred with the Stalinist brush. Socialism – though it entailed the nationalization of monopolistic industries and the establishment of a comprehensive national economic plan – meant neither state-capitalist public ownership nor the confiscation of industries, the nationalization of farmland, or the operation of industry by civil servants.

Socialized industries would in fact be administered not by government departments but by responsible autonomous boards of directors – appointed by the government (probably from panels drawn up by the trade unions, technicians' associations and the cooperatives), carrying out a policy defined in its general lines by the community and answerable to the community for the results; but free within the limits of the national plan to conduct the management with a single eye to efficiency, free from what we ordinarily call "political" interference, patronage and the like.[150]

CONCLUSION

It is not necessary for our purposes to engage in a detailed analysis of the economic policy proposals of the FCSO, which are basically in line with the League for Social Reconstruction and its comprehensive plan for a democratic socialist society outlined in *Social Planning for Canada*.[151] But it is important here to reflect on how and why the FCSO appropriated Marxist social analyses to develop their economic policy proposals (in contrast to Reinhold Niebuhr) and on the consequences of this.

First, the FCSO share to some extent Marx's anthropology of what Schlomo Avineri calls "social man,"[152] that is, a radically interactive view of the relationship between individual and society. Particular human identities are constituted through participation in social, political and historical realities. People's ideas and actions are shaped (though not rigidly determined) by their relationships to others in society and to nature. Given the interdependence and reciprocity of these relationships, their mediation through totalitarian structures or institutions of domination violates the social nature of humanity and reduce human agents – in the case of capitalism, human workers – to instrumental means for alien purposes. Private ownership of the means of production entails such an alienating institution of economic domination, and it leads to widespread inequalities, the systematic suppression of the development of creative human capacities, and a bitterly conflictual class struggle. Like Marx, the FCSO opposed what they took to be ahistorical anthropological models, models that reify the acquisitive notions of freedom and possessive individualism of liberal capitalist societies as normative human nature,[153] and then adopt moralistic reformism as the only "realistic" form of political action. A change in social relationships will entail a change in what is normative for human action, since human nature is not an abstract or eternally fixed "given" but is significantly affected by the concrete ensemble of socially and historically constituted relations. Hence a critical understanding of material, socio-historical relations – which in capitalist society are organized around economic forces and relations of production – will have a strategic implication. It will affect how people understand their context, and consequently, how they will act within and upon it.

Unlike most forms of Marxism, the FCSO abandons the narrowly economistic view of historically invariant material interests, arguing only that in modern capitalist democracies it is the objective contradiction between the capitalist project for society and the democratic vision of society that constitutes the locus of the social crisis and that demands a choice. There is an important sense, however, in which the FCSO succumbs uncritically to Marxist revolutionary or utopian aspirations and thereby stumbles into a social gospel pitfall. While the FCSO, with its theocentric religious ethic, attempts to overcome the ethnocentrism, immanentism, and liberal idealism of the social gospel's view of history, it nevertheless retains a residual anthropocentric utilitarianism in its view of nature. Most explicitly and naïvely expressed in Eric Havelock's writing, but also present in various ways in the work of John Line, Gregory Vlastos, and Eugene Forsey, there is the notion of overcoming the constraints of and struggle with the forces of nature so as to achieve collective human purposes in a culture of abundance. In transforming the capitalist "planning for scarcity" into a socialist "planning for abundance"[154] by overcoming the obstacle of socio-economic injustice, the free spiritual life of humanity in fellowship can be attained.[155] The benefits of modern technology (currently blocked or diverted only to the oligarchic few by capitalist economic organization) could be appropriated to serve higher human goods if only they were controlled by the community in structures of democratic accountability.[156] Citizens of such a society could then turn their primary attention from material production and accumulation (the brute animal concern for security) to the cultivation of creative human goods and capacities that enrich the common social and cultural life.[157] Gregory Vlastos articulates the anthropological assumptions behind this perspective:

First of all, let us be perfectly clear that human equality has nothing to do with inequalities of natural endowment. Hereditary inequalities belong to the level of fate; personal equality belongs to the level of freedom. Man's heredity is, strictly speaking, a zoological fact. His freedom has absolutely nothing to do with determining it. It is sheer fate. It belongs to the same category as a landslide or a thunderbolt. In relation to such facts as these, man does not behave with his full powers as man. His power of self-determination, which is his unique and distinctive possession, is not involved ... Only when his power of self-determination comes into play does he behave as a fully human entity. This does happen in the field of moral conduct.[158]

It is one thing to argue for a conception of citizenship and social membership in which distributive equality and genuine equality of participation and opportunity goes beyond inequalities of natural endowment (however that be understood). Judgments about relations of reciprocity and mutual indebtedness in a community-oriented conception of human needs and action (rather than grounded in individual rights or on one's economic productivity) are far more difficult to quantify than those same needs commodified in market exchange.[159] But it is quite another matter to make the claim that human freedom *qua* human has nothing to do with natural determinations. Vlastos seems to be dangerously close to attributing god-like powers to human freedom to overcome natural constraints; indeed that only by such a radical freedom are we truly human. This no doubt explains in part his enthusiasm for the liberating possibilities of modern technologies when controlled by a cooperative, democratic community.[160]

To believe that human beings are not merely creatures of fate but also in some sense creators of their destiny is of course necessary if one is to affirm human freedom and moral agency. But it is equally necessary to recognize the limitations of that freedom precisely because human beings exist in relationships of mutual interaction and interdependence, not only with other human beings, but also with nature in the larger order of creation. And nature in itself – as Vlastos' own putative theocentric vision should be able to recognize – does not necessarily or primarily serve human purposes. A situated freedom, not only in relation to one's historical, cultural, and social identity and context but also in relation to nature in general, is truly human freedom. The context within which human beings have the freedom to think and act fittingly or unfittingly, realistically or unrealistically, is not only the horizon of historical societies, but also of nature. This will affect the way in which issues of political economy are considered. The productivist paradigm – the domination of nature for human purposes and the proliferation of material needs – that lies behind the FCSO's anthropology is itself in need of critical attention.

As I pointed out above, Reinhold Niebuhr criticized the FCSO for linking the quest for political and economic justice with the overcoming of human alienation. I have also indicated that Niebuhr's theological anthropology produces an important awareness of the limitations of all human historical and technological achievements. Does his approach here provide a corrective to FCSO illusions? In my view it does not. Niebuhr's primary criticism is that the FCSO "Marxist Christians" do not do justice to the true, trans-historical essence of human life and thus they "eviscerate the human spirit." They attribute too much to material history and not enough to the transcendent orientation of the human spirit, thus losing the permanent tension in the human soul between the ideal and the historical that constitutes the paradoxical meaning of human existence. Niebuhr's focus remains too rooted in a dualistic account of the human self. I believe the productivist paradigm could be relativized within the FCSO's own theocentric religious vision by including nature within its purview of significant interdependent interactions. God, in such a view, would be understood to be present not only in the sphere of human interaction in history and society but also in the limiting constraints and inner goods of the natural world (not only its creative possibilities for human self-realization). To discern this, however, would require an understanding of the *imago Dei* of human beings from within a more adequate theology of creation. Such a realism, as I will try to show more fully in the concluding chapter, would require some considerable revision of anthropology and of social and political theory.

Let us reflect briefly on this issue in conclusion to this chapter. I have tried to argue that the FCSO's religious social theory provides an important alternative to Niebuhrian realism in addressing economic issues. The FCSO recognized, through their socio-historical analyses of North American capitalist democracies, that economic rationality constricts public choices into the political pursuit of short-term, self-interested material gain and that this undermines democratic culture, a substantive long-term vision of the common good. They recognized that these cannot coexist harmoniously in a stable compromise or equilibrium, but that at some point a political decision must be made between these contrasting visions of society, human agency, and "reality." Finally, they recognized that this is not a permanent tension pregiven in the structure of human nature, but rather a socio-historical development that can be changed – changed not into the kingdom of God on earth, but at least toward a less crisis-ridden political economy in which both particular and more general needs can be addressed in a democratically accountable community of moral discourse.

There is in the FCSO's view a highly interactive relationship between religion and social theory or practical reason as our interpretations, commitments, loyalties, and practices are constantly revised and expanded by the "real" claims of other persons or communities, and of philosophical, historical, and scientific analyses we have hitherto ignored or failed to see. Such a religious understanding gives priority to the elaboration of a public practical discourse about the common good rather than to a utilitarian compromise between an inner religious ideal and the conflictual realities of external political morality. The FCSO gets beyond the language of "ideals" that is too easily reified either in terms of a particular conception of the kingdom of God on earth or of the human self. What is at stake here is precisely the construal of reality to which persons in community must respond, and here religious faith and public reason cannot be separated – both are relational and community centred, both involve loyalties and commitments. This is not an attempt to elaborate an Archimedean point, nor does it employ a religious ideal which comes from beyond the social and historical processes of human culture. Rather it is the historically and culturally mediated movement toward an expanding community of being – and here we have noted an important deficiency in the FCSO approach, namely that its view of community lacks an adequate account of the human relation to nature within a larger order of creation – which orients human identity and action, and which must be taken into account in the setting of political economic priorities and policies.

What is lacking in both forms of Christian realism is an adequate theology of creation, and this prevents them from being able to discern the inner meaning of nature and the proper or fitting human place within it. Niebuhr and the FCSO both see "spirit" as the exclusive possession of human beings – for Niebuhr the vertical relation of the self-transcendent self to the supernatural divine ideal, for the FCSO the socially and historically mediated purposes of God discerned in covenant community. In the case of Niebuhr, the whole immanent "outer" or material realm of nature is therefore conceded to the modern sciences, to power politics and technological develop-ment, to the pragmatic calculations of a purely technical reason. Spiritual meaning and truth is not mediated by nature in a manner accessible to historical reason, but comes from beyond nature and history in the transcendent, "religious" realm of the spirit present only to the faith of individual moral subjects who exist amid an impersonal, value-neutral world of powers and things. In the case of the FCSO, the spiritual subject is rooted in community and its rela-tions, leading to a more participatory and positive conception of public reason as rooted for its meaning in the historically mediated purposes of God. However, here too the *imago Dei* of human nature is too narrowly construed in terms of the socially constituted pur-poses of human beings who use nature instrumentally to fulfil them. There must be a larger framework of meaning and accountability than community or democratic society if human beings are to under-stand themselves in relation to the divine purposes for creation and are to mediate those purposes in history. Moral considerations and judgments must be grounded in response to the divine purposes throughout the whole order of creation. History, in fact, represents the ongoing human search for and response to this divinely created meaning.

The modern "social crisis" is in the first place not economic or political but "spiritual" – a failure to understand the vocation of human beings in creation. The problem of social order and the common good is a spiritual matter not discerned so long as one is oriented toward the external power struggles of those whose only aim is to conquer and control reality for their own purposes. The true nature of political and economic reality can be discerned only by those who look beyond their own interests and the immediacy of social forces to the invisible yet present divine order of creation. There is no external political substitute for the rightly ordered spirit. Politics and justice are therefore not merely a matter of the pragmatic man-agement of external forces (in a power struggle or "balance of power" or technological domination of nature) but rather the practical medi-ation of divine wisdom that binds the world together in a meaningful order.

4 Human Dignity and Labour: The Catholic Bishops and Economic Policy

In recent years Roman Catholic bishops in North America have added their widely publicized voices to the growing choir of ethicists who seek to contribute to public debates on ethics and economics. This is both admirable and courageous, for although this choir boasts many skilled voices, there is little harmony among them. Given the breakdown of the postwar "Keynesian consensus" in the face of economic recessions and the simultaneous rise of inflation and unemployment, a variety of competing theoretical and ideological positions have arisen to interpret and address the situation. The bishops of Canada and the u.s. have entered this polyphonic setting with the claim, not to resolve the technical debates on how the economy works, but to sound the principal moral themes that ought to guide and inform those debates if there is to be social harmony and economic justice.

My analysis of the Canadian bishops will attend primarily to the statement issued in January 1983 by the Episcopal Commission for Social Affairs of the Canadian Conference of Catholic Bishops (cccb), "Ethical Reflections on the Economic Crisis." When examining their policy proposals, I will also refer to the cccb's more recent "A Statement on Social Policy." My interpretation of the u.s. bishops will focus on the final draft of their pastoral letter: National Conference of Catholic Bishops (nccb), *Economic Justice For All: Pastoral Letter on Catholic Social Teaching and the u.s. Economy.*

In making the transition from Protestant social ethics to Catholicism, it will be necessary to chart briefly the distinctive theological ethical tradition of Catholic social teaching in the past century. I shall argue that while the Canadian and u.s. bishops share the same basic model of religious ethics (the grounding norm of human dignity in community, leading to the principles of the preferential option for the poor and the dignity of human labour), the concrete ethical positions and policy proposals they adopt differ significantly due to their distinctive social theories and economic analyses. While the statements of both Canadian and u.s. bishops employ the language of economic "crisis," their understandings of what this means, of how to interpret and address it, diverge.[1] Whereas the Canadian statement deploys a more radical social democratic discourse, the u.s. bishops end by implicitly supporting a liberal corporatist position – so I shall argue. However, beyond these important differences, both documents share an optimism about economic growth and productivity that is rooted quite obviously in a liberal understanding of the human good tied to the more traditional theological anthropological language of *imago Dei*. This provides, in my view, an implicit religious legitimation for the modern domination of nature, a principle vital to the expansionist ethos of advanced industrial societies and the North American dream of unlimited prosperity for all.

ROMAN CATHOLIC SOCIAL TEACHING

Both the Canadian Conference of Catholic bishops (cccb) and the u.s. National Conference of Catholic bishops (nccb) begin with the assertion that their concerns about the economy are not based primarily on specific political considerations or economic theories but are religiously rooted in "fundamental gospel principles" as interpreted within the Catholic social tradition.[2] These are, first, a "preferential option for the poor, the afflicted and the oppressed," and second, an affirmation of the "special value and dignity of human work in God's plan for creation."[3] The first principle is prophetic, in that it identifies with the marginalized victims of social injustice, seeks to expose unjust attitudes and structures, and supports the need for social change. The second principle is taken from the *imago Dei* theology of the Catholic tradition, in that it affirms human participation in creation through work as the source of human dignity. Although they appear within different theological, ethical, and social frameworks, both principles are fundamental to the Catholic social tradition of the twentieth century, and it is helpful to consider the North American statements in the context of that tradition.

The main features and developments of the Catholic social tradition have been well documented,[4] and a comprehensive analysis of the documents comprising that tradition is beyond the scope of this study. However, it is important to note here those major themes and shifts in the theological bases and socio-economic assumptions of the tradition that are most relevant to the statements under consideration in this chapter. The earlier documents, beginning with Pope Leo XIII's *Rerum Novarum*, are rooted more firmly in a neo-scholastic reading of the classical natural law tradition, where the human dignity of the *imago Dei* is preeminently expressed in the rational capacity of human beings to know the fundamental structures of human existence and to dispose of natural resources in a manner that serves their own basic needs and those of the common good. Hence the insistence on the inviolable right of private property, for "man precedes the State" and all other material and temporal institutions[5] – human beings must have the right to dispose of the products of their own labour, since all things are oriented toward rational human control. However, this personalist principle (rooted in the spiritual primacy of persons) is quite different from liberal individualism, since persons and their property are oriented by nature and the objective, rational principles of justice toward the common good (*Rerum Novarum*, 14ff.; *Quadragesimo Anno*, 81, 87).

In these early encyclicals, the fundamental socio-economic problem (and both Leo XIII in 1891 and Pius XI in 1931 addressed situations of economic crisis)[6] is understood in terms of disorder, especially as manifested in the class conflict between labour and capital. And the disorder is interpreted primarily in moral terms, as the reduction of spiritual persons to material ends in both capitalism and socialism. Liberal capitalism breeds an unrestrained competitiveness between self-interested individuals that concentrates economic power in the hands of a few, undermines the common good, and violates the spiritual dignity of persons who are used as instruments to serve selfish material interests. But the proposed solutions of socialism are even more reprehensible, since they violate the natural order itself. Both Leo and Pius emphasize the dignity of *imago Dei* in human persons in the development of human powers through the rational disposal of natural, material resources in the service of personally determined needs or ends. Hence the moral inviolability of the right of private property, which socialism undermines in its call for the socialization of the means of production. Furthermore, human spiritual dignity is repudiated in principle by the materialist dialectic of socialism, which leads to a disordered strategy for social change through class struggle and to the "confusion" between political (state) and economic (market) realms.

Both popes seek the reestablishment of a harmonious common good through the application of natural law principles and the reform of Christian morality. Leo argues that there is a "natural harmony" between labour and capital, which will be realized if all people fulfil their mutual duties and obligations to one another as prescribed by the judicial order upheld by the state (the "guardian" of the common good). In Leo's view, while all people have an equal spiritual dignity, their social and economic roles and status – contra democratic liberalism – are not and cannot be equal. And since human nature is permanent, it is necessary to recognize and accept these inequalities as unchanging in an orderly organic hierarchy, which is meliorated by "Christian attitudes" of charity (especially by the rich) and cooperative acceptance of one's role (especially by the poor). However, there are also certain fundamental rights backed by the state. While private property is a basic right, workers must also be given a just or "living" wage, so that they too can acquire the basic necessities for themselves and their families. Indeed, in this way the concentration of economic power and ownership can be broken down as workers are enabled to purchase more property for themselves. Workers are also to be given the right to form associations in which they improve their lot, not through strikes and confrontations, but through education and character-building.

The role of the state in this is to judicially oversee the common good. This means that the state ought to stay out of the economic realm as a direct actor, although it can legislate workers' rights and thus protect the weak. It can also intervene, if necessary, in order to correct injustice, but never through the expropriation of private property, and only if persons or smaller groups cannot accomplish it by themselves (according to the principle of subsidiarity). The role of the church is the renewal of Christian spirit and moral values, without which there can be no "cure" of social disorder. Thus the economic crisis is above all to be viewed as a moral failure due to the abandonment of belief in God and spiritual values, and both Leo XIII and Pius XI call for a re-Christianization of the culture.

Pope Pius XI's proposals in *Quadragesimo Anno* reflect a theological perspective that is similar to Pope Leo XIII's, but there is present in the former a more dynamic understanding of social anthropology which leads to a greater openness to democracy and institutional social change. Rather than calling for the entrenchment of a hierarchical and paternal state, Pius proposes a "third way" between capitalist individualism and socialist totalitarianism: a Christian "corporatism" in which people are organized into workers' guilds or vocational groups and pursue their interests cooperatively under the supervision of a neutral state.

The social encyclicals of Pope John XXIII, notably *Mater et Magistra* and *Pacem in Terris*, retain the natural law foundation for socio-economic ethics, but with some important changes from *Rerum Novarum* and *Quadragesimo Anno*. In contrast to the hierarchical paternalism of Leo XIII and the abstract "corporatism" of Pius XI's "third way," John XXIII's understanding of human dignity and its social ethical implications is more concretely developed, with an awareness of the social and structural nature of human dignity and the common good (*Mater et Magistra*, 65). Pope John also recognizes that human institutions and social orders are subject to historical change, and that a growing global interdependence has rendered social relations more complex. Leo's organic hierarchical society in which politics and economics are rigidly separated is no longer relevant in a global situation where economic and technological development are inextricably linked to political concerns. Nor is human dignity viewed merely as a spiritual reality unrelated to one's social location. In John's view, human nature is fundamentally social and human dignity must therefore be concretely specified in a social structural way. He consequently advocates the formation of intermediary bodies, not only to cultivate Christian morals, but to create "true community" in which all persons are encouraged to participate (*Mater et Magistra*, 91ff.; *Pacem in Terris*, 31). In *Pacem in Terris*, he goes on to argue that the fundamental moral norm of intrinsic human dignity implies a series of natural human rights and duties that address the whole range of personal, social, and institutional relationships. Furthermore, although the created moral order and its principles of justice are permanent and absolute, these must continually be adapted to the changing social and economic conditions within which human dignity is concretely defined and realized (*Pacem in Terris*, 37–8).

John XXIII also adds a fourth fundamental moral norm – freedom – to the traditional norms of justice, charity, and truth. It is in this value that he seeks to retain the truth in Leo XIII's dictum that "man precedes the State" (*Rerum Novarum*, 6) – that people have the right to the self-development of their capacities and powers. Pope John applies this not only to individuals, families, and smaller groups within society, but also to nations, and especially those less developed than Western nations (*Mater et Magistra*, 151ff.). In his perspective, then, the traditional principle of subsidiarity, which recognizes the fundamental right of private property and the need to avoid state totalitarianism, must be supplemented with a stronger claim for "socialization," in which human self-development proceeds by way of cooperation on a large scale and therefore often requires the intervention of the state in socio-economic affairs. Indeed such intervention is demanded by the comprehensive specification of human rights and duties overseen by the state in the new global situation. Pope

John's proposed solution for the economic problem, which he understands to be an international structure of disparity, generally accords with a Western model of economic development through the generosity of the rich and attention to economic efficiency within a gradualist and cooperative model of social change.

Despite this growing awareness of the social, structural, and dynamic character of human nature, the basic elements of natural law theology and ethics persist. The assumption that objective and universal norms of justice and equity are self-evident to all "people of good will" who reflect upon the natural created order appears throughout these encyclicals and is most clearly expressed in the early paragraphs of *Pacem in Terris*. An organic understanding of the common good, rooted in natural harmony and cooperation, expresses itself in calls to responsibility and the proper use of reason to solve the imbalances and injustices of the social order (*Mater et Magistra*, 80, 163ff.; *Pacem in Terris*, 85, 93). The process of social renovation and reconstruction is not conflictual or revolutionary, but a gradual betterment of human institutions from within, in "evolution through concord" (*Pacem in Terris*, 162).

I shall argue that some crucial elements of the social theory present in the preceding documents are also present in the proposals of Pope John Paul II and the u.s. Catholic bishops. But first it is necessary to point out a shift in the theological assumptions grounding Catholic social ethics heralded by the Vatican II document, *Gaudium et Spes*, and further developed in the social encyclicals of Pope Paul VI. *Gaudium et Spes* seeks to address all people, not in the light of universal reason or natural law, but "in the light of Christ" (10). Human dignity is found in the *imago Dei*, that is, "all things on earth should be related to man as their center and crown" (12), but human nature and society are not unequivocally constituted and known – divisions, conflicts, and mysteries are present (10, 12ff.). Therefore human being in all its dimensions can only be illuminated with reference to Christ, the "new man" in whom the *imago Dei* is historically and ontologically perfected and fulfilled (22, 38, 41). Hence it is "by virtue of the gospel" that "the church proclaims the rights of man" (41), not by virtue of natural law or universal reason. Because humanity is recognized as sinful and also as a fundamental mystery known in various dimensions through the variety of sciences employing different methods, reason itself can no longer be considered univocal. Not only is there a plurality of legitimate sciences, there is also a plurality of cultural contexts in which human beings come to know and define themselves. As a result, *Gaudium et Spes* appeals to Christ as the only adequate interpretive key to human nature, thus grounding a "Christocentric humanism" by which to approach various issues and situations in dialogue with the sciences and with the cultural milieu.

The Christological unity of love of God and love of neighbour also reveals the social character of human nature, and *Gaudium et Spes* closely correlates personal development and destiny with the development of social structures and institutions (25). This incarnational, theological perspective which Christologically affirms humanity and the world, socialization, and history, also affirms the pluralism of cultures, of political, social, and economic systems, and of branches of knowledge (42, 53–6). The relation between the church and the world in this pluralistic situation is one of mutual dialogue, in which the church uses the tools provided by historical, cultural developments in order better to understand reality, and then to address that reality in the light of the gospel message, rather than promulgating a universal "cure."

This incarnational, Christocentric humanism also informs Pope Paul VI's encyclical on development, *Populorum Progressio*, which calls for a struggle against those structural injustices that prevent human development and thus violate human dignity (6–21). Once again, it is assumed that true human development or "complete humanism" can only be accomplished through human solidarity, especially with the poor, to build a world in which all people can live fully human lives in accordance with their dignity (42–55). And, as in *Gaudium et Spes*, although *Populorum Progressio* recognizes conflictual situations deriving from socio-economic inequalities, the proposed model of change is one of dialogue and "world-wide collaboration," of the integral development of all peoples in cooperative solidarity.

In *Octogesima Adveniens*, Paul VI recognizes the many structural injustices in the world, but he also notes the diversity of situations in which the church finds itself and the plurality of social options available to Christians. He therefore asserts that his magisterial role is not to "put forward a solution which has universal validity" (4, 42). Solutions to social, political, and economic problems are to be worked out by local Christian communities who analyze their particular situations in the light of the gospel's teachings and the church's social teachings, and selectively employ the tools and resources of various ideological systems and the human sciences (32–40). Consequently, *Octogesima Adveniens* affirms the principle of self-determination for the common good, where people participate in and share responsibility for regional socio-political and economic decisions and strategies, thus building up truly human communities that serve the well-being of all.

This shift in theological bases for social ethics, from a form of the natural law approach in the earlier encyclicals to the Christocentric approach in the post-Vatican II documents, is characterized by David Hollenbach as a shift to a "dialogically universalist ethic."[7] By grounding social ethics in an incarnational theology, these later documents can still make universal ethical statements to "all people of good will," given the ontological unity of God and the world through Christ which constitutes the foundation of human dignity. But at the same time these writings affirm historical and social change and a legitimate plurality of socio-political, economic, and scientific options which precludes any univocal Catholic social ethic deductively derived from an unchanging natural moral order. Rather, they call upon church communities to interpret the "signs of the times" in the light of gospel principles and to develop concrete norms and strategies of social action that will promote and protect human dignity within their particular social situations. Because the gospel and salvation history are not restricted to the "spiritual realm," but are an integral part of human history in all its dimensions, the resources of biblical theology and religious symbols must critically inform socio-economic and political thinking.

Pope John Paul II and Laborem Exercens

Karol Wojtyla's accession to the papacy in 1979 was a unique departure, not only because he became the first modern non-Italian pope, but also because he was called from a career in the university as a professor of philosophy and ethics. So we have the first professional philosopher Pope. His encyclicals, particularly Laborem Exercens, have had a great influence on the pastoral letters of the Canadian and u.s. bishops, and it is therefore important to give them careful attention here.

A distinctive factor in the political philosophy of the current Pope that should be mentioned at the outset is an influence much emphasized in the superb intellectual biography of John Paul II by the Harvard historian of Christianity, George Williams – the influence of Polish Messianism. States Williams: "It is evident from much that he says that the awesome fact of the opening of the third millenium of the Era of the Saviour, as he approaches the close of his own pontificate, has aroused in the Polish poet, deeply imbued with the Messianism of the great poets of his long-tripartitioned nation, powerful emotions."[8] The Polish poet considered by John Paul to be the most profound is Cyprian Norwid, who represents Poland as a "son of Prometheus," representative of a humanity creating itself by the energy of thought and inspired by love, the harbinger of a universal Christian humanism.

In his first papal encyclical, *Redemptor Hominis,* John Paul II speaks four times of the third millenium as a "new Advent" for humanity and the Church, an advent of redemption in which the tremendous technological progress of the modern world is "humanized"; that is, it is subordinated to the human spirit, the transcendent truth and dignity of human personhood. As John Paul puts it in the section titled "authentic human development" in *Solicitudo Rei Socialis,* divine redemption incarnated in Christ as the perfect *imago Dei* is the foundation of any true progress, and this is a matter of spiritual "solidarity" in a context of growing global interdependence. The "new humanity" John Paul II envisions is that of human beings as co-creators with God of a transformed, humanized world in which the human vocation is fulfilled. Of course, the Pope interprets these Messianic motifs in conformity with orthodox Roman Catholicism. John Paul II stands clearly within the modern Catholic social tradition in his affirmation of human dignity rooted in a theology of *imago Dei* as the foundation of the church's social teaching. A true political philosophy and social theory must be grounded in a correct view of the human person – the fundamental errors of modern political theories and ideologies are rooted in faulty anthropologies (*Centesimus Annus,* 11, 13, 57). However, the interpretation of the *imago Dei* symbolism changes in some significant ways in John Paul II's writings, affecting the understanding of human nature, and this has important consequences for the political implications of "human dignity." This is especially evident in his most important encyclical on the economy, *Laborem Exercens.*

In his encyclical commemorating the ninetieth anniversary of *Rerum Novarum,* John Paul II follows in the church's social tradition when he asserts that the church's concern is for human dignity and rights. But what is novel in his approach is that he views human work as "probably the essential key to the whole social question" (*Laborem Exercens,* 3), that is, labour is the key to human dignity. John Paul II locates the biblical theological grounding for this thesis in the early chapters of Genesis and the doctrines of creation and the *imago Dei.* Human beings acquire their dignity as images of God through the divine mandate to subdue and dominate the earth through the process of work, understood as co-creation with God (25). This process of work can be seen both in its "objective" aspect as the technological means of production, whereby people appropriate the resources of nature and adapt them for human use (5), and in its "subjective" aspect as the process of human self-realization, which is the more important value of work – namely, that humanity decides about itself and fulfils its nature and dignity through work (6, 9). Work, as the foundation of human dignity, is not only co-creation with God, it is also to be understood as participation in the redemptive work of Christ (27). By enduring the toil of work, humanity "in a way" carries the cross of Christ, and through this toil brings the glimmer of resurrection hope and contributes to a better ordering of human society. From this theological perspective a number of ethical principles follow, the major one being the priority of labour (in the subjective sense) over capital, over the instruments and means of production (12).

On the basis of this ethical principle, John Paul goes on to condemn the errors of economism and materialism, which subordinate the spiritual human subject of work to his or her objective, material function (13). In John Paul's view, this "error" derives from the opposition between labour and capital conceived as two impersonal productive forces. This error has arisen from the practice, in a rapidly industrializing world, of viewing the world in purely economic terms, that is, seeking to increase wealth and the means of wealth without consideration of the *end* of wealth – humanity and the common good. In other words, the economistic opposition and conflict between labour and capital is not built into the production process, since the natural human "workbench" assumes a harmonious cooperation between the two, nor is it a problem of sinful distortion and wilful disorder. It is rather the result of a practical and theoretical *error* which can only be overcome through the practical and theoretical change of priorities toward the primacy of labour and the human subject over capital and material production.

In my view, there are two problems with this interpretation, and both can be traced to the theological assumptions of the encyclical and perhaps of the entire Catholic social tradition. The first problem is reflected in John Paul's choice of the term "error" rather than "sin" as the source of the conflict between labour and capital, the ethical disorder in modern society. To call economism and its conflict an error is to emphasize a particular conception of the rational and cognitive dimensions and possibilities of human agency, and represents a fundamentally organicist, harmonious model of society. This leads to an idealistic solution to the problem: changing the practical and theoretical principle of the social order to the priority of labour over capital. Such a solution downplays the possibility that sin and perversity characterize human agency and social structures, causing conflict and opposition, and affecting the possibilities and strategies for social change.[9]

This first problem is related, I believe, to the theological centrality of a particular interpretation of the doctrine of the *imago Dei* in *Laborem Exercens* and in the whole corpus of official Catholic social teaching. Despite the greater awareness of the realities of conflict and sin in *Gaudium et Spes*, Paul VI's social encyclicals, and the Canadian bishops' statement, the Christological focus of these documents is still rooted in an ontological *imago Dei* view of the world where human development, fulfilment, and salvation constitute the primary goal of creation. Human beings are seen as co-creators with God who, through cooperative labor, can build up a "new humanity" and bring about the perfection of creation. *Gaudium et Spes* avers: "God intended the earth and all that it contains for the use of every human being and people. Thus, as all men follow justice and unite in charity, created good should abound for them on a reasonable basis" (69). In *Populorum Progressio*, Paul VI writes: "'Fill the earth and subdue it': the Bible, from the first page on, teaches us that the whole of creation is for man, that it is his responsibility to develop it by intelligent effort and by means of labour to perfect it, so to speak, for his use" (22). There is in these writings[10] a Christologically grounded optimism about human possibilities for perfecting creation which downplays the limitations to human possibilities and the destructive potential of human action in the world.

The second, related problem that I see in *Laborem Exercens* derives as well from this doctrine of the *imago Dei*: the emphasis on human beings as the summit of creation[11] and the *telos* of the production process who realize themselves through the domination of nature via work. This theological anthropology, with its assertion that labour is the self-creation of human beings through the domination and mastery of nature, leads inevitably to a concentration on the universal process of production – not only the production of material objects but also the production of human value and dignity via the transformation of nature. Human existence is no longer a matter of "being" oneself but of "producing" oneself. It is instructive to notice that while John Paul speaks of the human person as subject and maker (*homo faber*), he goes on to specify that as such the human person is the true purpose and end of the whole process of production (*Laborem Exercens*, 7). In my view, this anthropocentric utilitarian concept of work – the domination of the earth in the productive process of human development and fulfilment – contributes to the "economistic error," the opposition and conflict between labour and capital, between the subject and object of work, between humanity and nature. Perhaps it is not the primacy of capital over labour that lies at the heart of the social problem, but rather a particular understanding of the primacy of the human over everything else, and the identification of the *imago Dei* with labour as the productive transformation and mastery of nature for human ends.

This point may be clarified further with reference to Hannah Arendt's illuminating distinctions among labour, work, and action.[12] In Arendt's terms, to define humankind as *animal laborans* is to refer all things to the human life process and its necessary requirements. All of life is then structured upon the dialectical foundation of the productive process, namely human needs and human labour, which constantly reproduce each other. In this human-oriented rather than world-oriented perspective, all value is found in human labour power, not in the natural "raw materials" or the finished products, which are simply appropriated for human consumption in the infinite process of human self-production and reproduction. When this perspective becomes universal, the result is what Jean Baudrillard calls the "mirror of production": "confronted by Nature 'liberated' as a productive power, the individual finds himself 'liberated' as labor power. Production subordinates Nature and the individual simultaneously as economic factors of production and as respective terms of the same rationality – a transparency in which production is the mirror, directing articulation and expression in the form of a[n abstract] code."[13]

When *animal laborans* controls the public realm there is no true public in the sense of a stable common world where human action and symbolic exchange – gift, sacrifice, play, story – can occur within a complex and diverse web of relationships. There is only the open display of private enterprises, the never-ending process of production and consumption extended to all areas of life, so that culture becomes mass culture and society becomes a consumer society.[14] Everything is subordinated to the economistic code of production, including human beings who are generically defined as consumers and labour power. John Paul II abhors such an impersonal understanding of human labour which reduces it to an economic factor of production. In *Laborem Exercens*, not *animal laborans* but "man the maker" or *homo faber* constitutes the meaning and dignity of human labour.

To define humankind as *homo faber* is to shift the focus from productive labour to the creative work of fabricating a meaningful stable world. This perspective is not determined by the categories of production and consumption – the infinite life process – but rather by the categories of means and ends. The process of production is but the instrumental means to a more permanent end: the human end of the product. In contrast to the all-consuming concentration on the "necessities" of life by *animal laborans*, *homo faber* is predicated on the freedom of human mastery, the human domination of nature and of itself. All things are evaluated in terms of their suitability and usefulness for the desired human end, which gives them their meaning. As Arendt points out, this ultimately results in a "subjectivity of use" or an "anthropocentric utilitarianism" where all things are instrumentalized into means, lose their independent inherent value, and humanity becomes the measure of all things.[15] This emphasis on the instrumental value of all things in the service of humanity, the subject of work, is strongly present in *Laborem Exercens* (see especially 12). In a telling shift from traditional language, John Paul speaks of the common *use* of property (*Laborem Exercens*, 14), rather than the orientation of private property to the common good (a more objective concept), without apparently recognizing that in capitalist societies, use values can only be expressed as exchange values.[16] If this perspective of "man the maker" and "man the measure of all things" is universalized in a historical context where humanity is not something predefined but is in the *process* of self-realization through world domination (*Laborem Exercens*, 4, 6), then the production process once again becomes primary.[17] This is precisely what one finds in John Paul's *Laborem Exercens* – the attempt to humanize or personalize the process of production, to show that its proper end is humanity, not vice-versa. Hence he calls for the increased participation of all workers in the production process so that they might feel more like "subjects of work," as working "for themselves" (*Laborem Exercens*, 15).

But the question remains: what is the end of *homo faber* who produces him/herself through subduing the earth in the process of production? When the world is construed from such an anthropocentric perspective and human dignity is derived from labour, then how are the conflicting claims as to what this might mean adjudicated?[18] To argue, as *Laborem Exercens* does, that there is a natural harmony in the structure of production (13) or that "it is characteristic of work that it first and foremost unites people" (20) is empirically false.[19] And to assert that the conflicts present in the process of production can be overcome by adherence to the priority of labour over capital and respect for "personal values" requires a much more detailed, concrete analysis and strategy than is or can be given by John Paul in *Laborem Exercens*. It also requires an understanding of human action as not only doing but suffering, not only initiating but also responding, within the broader web of relationships in the world. It requires a view of the world not only in terms of human ends and material means, but in terms of larger processes and powers – social, psychological, natural – that order and shape human possibilities and limitations. The Pope's (and the North American bishops) instrumentalist conception of the technological means of production as a value-neutral tool remains in the thrall of the liberal promise of technology. It fails to discern that economic institutions and technological instruments have a goal, the production and consumption of commodities. The ends are present within the means and they affect the ways in which we take up with the world,[20] including our understanding of morally weighted terms such as "participation," "solidarity," and "fulfilment." The fact that religious and moral terms and principles are coopted by the "means" of labour to serve commodified ends (focused on the procurement and distribution of external, consumer goods) is indicative of a deeper spiritual crisis, the loss of meaningful orientation toward the transcendent good in modern liberalism. I will return to this point, but turn now to a closer examination of the Canadian and u.s. pastoral letters themselves.

THE CANADIAN BISHOPS

The incarnational, Christocentric theological approach that characterises post-Vatican II Catholic social thought also provides the grounding for the Canadian bishops' social ethical reflections, and it is well expressed in the following passage from "Ethical Reflections on the Economic Crisis": "We believe that the cries of the poor and the powerless are the voice of Christ, the Lord of History, in our midst. As Christians, we are called to become involved in the struggle for economic justice and participate in the building up of a new society based on gospel principles. In so doing, we fulfill our vocation as a pilgrim people on earth, participating in Creation and preparing for the coming Kingdom."[21] The primary principle by which the bishops interpret the economic signs of the times and make their policy proposals is the preferential option for the poor and marginalized people of society. This preferential option is defined in the following terms: "As Christians, we are called to follow Jesus by identifying with the victims of injustice, by analyzing the dominant attitudes and structures that cause human suffering, and by actively supporting the poor and the oppressed in their struggles to transform society. For, as Jesus declared, 'when you did it unto these, the least of my brethren, you did it unto me.'"[22] As these quotations indicate, this principle derives from the central themes of the norm of love and human solidarity in incarnational theology, which demands that all people must be participants in and beneficiaries of the common good (defined by "gospel principles"), and that the dignity of all people must be realized within concrete socio-political and economic structures if the common good is truly to exist. Thus this principle issues in the proposal of alternative socio-economic models and new policy strategies which oppose the unjust structures and values of current economic ideologies.[23]

The second theological principle informing the Canadian bishops' statement, concerning the special value and dignity of human work as participation in creation (which gives rise to the priority of labour over capital), is more difficult to identify as a "gospel principle." To argue that this principle is illustrated in Jesus' life, as the bishops do, following Pope John Paul II,[24] is an overdetermination of the gospel texts.[25] This principle is more immediately rooted in the personalist philosophy of the recent Catholic social documents, most clearly expressed by John Paul II in *Laborem Exercens*. Despite the fact that the Canadian bishops' statement takes its second theological principle on the value and dignity of human work and its call for the priority of labour over capital from *Laborem Exercens*, and therefore shares the problematic theological assumptions outlined above, it is less idealistic and abstract than the papal encyclical. It is rooted more in a concrete analysis of socio-economic realities and it reflects the awareness that "true community" is not a natural byproduct of human labour but demands vision, public debate, and certain kinds of social structures and policies.[26] The bishops also recognize that economism is not just an "error" but is rooted in ethical choices which they consider to be morally unacceptable, and this judgment is based on a set of ethical priorities that function as norms for formulating economic policy. These priorities are: (1) the needs of the poor over the wants of the rich; (2) the rights of workers over the maximization of profits; (3) the participation of marginalized groups over the preservation of a system which excludes them.[27] These "middle axioms," based more on an interactionist than an organic or individualist view of society, are very similar to those found in David Hollenbach's "strategic morality"[28] and go beyond the abstract principles characteristic of the social encyclicals in order to provide concrete strategic direction for social action and public policy.

Economic Analysis and Proposals

The bishops' middle axioms come not only from their theological assumptions and "gospel principles" but are also informed by their concrete socio-political analysis.[29] The bishops wrote "Ethical Reflections on the Economic Crisis" at the end of 1982, when the Canadian economy was in its worst slump since the 1930s. They argue that the recession is part of a larger structural crisis in the international capitalist system characterized by the dominant power of multinational corporations and the growth of capital intensive high technology.[30] Briefly stated, the problem with transnational corporations on this view is the concentration of capital and power in the hands of an elite group of private corporations which are able to maximize their profits by moving their investments all over the globe in response to cheap labour, low taxes, monopoly markets, and the availability of cheap resources.

In the bishops' view, these large corporations primarily base their decisions regarding production and investment on one overriding concern, profitability.[31] Thus when economic expansion fuels inflation and wages begin to squeeze profits, these corporations can create a recession by cutting back production, laying off workers, and investing in capital intensive technology which increases the output of production per worker while bringing the economic expansion to a halt. Such a tactic is sometimes termed "capital strike."[32] Although recessions result in a lower rate of consumption due to a decrease in the purchasing power of wage earners, a recession also allows businesses to reduce inventories, it wipes out weak companies whose assets are transferred at bargain prices to the larger, stronger corporations,[33] and it lowers wage demands as people fear job loss and take lower paying jobs.[34] In effect, "recession or depression is a necessary phase to create the preconditions for a new period of expansion."[35] But a recession does not necessarily mean a drop in monopoly prices, only higher unemployment and a lack of private corporate investment. Thus the costs of inflation and recession are ultimately passed on to consumers and workers, while corporate profits are preserved.[36]

Ever since the massive social costs ultimately demanded by the vicious "boom and bust" cycles of a laissez-faire capitalist economy were realized in the Great Depression, governments have endeavoured to stabilize their economies so as to avoid recessions and their negative effects. The traditional Keynesian solution to recession is government deficit spending in order to stimulate the economy toward growth. Liberal welfare states have attempted not only to facilitate economic expansion but also to ameliorate the social costs endemic to a capitalist economy through social security programs and labour laws. The result has been an inflationary spiral that has exceeded economic growth, causing "stagflation," a combination of stagnation and inflation.[37]

At the same time governments view the private business sector as the "engine" for economic recovery, ignoring the effects of monopoly pricing on inflation and calling for labour rather than capital to make the requisite sacrifices. Thus, even while calling for monetary and wage restraint and social service cutbacks, governments offer tax breaks, investment guarantees, and huge financial incentives to the large private corporations with the hope that they will generate capital investment and economic growth. Yet the bishops point out, although working and unemployed people are required to sacrifice most for this attempt to bring about economic recovery, there is no reason to believe that they will benefit from it. "For even if companies recover and increase their profit margins, the additional revenues are likely to be reinvested in some labour-saving technology, exported to other countries or spent on market speculation or luxury goods."[38]

The Canadian bishops oppose such economic strategies because they do not address the structural problems in advanced capitalism and thus fail to address the moral crisis created by those problems – growing unemployment and the socio-economic marginalization of more and more people.[39] As long as maximizing the interests of the large private corporations is viewed as the fundamental key to economic success in a market-oriented industrial strategy, the basic needs of the human community will not be met.[40] Rather there will be a growing concentration of wealth and power in the hands of private corporations that make society's financial decisions on the basis of how they will affect private profits, not the quality of life of workers and their communities. Such patterns of domination and inequality in which human beings are viewed simply as factors in the process of production dedicated to the service of capital rather than the human community, violate the basic norms of human dignity. The bishops reject the dogmatic assumptions of the economic status quo, which accepts the structural problems of the current system as "natural," and call for a reordering of values and priorities in economic life: "The goal of serving the human needs of all people in our society must take precedence over the maximization of profits and growth, and priority must be given to the dignity of human labour, not machines."[41]

In keeping with this basic shift in focus, the bishops suggest an alternative industrial strategy and economic model to the current capital intensive, foreign controlled, export oriented Canadian model.[42] The traditional industrial identity of the Canadian people is that of "hewers of wood and drawers of water," and the Canadian economy is based on the production and export of raw and semi-processed materials. In contrast to manufacturing industries which are labour intensive, the production of raw materials is capital intensive and thus requires foreign investment. Canada also lacks the resources for industrial research and development since both its small manufacturing sector and large natural resources sectors are dominated by foreign (mostly u.s.) branch plants. As many economists (employing a variety of explanatory models) have noted, this makes Canada essentially a resource satellite of the u.s. political economy.[43] Such a "continentalist" industrial strategy of dependence on resource exports (a "staples" economy) has led to a dependence on foreign capital which ultimately places heavy burdens on Canadian workers and local communities. Regional economies are at the mercy of the large transnational corporations whose priorities are not oriented toward the welfare of local communities.

When the Canadian bishops published "Ethical Reflections on the Economic Crisis" in early 1983, the prevailing political currents – under the pressures of the growing prospect of deindustrialization and economic recession – were also increasingly challenging the traditional continentalist, resource export based strategy of postwar Canadian economic policy.[44] The alternative industrial strategy receiving the most attention at the time was what Rianne Mahon calls the "liberal nationalist, technological sovereignty option."[45] This strategy proposed state intervention to strengthen Canadian manufacturing industries, particularly those in the high-technology sectors, through the development of growth-producing "megaprojects" (oriented toward high-technology resource development). The bishops cite this alternative strategy, promulgated by the Science Council of Canada, in order to reject it as ultimately capital and resource centred rather than employment and community centred.[46]

In contrast to this liberal nationalist industrial strategy, the bishops call for "a fundamental reordering of the basic values and priorities of economic development"[47] away from both the continentalist and the nationalist approaches toward a full employment, regionally based strategy. Following the proposals of the Canadian Labour Congress, the bishops make the following suggestions:

In our view, it is important to increase the self-sufficiency of Canada's industries, to strengthen manufacturing and construction industries, to create new job-producing industries in local communities, to redistribute capital for industrial development in underdeveloped regions and to provide relevant job-training programs. It is imperative that such strategies, wherever possible, be developed on a regional basis and that labour unions and community organizations be effectively involved in their design and implementation.[48]

In effect the bishops call for Canadian people throughout the society to have a greater role in setting the economic priorities of the political economy.[49] They propose a decentralization of decision-making in which labour unions and community organizations become involved in the design and implementation of industrial strategies. The bishops seek the elimination of the concentration of economic power in the profit sector in order to render the entire economic policy-making process politically and socially more accountable to all levels of society. This is, in their view, the only way to forge a true community in which human dignity is respected and the common good developed. They envision a planned economy informed by public democratic debate concerning the basic moral values and priorities of economic development.

The bishops voice a radical critique of advanced capitalism and its structural inability to build genuine human community, and they call for participatory economic planning in which all levels of society are represented. Their model of participatory democracy is, as we shall see, different in certain respects from the u.s. bishops' model and leads to different economic policy implications. However, because the Canadian bishops reject the two dominant strategic alternatives for industrial development in Canada – the traditional continental trade liberalization strategy and the nationalist high-technology strategy – the question of policy implementation becomes especially crucial. This is not merely a question of "public debate" or "political will," for policy instruments and alternatives are mediated in and constrained by patterns of institutional organization, legal structures, jurisdictional limits and interactions of state agencies and departments, and so on. The Canadians recognize this to some extent in their more recent "Statement on Social Policy," where they link their alternative vision of society and an economy based on "social solidarity" with the need to develop a social movement comprised of "popular groups" that coalesce around a common vision of strategic change for an alternative set of institutional realities that make possible the formulation of alternative economic policies.[50]

However, to call for a "people-oriented" as opposed to a "market-oriented" society[51] leaves open the question of what people are fitted for and what the human vocation in the world really is. The biblical and classical religious understanding of justice – including economic justice – is rooted in an understanding of the "goodness" of the divinely created order of reality, and social justice is related to the "righteousness" of human agents fulfilling their created purposes. Such justice is not primarily a matter of law or policy or external convention but a way of life nourished by discernment into the meaningful moral order and truth of things in the real world. The root of injustice, in this view, is not faulty organization or social process but a faulty vision of reality. Politics without a substantive understanding of these matters is reduced to ideological warfare, the purely external power struggle of special interest groups.[52]

Furthermore, although the bishops criticize the narrow, competitive self-interest of profit maximization as an inadequate basis for economic policies, they do not challenge the implicit assumption of the productive process itself: that growth and consumption are infinite. Although they argue that the market-based orientation of the productive process toward capital is disordered, they do not challenge the idea of what I have called the "productivist paradigm" and its exploitative impact on nature as well as its social limits and negative "externalities." The economist Paul Hawkin points out that our maximizing, expansionist economy has refused to deal with "the inherent limitations of the mass economy," that is, its relatedness to the environment as a whole.[53] Capitalist economies, predicated on the maximization of profits and material expansion, have resulted in waste economies that seek to sustain consumptive behaviour without consideration for the resulting spoliation of nature and its resources, and without careful attention to the objective character and qualities of human needs and social goods.[54] In other words, the fundamental disorder of our economic life may not only be the priority of capital over labour, as the Canadian bishops argue, but may reside also in the whole current process of production and consumption, which seeks to dominate nature and thereby violates it.

That the Canadian bishops fail to address this problem adequately has to do with their theological perspective.[55] I have earlier noted an important theological inadequacy in the Catholic social tradition, particularly evident in John Paul II's *Laborem Exercens*, namely human self-centredness, an anthropocentric construal of reality. This narrowing of the common good to the human subject who "conquers" nature in order to become more human as the "crown of creation" cannot finally provide an adequate perspective from which to address the distortions and disorder of liberal societies. Although the Catholic tradition makes an important contribution to economic ethics by widening the terms of reference beyond individuals and corporate profits to the human community, this is subject to its own distortions if it ignores the larger context of human action in the created order.

Victor Ferkiss says that the most basic value change required is "one of deciding that the common good requires us to give up the attempt to 'conquer' nature and to accept the necessity of living in harmony with it."[56] The common good is not served by dominating nature for human use in a subject-object dualism but means living in a reciprocal, moral interaction with the natural world. The emphasis on a personalist understanding of human labour is too narrow an orientation; the debate about socio-economic values must broaden the context in which human action is understood so that human limitations and responsibilities can be taken into account more effectively in formulating the proper ethical ordering of society. The cccb statement on the economy is an improvement over the abstract personalism of *Laborem Exercens*. It seeks to address critical economic issues not through universally valid solutions authoritatively promulgated from on high but through local, community-centred strategies in which theological ethical commitments and concrete social analysis mutually inform a set of mediating norms and priorities for guiding public policy. In so doing it contributes important critical insights and alternative proposals to the public debate on economic policy. However, in order to address more adequately the current disorder in economic life the orientation of ethics and social theory must be extended beyond an "anthropocentric utilitarianism" to the wider created order of nature and history.

THE UNITED STATES BISHOPS

The u.s. bishops envision their task as more than simply contributing to the public debate about the economy, which is the Canadian bishops' focus. They wish to advance the development of a common cultural and moral vision,[57] a common ground founded on the "dual heritage" of Catholic teaching and "traditional American values" (preface, 7–9). The pastoral letter also includes a chapter on "A New American Experiment: partnership for the public good" (chapter four), in which the bishops argue for a continuation of the "American dream" or "experiment" (preface, 9; 6ff., 14, 363) by extending democratic ideals – understood in terms of rights and cooperation – into economic life.

Do the bishops achieve this stated aim? David Hollenbach thinks that in large measure they do. He argues that the letter does embody a coherent moral theory that offers the framework for an impasse-breaking synthesis between liberal and communitarian theories of justice.[58] Considerable attention has recently been paid to liberalism and communitarianism as contrasting normative approaches to questions of social justice.[59] Briefly stated, liberal theorists employ rights language, arguing that in a pluralistic democratic society there can be no normative consensus on a substantive vision of the common good. Democracy is understood as an institutionalized set of procedures in which competing individual or group interests are equilibrated in order to prevent the hegemonic tyranny of any particular vision of the human good over the whole of society. Communitarian theorists argue, on the contrary, that rights language cannot express the human need for community as constitutive of moral agency and of the values embodied in the practices and institutions of justice in our society. For this we need a shared language of the historical goods and traditional values to be preserved in a just and humane society, and this implies a substantive conception of democracy as a community of moral discourse and judgment.

Hollenbach argues that the bishops' synthesis of these positions in a theory of participatory justice entails the following normative proposals: the endorsement of institutional pluralism and social differentiation, minimum levels of socio-economic participation, and the proper role of government intervention in securing economic rights. *Economic Justice for All* moves beyond the liberal position, he claims, in linking human dignity to participation in social community and in calling for the cultivation of the personal and civic virtues necessary for a society to promote the common good. Hollenbach concludes: "In contrast to liberalism, the letter also assumes that there is a fundamental coherence among the diverse dimensions of modern social life. Its moral argument presupposes that the religious, political, economic, familial, technological, and other kinds of relationships that bind us together or drive us apart in advanced industrial societies can be brought into an imperfect but tolerable harmony with each other."[60] This statement reveals just how entrenched the liberal paradigm has become in modern social and political theory, religious or not, communitarian or not. The presumption that tolerable harmony can be achieved within diversity lies at the heart of liberal theory, from Hobbes, Locke, and Rousseau through Adam Smith, J.S. Mill, and John Dewey to Keynes, Reinhold Niebuhr, and C.B. Macpherson. The real question is what kind of harmony do we mean, what is the substance of the common good and the language of participation, and how is this concretely related to the institutions and practices of advanced industrial political economies?

In contrast to Hollenbach, I shall argue that the bishops' "synthetic" vision is fundamentally liberal and is therefore unable to resolve the spiritual moral crisis it seeks to address. The bishops remain captive to what Albert Borgmann calls the "irony of technology"[61]: the technological promise to provide access to liberating human self-realization for all by making available the instruments of control over nature leads rather to Nietzsche's "last men" – bourgeois citizens disengaged from reality in the mindless production and consumption of consumer commodities. Indeed, it is worth noting that both "liberal" and "communitarian" theories are modern historicist positions rooted in the division between facts and values (instrumental means and moral principles),[62] committed – as the bishops are – to the growth of technology and economic production as the means of "liberty and justice for all": "We are proud of the strength, productivity, and creativity of our economy, but we also remember those who have been left behind in our progress. We believe that we honor our history best by working for the day when all our sisters and brothers share adequately in the American dream" (preface, 9). As this quotation indicates, the bishops accept the progressivist assumptions of liberal political economy, so that the basic problem becomes one of helping those "left behind" to gain access to the American dream. The policy proposals the bishops recommend, furthermore, are compatible with the aims and assumptions of liberal corporatism – a synthesis of liberalism and communitarianism, to be sure, but hardly compatible with the religious and moral vision of the common good as represented by "traditional biblical principles." At issue here is the meaning of "participation" in human community, which is central to the bishops' understanding of human dignity, justice, and the common good. By linking participation to "labor" in modern industrial society, the bishops uncritically link their moral vision to an economistic social theory and end up giving moral support to democracy and the common good "enacted as technology."[63]

Theological Ethics

I begin with the theological assumptions of the pastoral letter, for I believe that it is there that the decisive moves are made. The u.s. bishops state their basic source and goal to be the biblical conception of justice, rooted in the focal points of Hebrew religion – creation, covenant, and community. Central to the bishops' creation theology is the doctrine of *imago Dei*, the very heart of Catholic social teaching in which human persons are understood to possess an "inalienable dignity" deriving from their divinely endowed status as the "summit of creation"(32). This dignity is expressed and fulfilled through participation in human community, preeminently through cooperative labour (96ff., 102) by which human beings share in the creative work of God (32). Justice entails the protection of those basic human rights that enable and ensure the active participation of all in the life of society (71, 77), thus making social and individual fulfilment possible.[64] The fundamental form of injustice, consequently, is "marginalization" or the exclusion of persons from social life.

Participation, then, as the essential expression of the social nature of human beings is the primary characteristic of covenant community

(35ff., 78). But what do the bishops mean by "participation" in concrete terms? How are these universal basic rights of each person to be institutionally embodied, particularly with reference to economic justice? Here the bishops rely heavily on Pope John Paul II's novel contribution to Catholic social teaching, his emphasis on labour as the key to the whole social question,[65] that is, that work is the fundamental expression of human dignity and solidarity with others (96, 102). Hence, for the bishops, full employment is the number one priority, the foundation of a just economy (136, 151ff.): "Work with adequate pay for all who seek it is the primary means for achieving basic justice in our society"(73). From this follows also the "litmus test" for the quality of socio-economic justice, the lot of the disadvantaged (Preface 8, 16; 24, 38, 52, 85ff., 123); and the "preferential option for the poor" is presented as the primary moral criterion for choosing policy positions (260, 319).

When the fulfilment of the "basic needs" of the poor becomes the highest priority within existing political economic structures – and the bishops accept the non-ideological "givenness" of American welfare capitalism, calling for "pragmatic reform" in selected policy areas (127–35) – then society will be required to commit itself to greater economic development and growth so that the poor can also be raised on the tide of "progress," primarily via job creation and welfare programs. In a society dedicated to the industrial marketplace, "participation" and "citizenship" come to be defined largely in economic terms – as employment. Hence the bishops' theological ethic and anthropology contribute – perhaps against their intentions – to an economistic and technological conception of justice and democracy.

Liberal Corporatism and the Common Good

We turn now to the policy framework of the pastoral letter, which fundamentally shapes the concrete meaning of labour, participation, democracy, and the common good in the pastoral letter, and which I shall argue is compatible with liberal corporatism. Two comments about liberalism are necessary at the outset. The first concerns the discourse of "values." Recall the bishops' aim to bring together the dual heritage of Catholic social teaching and traditional American values. Although the bishops use language of "vision" when writing about the Christian understanding of human life in the world, they are quick to translate the *symbols* of creation, covenant, kingdom of God, and discipleship into the abstract universal and permanent moral *principles* of the Catholic social tradition. And these in turn are applied rather directly as functional "values" to the existing institutional needs and problems of a progressive liberal political economy.

The assumption here seems to be that there is no real conflict or tension between the religious vision and its moral principles on the one hand, and the vision and values of modern liberalism on the other. What the bishops fail to consider is that the practices and institutions of American political economy entail the commitment to a vision of human purpose and the common good rooted in the "paradigm of productivity," the technological promise of liberation via the efficient production and distribution of commodities. Such a commitment calls for a quite different consensus about the ultimate meaning of human and social reality than is present in the visionary language of the bishops concerning Christian love and discipleship. Consequently the religious moral language of the bishops comes across as moralistic, spoken in lofty abstraction from the "real" issues of economic policy.

Consider, for example, the bishops' statements on the need for the conversion of individual hearts to the discipleship of Jesus (45–7, chapter 5). This is expressed in a highly personalistic and moralistic language of piety: "Renouncing self-centered desires, bearing one's daily cross, and imitating Christ's compassion, all involve a personal struggle to control greed and selfishness, a personal commitment to reverence one's own human dignity and the dignity of others by avoiding self-indulgence and those attachments that make us insensitive to the conditions of others and that erode social solidarity. Christ warned us against attachments to material things" (328). The focus here is on patterns of individual behaviour and on a kind of moral heroism – following Jesus in the "way of the cross" by taking seriously alternative or "countercultural" lifestyles, such as the practice of evangelical poverty (50), the service of compassion (43), simplicity in private consumption (334), the avoidance of greed (75, 342, 365), the commitment to family values (209, 344ff.), and the need to make sacrifices (336, 365). However, these moral exhortations and "values" are not coherently related to the socio-historical institutions and structures of choice within which people experience their daily lives. Nor do the bishops seriously relate them to matters of policy, for obvious reasons.

This brings us to the second comment about the liberalism of the pastoral letter, the observation that commitment to a particular set of institutions is also commitment to a public conception of the good,[66] that prescribes and limits the range of possibilities for thought and action. In modern liberal societies technological production and progress orient these institutions, and public policy discourse accordingly uses

all "values" in the service of these material ends. In a liberal democratic order, "technology comes into play as the indispensable and
unequaled procurement of the means that allow us to realize our
preferred values."[67] Within the orienting liberal paradigm, such
values can only be realized through commodities. In such a context,
"humanization" comes to be seen as raising the "standard of living"
for all.

Consider here the bishops' view of work and how they translate
this into specific policy proposals. Following the theological anthropology of *Laborem Exercens*, the bishops claim that work has a threefold moral significance: it is a primary means for distinctively human
self-expression and self-realization, it enables people to fulfil their
material needs, and it is the way in which persons contribute to the
common good (97). However, in an advanced industrial society, most
jobs fit only the second category of significance – they enable people
to fulfil their social duty as consumers of commodities. This is presumably not what the bishops have in mind when they speak of
human self-expression and the virtues of citizenship, but it becomes
the functional consequence within the political economic conditions
that shape the meaning of employment in liberal capitalist democracies.

Andre Gorz provides the following definition of work in capitalist
societies: "It means an activity carried out: for someone else; in return
for a wage; according to forms and time schedules laid down by the
person paying the wage; and for a purpose not chosen by the
worker."[68] Work, in other words, is wage labour within the exchange
relations of large-scale markets, and it is understood primarily as a
means of earning money. It is defined in terms of *having* a job and is
often valued in direct relation to its remuneration (having a "good"
job), rather than in terms of the nature and purpose of what one *does*.
The full employment ideal, as John Keane and John Owens point out,
is a development of nineteenth century capitalist industrialization
and urbanization, the rapid growth of an "employment society."[69]
And under Keynesian reform measures, the goal of full employment
via the full employment of private capital became an ostensible
political objective of the state. The focus here is on distributive policies that benefit the working class, specifically, higher wages to enable
them to raise their levels of consumption. The Keynesian compromise
transforms the terms of ideological and political discourse toward,
as Bertil Ohlin puts it, the "nationalization of consumption" within
the constraints of capitalist relations of production.[70] This, of course,
results in a primary concern with increased productivity and economic growth which alone can protect both profits (a necessary
condition) and jobs.

In such a structure of choices, premised on highly uncertain outcomes, participation is oriented toward the realization of short-term material interests. Workers "participate" in democratic political institutions (i.e., they vote) and "cooperate" with corporations in order to improve their material conditions.[71] All this is implicit in the policy recommendations of the bishops: in their reliance on continued economic growth to solve distributional problems (156ff., 196, 278); in their emphasis on a full employment policy through cooperation among labour, business, and government; in their focus on institutional pluralism and the functional consensus of social groups and their rejection of class struggle (100ff., 128ff., 298ff.).

There are problems with this approach, both in terms of the bishops' own religious ethical vision and on external grounds. The most apparent tension exists in the bishops' critique of consumerism, which they conclude is a form of greed. They make the following appeal: "Americans are challenged today as never before to develop the inner freedom to resist the temptation constantly to seek more" (75, cf. 248). Such an individual moral appeal ignores the structure of choices and rationality present within the dynamics of production and consumption in advanced industrial economies. Similarly, the appeals to corporations ("owners and managers") to make a commitment to the "common good" (what this might mean the bishops never really say) and to develop the virtues of citizenship (110–18, 298ff.), amount, in the absence of specific institutional analysis and recommendations, to an amorphous plea for corporate responsibility.[72] And in practical policy terms, this amounts to a plea for corporations to "do good" through the expansion of productivity, "good" determined, of course, by the bottom line of profitability (278, 300).[73] In fact (to make the point even more sharply), by calling for greater commitment and participation within the existing economic order, do not the bishops actually contribute to the marginalization of non-material aims as constituting the good? Participation becomes a matter of providing jobs and economic growth via technological progress.

It is significant that the bishops appeal so frequently to the primacy of building cultural consensus and cooperation (83, 124, 153, 321) to mobilize the "political will" of various groups in order to attain the goals of basic justice. Above all, the bishops are concerned about the need to reduce adversarial relations between labour and capital (298, 88) in order to establish an orderly and functional cooperation between the various "groups" (298, 100) that play important economic roles. It is no accident that *Rerum Novarum* is referred to at strategic moments in the document (103, 114, 123, 299) – the bishops share Leo XIII's yearning for the harmony and order realized when all people play their economic roles in a cooperative, non-conflictual way. Like Reinhold Niebuhr, the bishops adopt a pragmatic liberal functionalism as their implicit social theory, but unlike Niebuhr's realism, they deny class conflict and they display a much more optimistic view of the possibilities for moral persuasion and rational consensus on the common good (61).[74] This is why in practice their approach resembles more a form of corporatism than does Niebuhr's equilibrium pluralist approach, even though the bishops share Niebuhr's preoccupation with stability. Corporatist social thought has existed in various forms since the late nineteenth century, as a "third way" between liberalism and socialism, and Leo Panitch describes its general features:

Decrying on the one hand the individualism and competition of capitalism, and on the other the class conflict and socialist movements to which it gave rise, corporatist theories contended that class harmony and organic unity were essential to society. Looking backwards to the mutual rights and obligations that presumably united the medieval estates, they proposed a social and political order based on functional socio-economic organizations in civil society, operating largely autonomously in their respective fields, but united with each other and the state in sectoral and national decision-making bodies and committed to maintaining the functional hierarchy of an organic society.[75]

While corporatism as a social system – such as Pope Pius XI recommended in *Quadragesimo Anno* – has never succeeded and is highly problematic, it has become an important strategy for organizing business-labour relations within advanced capitalist societies.[76]

In suggesting that the bishops embrace a kind of corporatist political economic approach, it is important to be clear about what this does *not* mean. It does not mean that they advocate a "statist" approach to political economy, as the bishops insist on a distinction between state and society (121). The bishops understand democracy to be a form of political community comprised of a plurality of "mediating structures" in which citizens voluntarily participate to sustain the common good (99–100, 308). They resist both individualist and totalitarian conceptions of political power and authority, focusing on the duties and obligations of social relationships. But this broadening of the political is contradicted by the bishops' traditional liberal understanding of the distinction between "private" and "public" agencies or sectors, a view that implies different meanings of the "common good." In a capitalist society, "public" goods are understood to be those activities that are not profitable for "private" enterprise and yet are necessary for the economy as a whole – communication and transportation infrastructure, social welfare, military defense and security. And from this perspective, public goods are ineluctably perceived to be "inefficient" and "non-productive" even while they protect and secure private efficiency and profits.[77] Even more significant for this argument is the fact that these "public" goods are in fact commodities related to standard of living considerations. Public policy discourse leaves room for no other meaning of the common good – the *kind* of life to be secured for all, and the means to secure it, are already specified.

The bishops' call for pragmatic reform and civic cooperation leaves this background structure outside the framework of political discourse, so that the subordination of civic cooperation to the constraints and imperatives of liberal capitalism is simply taken for granted. The question remains: is this a conception of the common good that can sustain meaningful human community, citizenship allegiance, and civic virtue? Are these structural or institutional constraints justified with reference to the substantive meaning of democracy? Do they satisfy the social preconditions for just participation in a democratic society? Or do they not rather sacrifice a genuinely pluralistic, participatory public life for the need to mobilize participation in a political economy uniformly devoted to technological advance and oriented toward economic growth and the maintainance of a "good business climate"?[78]

It seems that the bishops are less concerned, in their eagerness to affirm an overall cooperative consensus rooted in the hegemony of liberal capitalist interests and ideologies, to address the institutional and ideological constraints upon the articulation of human needs. Given this material and ideological hegemony, the real structure of choices remains oriented toward short-term profits, the satisfaction of consumer needs, and the necessary expansion of productive capacity. The bishops oppose short-term profitability as the only bottom line (112ff., 280), but the structural constraints of a capitalist economy force them back to it time and again in their policy proposals, which require a "healthy" economy characterized by economic growth (156, 196, 256, 278ff., 300, 309).

This is a highly economistic and utilitarian conception of the "common good," in which collective technological means are developed for economic ends. Clearly the u.s. bishops themselves mean something else by the common good, but they continue to accept this definition of public and private quite uncritically in their policy recommendations.[79] We have already seen that the bishops define the common good as the conditions of social life that allow individuals and groups access to their own fulfilment (see note 8 above). This fulfilment, the bishops affirm, has a religious dimension in that "human life is fulfilled in the knowledge and love of the living God in communion with others" (30; cf. 64ff.). However, rather than asking whether and how modern industrial society serves the transcendent good, the spiritual destiny and meaning of life, the bishops assume that there are no fundamental conflicts here. They simply relate transcendently authorized "values" to the existing political economic structures, where they are functionally transformed into moral support for material and technological ends – the control of nature for human purposes, understood in commodified terms. The only possible public debate or reform then is the technical question about which procedures best provide access for individuals and groups to the socio-economic means of their fulfilment. No further public consideration of what we are fitted for is any longer appropriate, once this move is made.

CONCLUSION

The main burden of the argument I have attempted to make in this chapter is that the North American bishops' theological ethic is unable to address the crisis – finally a spiritual one – behind economic disorder in Canada and the u.s. The spiritual crisis, as I argued in the first chapter, concerns the centrality of the paradigm of productivity – the rationality, institutions, and ends of liberal political economy – in modern social life. The problem here is not primarily the dominance of capital and self-interested profit maximization over most other needs and goods, nor is it the absence of economic democracy or the full participation of all in the economy.[80] It is, more fundamentally, the entrenchment of an anthropocentric utilitarianism that fails to look beyond narrowly defined human needs and desires to the divine ordering of life, in which we are always already participants. It is a problem of orientation and self-understanding that constricts our vision of reality within a very myopic framework of interpretation and action – and thereby clouds our judgment, our ability to discern and to respond to meanings that are not humanly created but are part of the divinely ordered whole of reality.

Until this spiritual crisis at the heart of modern economic and political life is addressed, attempts to "humanize" the process of production – whether through democratic experiments or economic redistribution or the extension of human rights – will end in ironic failure. In my judgment, the *imago Dei* theology of the bishops and

Pope John Paul II is too anthropocentric a perspective from which to address the disorder. Perhaps this is not deliberate or intentional. Perhaps the Pope and the bishops understand labour as the concrete incarnation of the human spirit, oriented by the divinely created order, lovingly mediating those larger ends in the world by ordering "all things in a manner appropriate to their relations to God."[81] Such a theocentric understanding of labour would, I take it, also be compatible in certain respects with the natural law tradition.

Such a theocentric (as opposed to an anthropocentric or "humanizing") approach would, however, point out the sinful idolatry of the modern liberal political economic vision and its progressivist assumptions. This is what the bishops fail to do with any consistency or conviction. From a theocentric perspective, the true order of life is measured not by human beings but by God, and it can be discerned only by turning from instruments of control to the orienting religious symbols and meanings that enable us to respond fittingly to the larger whole of which we are parts. In this community of being we are linked together, not by participation in external processes of production and consumption or a shared commitment to technological progress; neither is our dignity derived from labour. Rather we are held together as responsive participants in the whole community of being, and our dignity is rooted in our self-conscious and responsive relatedness to the divine, enabling us to interpret and respond appropriately to (not create or control) the real world created by God. To articulate some understanding of the significance of this alternative approach to political economy, an approach rooted in a moral theology of creation, is the task of the concluding chapter.

5 Conclusion: Toward a Moral Theology of Creation

That the issues and problems of political economy have taken centre stage in modern North American public life hardly needs argument. Political economy, as Sheldon Wolin remarks, is "a conception striving for totalization" in our public discourse and social relationships, the constitutive and generally unquestioned paradigm in making political judgments about public policy.[1] The context for understanding this development, elaborated in the introductory chapter, is the shift from religious cosmology to scientism as the orienting pattern for public order. The totalization of political economic discourse, I have argued, is a symptom of the spiritual crisis that results from such a shift. This means that the "social crisis," the malaise of liberal political economy, cannot be addressed in a fundamentally moral way by policy proposals. For the parameters of policy making are always already circumscribed by the anthropocentric utilitarian vision of life embodied in modern economic practices and institutions. And it is precisely this vision of life that must be judged by a religious or spiritual measure to be foolishness, expressing as it does a lack of realism concerning the ultimate nature and purposes of worldly existence that can only result in social and political disorder. The practical atheism of a public life devoted to the expansion of external goods at the expense of the human spirit lacks, not knowledge in the guise of information, but wisdom and understanding.[2] It is precisely wisdom and understanding – insight derived from religious realism – that are most needed if public life is to be oriented toward the common good of the created order.

In this chapter, then, I will explore the connections between wisdom and the religious symbol of creation in order to articulate a moral understanding of nature and our responsible participation in its spiritual meaning, even in economic affairs. And I will attempt to do so, following Augustine's approach to political ethics, by thinking together the Platonic conception of philosophical theology and the biblical understanding of the meaning of creation. The purpose, then, of this chapter is not to prescribe an alternative economic ethic but to conduct a meditative exploration of a theological approach that might better address the set of moral problems outlined in chapter one. I proceed by developing a comparison between the classical liberal realism of Thomas Hobbes and the classical Christian realism of Augustine.

SYMBOL AND REALITY

The initial problem confronting such an exploration is, of course, that religious symbols are no longer regarded as representing publicly significant and comprehensible, shared experience. They have therefore become all but incommunicable private meanings holding little relevance for the common life world defined by production and consumption. Erich Heller describes it this way: "The predicament of the symbol in our age is caused by a split between 'reality' and what it signifies. There is no more any commonly accepted symbolic or transcendent order of things. What the modern mind perceives as order is established through the tidy relationship between things themselves. In one word: the only conceivable order is positivist-scientific."[3] The reigning anthropocentric utilitarian approach to reality in the technological order of North American public life is grounded in the positivist assumptions of the modern natural sciences. The reduction of reality to positive, scientifically ascertained "facts" (which alone are "objectively" true) and subjective values (representing the private preferences and constructed ideological opinions of individuals and groups) entails the loss of public religious and moral meaning. Spiritual experience and its symbolic articulation are exiled from reality – its truth claims cannot be publicly adjudicated since they do not refer to anything real or true "out there" in objective nature. Heller puts it this way: "As an unavoidable corollary of this state of affairs, religion and art lost their unquestioned birthright in the homeland of human reality, and turned into strange messengers from the higher unreality, admitted now and then as edifying or entertaining songsters at the positivist banquet."[4] The way we represent the world – the way we *see* it, as the classical term *theoria* originally referred to the process of interpreting reality – makes a crucial difference to the ways in which we respond to and participate in it. Our attitudes, judgments, and actions are oriented by our symbols. However, symbolic language becomes artificial and unreal when it loses its connection with lived experience and is hardened into reified abstractions without a relational context. On the existential level, one can understand the motivation behind scientific disdain for religious myths, when these myths are presented as if they were empirical objects and are turned into closed, opaque doctrines considered exempt from rational investigation. Where religion degenerates into the unthinking conformity to conventional habits and opinions and the uncritical repetition of myths as doctrines without insight into their originating meaning and their lived symbolic significance, there religion becomes an ideological tool destructive of thought and the human spirit. And when such ideological distortions of reality become socially powerful through political, cultural, and educational institutions, they become harmful to human life and the common good.

But this problem (which in chapter one I called the problem of idolatry) is not unique to religion. It is true of any reified doctrine that claims to possess the key to reality and to be able to solve the problems of human life. In our day it is not reified religious myths and doctrines that distort public life, since religion has relatively little social power or authority. In our time and culture this position of power is held by the reified myths and doctrines of modern science and technological expansion, institutionalized in an increasingly global economic order and intellectually propagated in the instrumentalist creed of positivist science. In order to gain power over nature, society, and ultimately over human destiny itself, this creed asserts that the key to reality is found in instrumental rationality based on knowledge of phenomenal objects and their causal relations. It is a creed concisely expressed in the Baconian conception of science or knowledge as power: "We shall put nature to the rack and compel her to answer our questions." Bacon of course scoffed at classical philosophy and theology, comparing them to pubescent sexuality: "It can talk, but it cannot generate." However, one could construe the analogy somewhat differently by comparing Baconian positivist science to adolescent sexuality: it can generate, but cannot talk meaningfully about the moral aims and spiritual meaning of the acts and fruits of generation.

The problem here is not altogether different from the problem in fundamentalist religious doctrines which also treat questions concerning human nature, spirituality, and morality as if they are technical, phenomenal matters. Positivists make the same category mistake as religious fundamentalists, that is, they analyze symbols as dogmatic propositions about objects in the empirical world, separating them from their experiential basis and invisible spiritual reference. On this basis it is rather easy to point to contradictions and distortions, to demonstrate logically what every true philosopher and theologian already knows: symbols lead to contradiction and obfuscation if they are misunderstood as propositions concerning phenomenal reality. But the positivists do not solve the problem when they identify reality with *physis* and assume that knowledge of material facts and the advance of instrumental power over phenomenal objects will resolve the problems and answer the questions of human existence. Positivists as well as fundamentalists shift the focus of philosophy, theology, and ethics from the concrete order of lived human experience and its symbolic expression to the polymathic order of empirical information, where education entails the accumulation and classification of external facts and opinions according to prescribed scientific methods rather than the search for wisdom, for the spiritual measure by which to make good critical judgments based on a knowledge of the true order of reality.

Plato in the *Phaedrus* (278d) states that the true thinker is not a *sophos* (one who "knows things") but a *philosophos* (one who loves wisdom and being). True thinking is not the possession and domination of being, forcing it to serve one's own selfish purposes, but is rather the loving attunement of the soul (*psyche*) to the invisible order of being. In the *Phaedo* Plato has Socrates give an account of how he was freed from the "physical" philosophy of Anaxagorus, Archaleus, and the other positivists of his day, showing that a knowledge of physical causes and processes cannot account for human motivation, judgment and action.[5] The physical sciences are not adequate to understand and orient human thought and action – this requires existential thinking, rational reflection on the spiritual substance and order of human existence in the world. Otherwise, what we talk about and what we generate will be fatally divided.

Here we may still learn from Plato's response to the religious and intellectual decay of his own time. Plato did not hold to the diplomatic immunity of religious myths from critical rational investigation, but neither did he exempt the uncritical assumptions of the positivists from dialectical consideration.[6] Plato coined the term "theology" in the *Republic* out of a concern to critically rethink the originating questions and experiences that gave rise to religious myths and symbols in the first place, questions concerning the spiritual order of reality which the simple collection and classification of "facts" cannot raise or address. Plato discusses true theology in the *Republic* in relation to the question, What is the truth concerning human existence in relation to God, nature, and society? Is it at bottom characterised by *pleonexia*, the desire to gain power and to master, control, and possess as much as possible (Book II)? And are the laws (*nomoi*) of the polis therefore simply external conventions constructed by the powerful so as to rationalize existing relations of power, and legitimated with reference to edifying stories about the gods and religious rewards and punishments? Or is the human soul fundamentally related to an eternal good "beyond being [*epekeina tes ousias*], exceeding it in dignity and power" (509b), a transcendent measure that cannot be possessed or humanly manipulated but which illuminates the true meaning of human existence and its proper order and thereby makes prudent moral judgment possible? If so, then true theology cannot be understood as a matter of doctrinal abstraction or the mere possession of factual knowledge. Rather, philosophy and theology pertain to a spiritual order, the ascent of the soul toward the truth, and the experience of the divine measure through the soul's participatory response to the good beyond being. This truth is attained dialectically, not by employing a particular method or believing a particular myth or systematizing particular bits of information but by an orientation of the soul – a soul that is turned around (*periagoge*) from the phenomenal world of becoming toward the divine wisdom (*sophia*), which enables it to exercise prudent judgment (*phronesis*) (518–19) within the phenomenal realm.

Misconceptions about the gods, states Socrates in the *Republic*, are not ordinary falsehoods but represent the "veritable lie" (*to hos alethos pseudos*), the lie in the soul about the things that are (382, 535d-e). Given Plato's understanding of philosophy, it is clear that this should be the case, for theology concerns the question of how to speak about the gods (*hoi typoi peri theologias*, 379a) by which the soul is ordered and enabled to mediate the true measure of real things and thereby to make critical judgments about the myths and about opinions concerning the nature of human existence. The lie of sophistic disorder, therefore, is not merely the possession of false knowledge but a wrong relation to the transcendent, the invisible Good. This is a spiritual problem, a disease in the soul characterized by ignorance of the things of the spirit. It leads to the ridiculous attempt to treat spiritual and moral substance as purely phenomenal, to conceive of knowledge (*episteme*) in geometric terms, and to seek control over reality via the imposition of artificial constructs.

Plato's approach to the problem of social justice and political judgment is compatible with the theological politics of the Bible, where wisdom is linked to an understanding of God's purposes for the created order. As the well-known text from Jeremiah puts it: "Thus says the Lord: 'Let not the wise man glory in his wisdom, let not the mighty man glory in his might, let not the rich man glory in his riches; but let him who glories glory in this, that he understands and knows me, that I am the Lord who practice steadfast love, justice and righteousness in the earth; for in these things I delight,' says the Lord." (Jeremiah 9:23–4) The problem of order and the common good in society is a spiritual matter not discerned so long as one is oriented toward the external power struggles of those whose instrumental aim is to conquer and control reality for their own purposes. The true nature of reality, including political and social reality, can only be discerned by those who look beyond their own interests and the immediacy of social forces to the invisible, divine order of creation. There is no technical political substitute for the rightly ordered *psyche* or spirit in the quest for justice. Politics – and political economy – is therefore not merely a matter of the pragmatic management of external forces but the practical mediation of transcendent wisdom that binds the world together in a meaningful order.

The conditions for true political community and justice must be established existentially – they cannot be forcibly imposed through external constraints. This ultimately entails the formation of character in the well-ordered soul or the responsive heart, formed in participatory relation to the transcendent Creator. Political philosophy or theology, therefore, is a matter of the proper symbolization of human nature and society in relation to the divine order of reality in creation. It is a matter of the human mediation of the divine measure within the concrete circumstances of social life by making prudent judgments, the ability to discern the meaning of particular concrete political realities in relation to the larger purposes of the created order.

The absence of meaningful moral discourse in North American public life is related to the banishment of religious and moral symbols from politics and political theory, so that "ethics" must conform to the instrumental criteria of the positivist creed. That is, ethical proposals, if they are to be publicly relevant and politically "realistic," must be translated into the technical, procedural measures of policy discourse. As I have argued throughout this study, it is precisely in this translation that the insights made possible by the religious symbols are rendered obscure and misunderstood. For religious symbols seek not to control reality and master the objects of experience but to reveal the inner meaning and relations between things in a reality that is ultimately beyond human control and to reveal also the inner meaning of human existence as related to the Creator – a revelation not only of the truth of human nature but also of the divine measure that human nature is uniquely equipped to mediate in its vocation to care for the earth.

The positivist scientific mentality has tended to reduce the dramatic action of a living creation to mechanical motion, leaving human moral judgment and motivation to the private realm of "belief" and "values." The instrumentalization and commodification of public life is a foregone conclusion in a cosmos construed as dead matter propelled by blind force, ordered by an impersonal causality. In such an order the human sciences are themselves reduced to the cold abstractions of their quantifying methods that allow them to "control" their materials and render them fit for policy application. As Eric Voegelin argues in *The New Science of Politics*, when theoretical relevance in the scientific search for truth in various realms of being (whose different objects require different methods) is subordinated to methodological conformity to the formal rules of the natural sciences, the meaning of the human sciences is perverted: "If the adequacy of a method is not measured by the usefulness to the purpose of science, if on the contrary the use of a method is made the criterion of the science, then the meaning of science as a truthful account of the structure of reality, as the theoretical orientation of man in his world, and as the great instrument for man's understanding of his own position in the universe is lost."[7]

The modern theoretical foundation for political science is laid in the writings of Thomas Hobbes. According to Hobbes, reality is fundamentally material, and nature, including human nature, is scientifically understood on Galileo's mechanistic geometric model, where everything is reduced to matter in motion.[8] Following Plato's lead in the *Republic* where the polis and its justice are understood as "man writ large," Hobbes sees the commonwealth as a gigantic "Artificiall Man."[9] But when human nature is construed in mechanistic terms ("For what is the *Heart*, but a *Spring*; and the *Nerves*, but so many *Strings*; and the *Joynts*, but so many wheels, giving motion to the whole Body"[10]), man writ large is best understood according to external motion – its causal relations and laws. Natural law for Hobbes is not linked to transcendent purpose or divine will; it is derived from the human desire to maintain oneself in motion by procuring what is needed to preserve physical life and to avoid death. This is the meaning of human power and the "state of nature" in which everyone is at war with everyone else.[11] There is no *finis ultimus* or *summum bonum* by which human power is oriented or ordered, only "a perpetuall and restlesse desire of Power after power, that ceaseth only in Death."[12] In this natural state there is not yet present a moral law, for there is no common power coordinating the motions of individual powers. However, this state of war is not conducive to the enjoyment of the fruits of life made possible when people cooperate socially in the production and consumption of commodities, and, even worse, because it entails the "continuall feare and danger of violent death"[13] (if motion is everything, then loss of motion is loss of everything). Because of this people have a rational interest in entering into a common agreement to restrain their individual powers of movement for the sake of self-preservation and a more contented (read "commodious") life.[14] This is the foundation of the commonwealth, and its conventional agreements (the social contract) enforced by a designated coercive power represent the origins of justice.[15] In Hobbes we find the rational reconstruction of social reality on the Baconian vision of scientific knowledge as power, the utilitarian mastery of nature for commodious human advancement. The common good is organized to serve individual interests, which are themselves understood as the frequently insatiable quest for possession. Politics is an instrumental matter of sorting out conflicts of interest and enforcing the procedural rules that regulate the field of external powers or forces that constitute the commonwealth.

Yet for all of Hobbes' reduction of human nature and social reality to material and mechanical as opposed to spiritual and "dramatistic" terms for the purposes of establishing a positive political science, certain dramatic vestiges remain. The most intriguing of these is the image taken from the Bible which gives Hobbes' best-known work its title and is artistically engraved on the frontispiece of the first edition of the *Leviathan*. "Leviathan" is the name Hobbes gives to the sovereign power that publicly represents the conventional order of the modern commonwealth and enforces its contractual justice upon threat of death.[16] The Latin inscription superimposed above the image of the gigantic "artificiall man," who rises imperiously above the natural landscape and is comprised of contractually joined individuals, is taken from Job 41: *Non est potestas Super Terram quae Comparetur ei* (No one on earth can be compared to him). In chapter 28 of *Leviathan* Hobbes identifies the source of the image and the inscription as the last two verses of Job 41 in which Leviathan is called "King of all the children of pride," who rules the proud with the power of fear.[17] It is a fortuitous irony that the inscribed reference to the Job 41 text, which appears in the Latin Vulgate at verse 24, reads as follows in the verse sequence of most English translations: "His heart is hard as stone, hard as the nether millstone."

It is no less ironic that the dramatic context of the Job passage is God's answer to Job's inquiry concerning the presence of divine justice in the experience of the suffering of the righteous. The divine response out of the whirlwind (Job 38–41) is to pose a series of counter-questions concerning the power of God in creation, a creation which ultimately bears witness to the divine purposes in creation. Those purposes are not subject to human judgment, for the goodness of creation is not simply good for human beings. Rather, human beings are but a part of the created order, the whole of which the Creator alone understands and measures (cf. Job 34:10–12). In contrast to the proud self-assertion of hard-hearted fools, wise human beings find and fulfil their place in creation. The fear of God, not fear of losing one's possessions or the external power of motion, is the beginning of wisdom and good judgment.

In his magisterial study in theological politics, *De Civitate Dei*, Augustine distinguishes between the society ordered by *amor Dei* (love of God) and the city centred around *amor sui* (love of self).[18] The latter is ordered by the autonomous rule of human will, corrupted by pride, and oriented toward the pursuit and possession of primary goods. To live according to *amor sui* is to live a lie, for human beings were not created to live only unto themselves.[19] Such a life ends up trapped by love of temporal objects, caught in the perversions of *lascivia* (lusts of the flesh – the quest for pleasure as mere satisfaction of desires), *curiositas* (lust of the eye – knowledge for knowledge's sake, lacking judgment), and *superbia* (pride of life – perverse imitation of God in the vainglorious desire to be feared and loved by others).[20] Such a city is characterised by the *libido dominandi* ("lust for domination") that Hobbes accepts as the natural human state, and which he believes can be curbed only by fear of death and the external constraints of contractual justice, a commonwealth devoted to the collective domination of nature via the cooperative production and consumption of commodities. The solution to the disordered life of *amor sui*, in Hobbes' view, is to ensure that its private desires be satisfied more efficiently and peacefully through the establishment of an external coordinating mechanism – the commonwealth.

In Augustine's view, the Hobbesian solution, by merely treating the symptoms of disorder, only feeds the disease, which is a spiritual one. The only cure for the disorder created by human life organized around *amor sui* is a reorientation of human desires by *amor Dei*, turning the will from a false and therefore harmful self-sufficiency toward a participation in God, in the love of whom is found the proper ordering of created goods. Such loving recognition of the meaning and end of the created order is required if transcendent justice is to be mediated in human life. The *ordo creationis* provides a quite different foundation for political science and political economy from that of the *ordo artificialis* of the Hobbesian commonwealth.

With the symbol of creation we enter the realm of symbolic action *par excellence*. Here the battle against the mechanistic, impersonal categories of positivist science concerning the true nature of reality is seriously engaged. Is the reality of human experience best understood in personal terms as a spiritual drama in which all creatures have their life through God's creative spirit? Is it possible to affirm with Job, "If [God] should take back his spirit to himself, and gather to himself his breath, all flesh would perish together, and man would return to dust" (Job 34:14–15; cf. Psalm 104:29–30)?[21] In Job, as indeed throughout the Bible, this spiritual relation is linked vitally to the possibility and realization of justice.

In the realm of economic justice, the symbol of creation implies the idea of stewardship as "usufruct," a term derived from classical civil law defined in the *Oxford English Dictionary* as "the right of temporary possession, use, or enjoyment of the advantages of property belonging to another, so far as may be had without causing damage or prejudice to this." This might be called a "theocentric utilitarianism" – using nature in a manner consistent with its created purposes. Such a moral economy is measured by the health of properties belonging ultimately to the Creator. To use properly and to enjoy fully the advantages of divinely created properties requires knowledge of their created purpose, their good, which is their true meaning. This the biblical literature calls wisdom. It is not mere technical knowledge that reduces good to "goods" or to the even more abstract quantitative measure of exchange, money.[22] Wisdom is characterized by love – only loving use of creation in relation to the mysterious, spiritual ordering power behind it can lead to enjoyment and what the biblical literature calls "blessing." In her speech in Proverbs 8 (17, 35–6), Wisdom states: "I love those who love me, and those who seek me diligently find me … For he who finds me finds life and obtains favour from the Lord; but he who misses me injures himself; all who hate me love death."

The term usufruct is comprised etymologically of two Latin terms – *usus* (use) and *fruitio* (enjoyment) – that are central to Augustine's creation theology.[23] Created in the image of God, human beings' *telos* is *fruitio dei*, to enjoy God by loving God, and the vocation of human beings is to mediate this *frui* in the world by referring all loves and created goods to the love of God. "Use" is therefore shaped by God's enjoyment of their created good, in which human beings can participate. "One lives in justice and sanctity when one is an unimpaired appraiser of the intrinsic reality of things. Such a one has an ordered love, who neither loves what should not be loved, nor fails to love what is lovable."[24] To love with an ordered love is to experience the transcendent measure of the divine Good (*ipsum bonum*) through the love of God, in whom is found "the goodness of every good" (*bonum omnis boni*). Since only what is good can truly draw one's love, true judgment concerning particular goods is found in one's loving relation to the "good Good" (*bonum bonum*) that transcends and yet indwells all particular goods.[25]

One who uses created goods in such a manner does not love them as private possessions, as one ordered by *amor sui* does, for the latter represents a shrunken self characterized by privation, unable to love even itself: "Therefore those who know how to love themselves, love God; while those who do not love God, though they retain the love of self which belongs to their nature, may yet properly be said to hate themselves when they pursue what is contrary to their own good and behave to themselves as an enemy. It is indeed a horrible delusion by which, though all desire their own advantage, so many do only what is most destructive to them."[26] By nature, goods are enjoyed only by being shared in the community of good that is created and enjoyed by God. In this manner love is seen to be creative; it builds up rather than destroys or diminishes the common good. As Augustine puts it in *De Civitate Dei*: "Goodness is in no way diminished when it is shared, either momentarily or permanently, with others, but expands and, in fact, the more heartily the lovers of goodness enjoy the possession together the more it grows. What is more, goodness is not merely a possession that no one can maintain who is not willing to have it in common, but it is one that increases the more its possessor loves to share it."[27] Precisely in this way do human beings become true imitators of the Creator, participating actively in the movement of earthly goods toward their intended purpose and *fruitio*. This is the uniquely human vocation – to mediate the purposes and therefore the blessings of the Creator, to be the instrument of God's creative work. "All these [created works] we see, and that they are very good, because you see them in us and it was you who gave us the Spirit by which we see these things and love you in them."[28] The measure of justice is the divine measure that understands the purposes of divinely created things. It is mediated by those persons who are related through love to the Creator and who mediate God's purposes in their responsible care and loving use of goods that participate for their meaning and enjoyment in a common goodness. Life lived according to the ordered love of *amor Dei* results in the true expression of the created meaning of human nature as *imago Dei*, capable of *imitatio Dei*.

Here we are brought back once again to the question of the proper symbolization of human nature and society in relation to the order of nature. Cosmologies, as Kenneth Burke points out, are "principles of governance" in regard to our understanding not only of nature but also of the conditions of socio-political order.[29] Hence "order" is an ambiguous word that can apply both to nature and/or to political society, and this is why the images we use to understand either realm are so important to our response and participation. The symbol of creation, in contrast to the mechanico-material vision of order, implies a moral order present in both realms, for both are ultimately ordered by God to whom human beings stand in spiritual, moral relation. Objects can but move or be moved, but people can act and therefore have responsibility – that is, they are able to respond in trust or distrust, in obedience or pride, in love or contempt of the One to whom they are related and whose image they bear. This is why biblical narrative always discusses creation in the context of covenant – the various relationships of the people to God in the ongoing dialogue (or lack of dialogue) between them. In true Augustinian spirit, Burke states this as follows: "Logologically, the statement that God made man in his image would be translated as: The principle of personality implicit in the idea of the first creative fiats, whereby all things are approached in terms of the word, applies also to the feeling for symbol-systems on the part of the human animal, who would come to read nature as if it were a book."[30] It is for this reason that the false images of false gods have such devastating consequences: they represent purposes and principles that destroy life, and human beings who image false gods therefore mediate destruction in their thought and action.

AUGUSTINIAN REALISM

I wish in conclusion to indicate what I take to be the most significant points of contrast between the Augustinian parameters of political theory rooted in a theology of creation and the various modern North American approaches examined in this book. My purpose here is not to contrast the modern approaches with one another; that I have done in the body of the book. Rather my aim is to show that Augustine's theoretical account of the nature of political reality as rooted in the order of creation provides him with principles of interpretation that differ fundamentally from the theoretical accounts offered by the influential North American approaches to religious social ethics that we have considered. Using these principles, Augustine, in his *De Civitate Dei*, elaborates a religious realism that discloses not only the spiritual crisis of the Roman Empire but provides resources for disclosing the spiritual crisis of the modern West as well. My argument will be that the failure of modern North American social ethics to take these resources into account has resulted in a failure to discern the extent of the crisis in the political economies and in the public life generally of liberal societies.

Perhaps the shortest and best path to the heart of this contrast is to consider the analysis of Augustine offered by the putatively most "Augustinian" of the ethicists considered in this book, Reinhold Niebuhr. Niebuhr's form of Christian realism has often been called Augustinian and Niebuhr himself adverts to this in an essay in *Christian Realism and Political Problems* titled "Augustine's Political Realism." In this essay Niebuhr identifies Augustine as "the first great 'realist' in western history,"[31] and he attributes this to the "dramatic-historical mode of apprehension" that characterizes Augustine's biblical conception of selfhood, as opposed to classical "rationalistic" conceptions of reality. Augustine's approach is able to comprehend the transcendent freedom of the human self beyond any rational or natural system of coherence. Augustine's realism is rooted in an analysis of loves, where the self's abandonment of its true end in the "love of God" (the guiding principle in the *civitas Dei*) leads to an inordinate "self-love" or *superbia* (pride) which is the root of evil, conflict, and injustice in the *civitas terrena* (the earthly city). Despite Niebuhr's appreciation for Augustinian realism, he makes some rather significant and self-revealing criticisms of Augustine's account of the different kinds of love that found the two cities.

Niebuhr credits Augustine with an "excessively realistic" account of the tensions, corruptions of self- interest, and forms of social and political domination present within all levels of community in the earthly city. It is an excessive realism rooted in an "excessive emphasis upon the factors of power and interest," which provides a welcome corrective to Ciceronian moralism (as articulated in Scipio's definition of the commonwealth),[32] but which fails to do justice to relative distinctions of true justice present also in communities belonging to the *civitas terrena*.[33] The problem here, suggests Niebuhr, is Augustine's normative conception of an "order of nature" rooted in a "primitivist" theology of creation that leads him to make indiscriminate socio-political criticisms of fallen human societies and does not adequately avail itself of relative "calculations of justice."[34]

Of course, when Augustine's discussion of the order of nature as tied to the divine act of creation is dismissed as a kind of "primitivism" and his discussion of the "order of loves" is isolated from the former and focused on the self-transcendent self whose mysterious freedom cannot find its norm in any natural or rational structures of ordered coherence,[35] a rather different kind of realism emerges.

Niebuhr's form of "biblical realism," in contrast to Augustine's, draws a radical distinction between nature and history.[36] Nature is the realm of mechanistic causality closed to divine intervention and is best understood through the modern natural sciences, whereas history is the realm of human freedom in relation to God, which cannot be understood within any rational or natural order and is ultimately mysterious. Hence historical events "presuppose an existential incoherence between human striving and the divine will" and can be understood only by faith, a faith that finds its meaning in the suprarational and supernatural divine suffering love for which "no reason can be given."[37] Niebuhr's interpretation of the biblical myth of creation supports this distinction and relates the creation myth to the unique, contradictory, paradoxical, and mysterious nature of free human selfhood in history: "The concept of creation defines the mystery beyond both natural and rational causalities, and its suprarational character is underscored when Christian theology is pressed to accept the doctrine of creation *ex nihilo*. Thereby a realm of freedom and mystery is indicated beyond the capacity of reason to comprehend. This is where reason starts and ends. The final irrationality of the givenness of things is frankly accepted."[38]

Love as "the harmonious relation of life to life" may be the law of human nature,[39] but this is not a rational harmony that links human beings to the created order of nature. Rather it is an "ultimate harmony" characterized by the paradoxes and contradictions of human historical experience. It is not surprising, then, that Niebuhr's second line of criticism against Augustinian realism concerns Augustine's account of the nature of love. Just as Augustine's account of justice too completely refers the meaning of justice to the perfection of divine ordering to recognise the relative possibilities of "calculative" justice in the earthly city, says Niebuhr, so also Augustine's account of love too consistently and comprehensively (one might say "too coherently") refers the nature and fulfilment of love to its ultimate end in *amor Dei*.[40] Such a radical theocentrism provides a safeguard against all forms of idolatry but "it hardly reveals the full paradox of self-realization through self-giving which [is] a scandal in the field of rational ethics as the Cross is a scandal in the field of rational religion."[41] Niebuhr attributes this problem in Augustine's thought to an excessive dependence upon a neo-Platonic eudaemonistic moral framework. Within such a rational cosmology love is too quickly integrated into an ultimate account of cosmic fulfilment, happiness, and harmony. This denies the mystery of suprarational, self-transcendent human freedom and obscures the radically sacrificial expression of *agape* in the love of neighbour, which can never be based on a rational calculation of the object and end of love. Indeed, asserts Niebuhr, Augustine fails to appreciate the equality of the love of neighbour and the love of God in New Testament *agape* when he subordinates the former to the latter as the more worthy object of love. Niebuhr maintains that Augustine has been influenced in the development of his conception of *amor Dei* too much by classical as opposed to biblical understanding. He therefore focuses excessively on conflict in the earthly city and attributes too much rational harmony to the *amor Dei* of the city of God.

The question concerning Augustine's understanding of the nature of love far exceeds the treatment it can be given here.[42] Several comments pertinent to our topic and to Niebuhr's criticisms, however, are in order. Augustine's interpreters are correct in emphasizing the inextricable connection between his account of the order of love and his understanding of creation.[43] Reality is ordered by the law of love as the principle of creative movement of all things toward their fulfilment. The doctrine of *creatio ex nihilo* preserves this connection, and it refers not to the irrational "givenness" of things nor even primarily to the incomprehensible mystery of self-transcendent human freedom. For Augustine it refers to the founding principle of created reality, that God created the world not out of necessity but in an absolutely free, gratuitous act of love out of the abundance of God's own goodness.[44] However, created nature is not simply an emanation of God's own being; it is therefore mortal, subject to change and comprised of various forms and modes of existence and their complex interrelations in a dynamic order of nature. In this order of nature the movement of creatures is governed by the inclination of each thing or being to find its fitting place in the harmony of the whole created order.[45] As rational creatures created in the divine image, human beings are drawn to their fitting end or supreme good by the weight of their love. And the fitting end for which human beings are created is the *fruitio Dei*, the loving enjoyment of God as the source of existence, knowledge, and love. This is the beatitude or happiness sought by all human beings, the attainment of which provides peace in the truly creative concord of love and justice.

Given the mortality and mutability of human nature, however, it is possible for human beings to turn away from their final end, from the supreme good, and to seek their happiness instead in the possession of temporal, contingent goods. This, according to Augustine, represents the defective, privative love of *amor sui* that leads to the loss of human integrity, health, virtue, and happiness; that is, a loss of goodness through perversion.[46] The perversion lies in the deliberate choice of a lower level of natural existence in which human creative power, rational intelligence, and will (loves and affections) are directed solely toward transient ends. Such an orientation can neither measure nor use created goods in a fitting, creative manner, and it leads inevitably to discord, violent conflict, and destruction.[47] The second important meaning of *creatio ex nihilo*, therefore, is the derivative nature of created existence. Human beings retain their rational freedom and creativity by adhering (*cohaerere*) in obedience to their supreme and true *principium* of existence, by participation in the true God.[48] Human beings fall away from their created nature when they turn away in pride from the true source of their good and attempt to establish themselves as their own *principium*. Such self-sufficiency turns out to be a deficiency, a diminished and defective mode of existence that seeks its happiness in the private possession of goods and ends up trapped by its own disordered, confused, and divided desires.[49]

The first point to be made against Niebuhr's interpretation of Augustine, then, is that for Augustine the supra-terrestrial or spiritual realm is not supra-rational or supra-natural. Indeed rational human nature must cling to the invisible divine power, the supreme Good which is common to all created goods, if it is to exercise its rational, affective, and bodily nature in an ordered way that brings happiness. For Augustine creation reveals symbolically the true *principia* or *archai* of reality as authored by God, and the roots of creative human authorship and rational or free agency in all spheres of existence lie in comprehension of that order. This comprehension – this vision or *theoria* – is made possible in love of God. One sees truly by adhering, cohering, or clinging to the Source of truth, who dwells in love and holds all things together in an order of love. This is the nature of wisdom, according to Augustine, that integrates the self (in its thoughts, affections, and actions) and all communities (households, cities, world, and universe) in the divine order of love,[50] which alone can preserve a "harmonious unity in plurality."[51]

On Augustine's view, therefore, the life of Christ which culminates in the Cross is not a message of incomprehensible, irrational divine suffering or sacrifice, as Niebuhr has it. Rather it is the revelation of the divine measure of humble love that purifies the mind (*mens*) – the natural seat of human reason (*ratio*) and understanding (*intelligentia*) – so that it may see reality properly and respond to it fittingly.[52] Augustine's realism is rooted not only in a "dramatic-historical mode of apprehension" but also in a "dramatic-natural" and "dramatic-rational" theology of creation. The humility of Christ evident in his self-sacrificial love is redemptive because it mediates the divine potency of creative love which reestablishes the proper ordering of creation, the community of good.[53] As the Mediator of divine goodness and wisdom, Christ simultaneously images the divine goal of human life – participation in God – and the human path to it – the way of humble love.[54] Christ therefore incarnates the *principium* or *logos* of existence and offers the way of purification by which human beings can return to their true good, identified by Augustine in his frequently repeated citation of Psalm 73:28, "*adhaerere Deo bonum est*" ("it is good to cling to God").[55]

This is the context in which to understand Augustine's eudaemonism, which is not focused primarily on *self*-fulfilment or happiness, but seeks the establishment of the true order of love by referring all thought, action, and desire to God as the supreme Good and end of all loves.[56] Of course, on this view Augustine would certainly consider Niebuhr's definition of *agape* as the equality of love of God and love of neighbour not only to be highly irrational but also profoundly mistaken – not a divine mystery. This is because Augustine affirms a rational order of nature, an ontological scale of good that corresponds to "rightly ordered love" (*ordo est amoris*), Augustine's definition of virtue which is the condition of the good life.[57] Hence his appeal to the canticle taken from the *Song of Songs* (2:4, LXX) sung by the City of God: "*Ordinate in me caritatem*" ("Set love in order in me").[58] Idolatry is precisely disordered love rooted in a false vision of reality. To equate love of God and love of neighbour is a confusion of unequal goods and their fitting relations in the order of creation. It is true that love of self and love of neighbour can be equated, since human beings are equal goods in the order of love and stand at the spiritual apex of the created order, created as they are in the image of God. But one cannot equate temporal, derivative, and dependent goods or beings and the eternal source and end of all good and all love.[59]

Indeed, to equate neighbour love and love of God leads to a confused understanding of sacrifice as well. In Augustine's understanding, it would be idolatrous and perverse to sacrifice oneself only for another human being without consideration for the larger ordering of love and the final meaning of life. Sacrifice is ultimately due only to God as the supreme and only Good common to all.[60] Sacrificial love, therefore, must always be directed toward God who alone has the creative power to establish the common good in the adherence to which the good of the neighbour can find its fulfilment as well. Such self-sacrifice is a rational scandal only to those whose reason is not rightly ordered by love. One who sees reality *secundum spiritum* or *secundum Deum* rather than *secundum carnem* or *secundum hominem*[61] understands that all created goods find their final rest by "cleaving to God" in whom their particular good and happiness is perfected in the community of Good, the peace of the city of God. "Cleaving to God," then, is not simply an individual matter of self-fulfilment but is the reference of all things to their final good. This insight distinguishes "rational consideration" in free judgment from ideological judgments rooted in mere "constraint of need" (*necessitate indigentis*) oriented to self-interest or in the "attraction of desire" (*voluptate cupientis*) oriented toward purely external enjoyment.[62] Truly rational judgments are oriented toward the common good of *amor Dei* whereas ideological judgments are oriented toward the privative possessiveness of the *libido dominandi*.

We are now in a better position to understand Augustine's political realism and the inextricable rational, natural, and moral relation of love and social justice in his creation theology. I shall argue, contra Niebuhr, that while Augustine does not adopt a kind of proto-Hobbesian conflict model of political realism with regard to the *civitas terrena*, neither is his vision of the rational harmony of created nature as an order of love to be understood as making love *rather than* justice the ultimate measure of social existence.[63] The dualisms that Niebuhr falsely reads into Augustine's formulations, and Niebuhr's resistance to Augustine's insistence upon a rational eudaemonism rooted in a coherent theology of creation are both related to Niebuhr's separation of nature and history, of reason and faith.[64]

It is precisely the conflict model of political realism that Augustine rejects as an inadequate theoretical basis for understanding human nature, historical causality, and political morality. In contrast to the classical historiographies of Herodotus and Thucydides, each of whom developed a distinctive causal account of the conflictual history of the Hellenic world rooted in material causality and power politics,[65] Augustine's account of conflict and peace, disorder and justice is rooted in his understanding of the order of love revealed in the divine *logos*. This alone establishes the conditions for creative peace and justice in the true commonwealth, the only adequate principle of political and historical interpretation. It is for this reason that Augustine opposes the Ciceronian Scipio's definition of the commonwealth (in the *De re publica*) and the theory of justice that it assumes. Scipio defines the commonwealth as not just any group (*coetus multitudinis*) but as "an association united by a common sense of right [*iuris consensu*] and by common advantage [*utilitatis communione*]."[66] However, a common sense of right assumes the presence of justice (*iustitia*), and under this definition there never was a true Roman commonwealth. For justice is "that virtue which distributes to each his due [*sua cuique distribuere*]."[67] Since human beings must give the

Creator his due to establish the proper order which alone leads to "a common pursuit of interest" and "agreement on what is right," Rome never knew the true measure of justice and had never been a true commonwealth.[68]

Augustine then provides an alternative definition of a "people" (*populus*) as "a group of rational beings associated by common agreement on the objects of their love [*dilectum*]."[69] The quality (*qualis*) of any community – not only a city or a republic but also a household or a friendship – can be measured by the object of the love or desire that unites and orients it. The conflict, chaos, and eventual fall of Rome can be attributed to the common love that unites it, a common love symbolized by the power struggle and fratricide of Remus by Romulus that founded the *pax Romana*.[70] It is a love that clings with self-interest to the possession of temporal goods, and its rule is therefore characterised by the lust for domination and self-glorification. Indeed, it is a self-love that seeks to make use of God in order to enjoy the world and thus abandons true justice for a lesser measure.[71] Remus and Romulus represent the division of the earthly city against itself in the power struggle over finite goods. To understand the division between the privative self-love of the earthly city and the ordered love of the city of God, says Augustine, we must consider another fratricide that symbolises a different kind of struggle. This is the murder of Abel by Cain, and it represents the hostility of the wicked toward the good, the "diabolical envy" by the unjust of those who enjoy partnership in the common good.[72] Cain, whose very name means "*possessio*," claims Augustine, and whose libidinous quest for possessive dominion leads to murder and conflict, becomes the founder of the earthly city in the biblical record.[73]

This does not mean, however, that the earthly city completely lacks justice. Even those who hate the just peace of God, the fellowship of human equality under God, who in pride and perverse imitation of God seek to impose their own unjust order or dominion on others – even they cannot help loving some kind of peace. For "no creature's perversion [*vitium*] is so contrary to nature as to destroy the last vestiges of its nature."[74] Even what is defective, then, must be at peace in some sense with the harmonious order of things if it is to exist at all. This is as true in the spiritual order of nature as in the material laws of nature, all of which is under the rule of the Creator and Ordinator who oversees the *pax universitatis*. This peace of the universal whole Augustine describes as the *tranquillitas ordinis*, the tranquility of order in which each equal and unequal thing finds its assigned proper place (*sua cuique loca*) in the whole.[75] For rational creatures this peace is found in the ordered agreement of thought and action in the will moved by *amor Dei*. Insofar as their love is properly ordered, human beings in society will enjoy the *ordinata concordia*, the harmonious order of the peaceful community.[76] However, even in improperly ordered communities there must be a *compositio voluntatum*, an arrangement of wills, that makes possible a certain measure of justice and concord necessary for any kind of community to exist.[77] This is not a Niebuhrian compromise between a transcendent ideal and historical ideological realities, but a concrete arrangement based on common objects of love or desire, a shared orientation of wills, and a shared pursuit of certain goods reflected in public rationality and institutions. Augustine then proceeds to formulate the implications of this redefinition of the commonwealth: the better the objects of the common agreement that unites a people, the better the people; the worse the objects of love that orient public rationality and justice, the worse the people.[78]

Peace and justice, in Augustine's understanding, are not tied to a static state of nature but to a dynamic ordering process in which the principle of movement is love. In this ordering no part can be considered in isolation from the larger whole since the purpose and place of each is found in the fellowship of all in the created order ordered by God. Peace is the universal longing of all creation according to the universal law operative throughout nature. The law of each part's nature is related to this universal law, moving that part toward the free and harmonious fulfilment of its purpose. All things are therefore ordered by love toward the fulfilment of their created capacities in that ultimate peace and perfectly ordered harmony of the supreme Good.[79] This ultimate peace or final end does of course surpass human understanding, says Augustine following Saint Paul.[80] But it is not thereby trans-rational or trans-natural, for we are made participants in this divine peace and know its perfection according to our mode of being (*pro modo*). It is a transcendent measure to which the nature and proper use of all temporal goods, peace, and justice should be referred for an understanding of their true meaning, and it is the measure of divine love. There is here no possibility of setting power, interest, or justice over against some ideal of love. A true and just order is rooted not in love of power but in the power of love that clings to the divine source and measure of created good. This is the fundamental principle for individual and social harmony and happiness.

Augustine's political realism and religious social theory are rooted in a rational anthropology situated within a theology of creation that understands both nature and history in terms of the order of divine love. This understanding supports the Christian realists' criticism of the social gospel analysis of the social crisis as representing a confusion of symbolisms. That is, the social gospel interprets a Remus-Romulus power struggle over finite goods and their just distribution too directly in terms of the struggle between Cain's self-love (the earthly city) and Abel's love of God (the kingdom of God). Such a formulation of the problem as a struggle between immanent political powers cannot disclose the spiritual or religious dimension of the political economic crisis. However, the Augustinian approach also offers grounds for criticizing both the Roman Catholic bishops and the North American varieties of Christian realism. In contrast to Niebuhr's "frank dualism" of morals which separates nature and history – correlatively reducing reason to the immanent and mechanistic calculations of natural phenomena and relating faith to a transcendent, mysterious ideal that does not attend to consequences – Augustine's realism relates nature and history to the order of creation in a wisdom that does not separate reason and revelation.[81] Nor does Augustine set self-transcendent individuals over against social and natural forces and relations. Human beings are social by nature just as they are rational creatures, set as corporeal and spiritual beings into a dramatic and interrelated order of nature. This whole web of created beings and their complex relations must be referred for their meaning, good use, and an understanding of their consequences to the divine order of love in which their existence is sustained and their purpose fulfilled. A politics and an economics rooted in love of domination and of the possession of commodities is destined to result in violent conflict, disorder, and destruction.

In contrast to the religious realism of Gregory Vlastos and the FCSO, who rightly challenge the elements of individualism and supernatural idealism present within Niebuhr's approach, Augustinian realism understands not just society but also nature in dramatistic terms. To represent the machine as (next to language) "the greatest instrument of cooperative community"[82] is to misunderstand the relation of justice to love in the order of creation. Vlastos substitutes here the external and artificial instrument for the rational insight rooted in love that he otherwise emphasizes, and it reflects a modern mechanistic understanding of nature and of the human use of natural goods. In Augustine's view a humanly made artifact can never become the proper basis for social concord, though of course artifacts and machines have their proper place in the order of goods when related to the just basis of social concord, the order of love. By contrast a technological basis for social concord as embodied in the practices and institutions of liberal capitalism is rooted in an economistic construal of the common good. When the Catholic bishops call for equal, democratic "participation" in such a common good as the very meaning of social justice then the meaning of human nature as created in *imago Dei* comes to be interpreted through the abstract and external measures of technical policy choices within the "productivist paradigm."

The problem here, from the standpoint of an Augustinian realism, is that a circumference of interpretation with wide scope (the symbol of creation) is reduced to a very narrow principle of interpretation (human production and consumption). This results in a misconstrual of the nature of reality itself as an outer set of material and social processes to be functionally subordinated to human purposes, defined as the progressive instrumental control and possession of nature. The consequences of this narrow vision of reality in the modern West were clearly evident already to Max Weber: the creation of an increasingly uniform, mechanistic, spiritless "iron cage" in which our choices and interactions are ever more narrowly constricted within short-term utility calculations and the collective slavery to material processes. In a cosmos construed as dead matter propelled by blind force, ordered by impersonal causality, we have lost the sense of belonging within a natural order charged with divine goodness.[83] In a utilitarian consumer society where possessive individuals are out to maximise their own interests and preferences, equipped with rights to protect their belongings, we lose sight of what it means to belong to one other in a community of trust. Having conceived our world as alien and abstract, we dare not trust it, and so we become preoccupied with securing ourselves against it – materially, emotionally, spiritually. Because we do not have a shared sense of a larger common purpose that unites various parts of society and nature into a meaningful whole, we seek security in a stifling formal equality of rights and in artifacts, which further preclude genuine communication through understanding in a common good. Such a world is strangely silent, empty of dialogue, trust, and shared purpose – as it was for Qoheleth: "All is vanity and a striving after the wind."

Such a reductive realism represents the loss of the experience of *amor Dei* that opens human beings to a trustworthy transcendent measure of things. This leads in turn to the privation of public life and a reductive understanding of the common good as the production and consumption of commodities. I have argued that such a measure, represented in the parameters of economic policy discourse, cannot disclose or address the spiritual crisis of modern liberal society. Only the recovery of symbolic language and the experience of the spiritual reality it represents can do so. To participate and understand such experience, however, requires that one give up the need to control it in order to love it, for it is ultimately not at human disposal.

Notes

1 On the "sublimation of politics" see Wolin, *Politics and Vision: Continuity and Innovation in Western Political Thought*, chapter 10. Wolin also has a brilliant essay on Weber, "Max Weber: Legitimation, Method, and the Politics of Theory," *Legitimacy and the State*, ed. Connolly, 63–87.

2 Weber, "Wissenschaft als Beruf," *Gesammelte Aufsatze zur Wissenschaftslehre*, vol. 3, 612. The English version is "Science as a Vocation," *From Max Weber*, 155.

3 See Weber, *The Protestant Ethic and the Spirit of Capitalism*, 24.

4 See the essays by Weber in *The Methodology of the Social Sciences*; see also the comparative essay by Löwith, *Max Weber and Karl Marx*.

5 "But it is above all the impersonal and economically rationalized (but for this very reason ethically irrational) character of purely commercial relationships that evokes the suspicion, never clearly expressed but all the more strongly felt, of ethical religions." Weber, *The Sociology of Religion*, 216. The paradox is, of course, that the ethical rationalization of ascetic Protestantism actually resulted in this contradictory situation (ibid., 218ff.).

6 Weber, "*Politik als Beruf*," *Gesammelte Politische Schriften*, vol. 3, 559. The English version is "Politics as a Vocation," *From Max Weber*, 128.

7 "Dass das Leben, solange es in sich selbst beruht und aus sich selbst verstanden wird, nur den ewigen Kampf jener Götter miteinander kennt, – unbildlich gesprochen: die Unvereinbarkeit und also die Unaustragbarkeit des Kampfes der letzten überhaupt möglichen

Standpunkte zum Leben, die Notwendigkeit also: zwischen ihnen sich zu entscheiden." Weber, "Wissenschaft als Beruf," 608.

8 Weber, *Protestant Ethic*, 104.

9 Weber makes these relevant comments in "Science as a Vocation": "All pietist theology of the time ... knew that God was not to be found along the road by which the Middle Ages had sought him. God is hidden, His ways are not our ways, His thoughts are not our thoughts. In the exact sciences, however, where one could physically grasp His works, one hoped to come upon the traces of what he planned for the world" (142). This religious and theological confidence in the natural sciences, of course, died out together with the piety that nourished it.

10 Weber, *Protestant Ethic*, 109.

11 I borrow the term from Hannah Arendt, *The Human Condition*, to describe Weber's interpretation of the Calvinist understanding of the doctrine of *imago dei* – that the "wonderfully purposeful organization and arrangement of this cosmos is ... evidently designed by God to serve the utility of the human race" (*Protestant Ethic*, 109).

12 Weber, *Protestant Ethic*, 163.

13 Ibid., 169.

14 Ibid., 165–6.

15 Ibid., 176.

16 Ibid., 181.

17 This is Weber's definition of the decisive aspect of any religious ethic, in *Sociology of Religion*, 209.

18 See Weber, "Science as a Vocation," 139ff.

19 Ibid., 151.

20 Benne, *The Ethic of Democratic Capitalism: A Moral Reassessment*.

21 Stackhouse, *Public Theology and Political Economy*.

22 Weber, *Protestant Ethic*, 182.

23 See Weber, "'Objectivity' in Social Science and Social Policy," *The Methodology of the Social Sciences*, 81; cf. 106–7.

24 Voegelin, *The New Science of Politics*, 131.

25 On this point see also Kohak, *The Embers and the Stars: A Philosophical Inquiry into the Moral Sense of Nature*, especially chapter 5.

26 Hans Jonas says this another way: "The expansion of [human] power is accompanied by a contraction of [human] self-conception and being" ("Technology and Responsibility: Reflections on the New Tasks of Ethics," *Philosophical Essays: From Ancient Creed to Technological Man*, 11).

27 See *Institutes of the Christian Religion*, Book I, chapter v, where Calvin states: "I confess, of course, that it can be said reverently, provided

that it proceeds from a reverent mind, that nature is God" (I,v,5; cf. I,v,9; I, xvi).

28 "When I see the blind and wretched state of man, when I survey the whole universe in its dumbness and man left to himself with no light, as though lost in this corner of the universe, without knowing who put him there, what he has come to do, what will become of him when he dies, incapable of knowing anything, I am moved to terror, like a man transported in his sleep to some terrifying desert island, who wakes up quite lost and with no means of escape" (Pascal, *Pensées*, 88).

29 Weber, "Science as a Vocation," 140–1. The German text reads: "Die Gedankenbilde der Wissenschaft sind ein hinterweltliches Reich von künstlichen Abstraktionen, die mit ihren dürren Händen Blut und Saft des wirklichen Lebens einzufangen trachten, ohne es doch je zu erhaschen" "Wissenschaft als Beruf" (595).

30 Jonas, *The Phenomenon of Life: Toward a Philosophical Biology,* 58ff.

31 This was first brought to my attention in Barfield, *Speaker's Meaning,* 114–15.

32 One can note a similar change in the lexical meaning of the word "objective" in its philosophical definition in the *Oxford English Dictionary.* Its obsolete meaning is "appearance" as distinct from "essence" (the obsolete meaning of "subjective"): "existing as an object of consciousness as distinct from having any real existence; considered only as presented to the mind (not as it is, or may be, in itself or its own nature)." Its modern meaning is reversed: "the object of perception or thought ... that is, or has the character of being, a 'thing' external to the mind; real."

33 Arendt, "The Concept of History: Ancient and Modern," *Between Past and Future,* chapter 2.

34 This is true also of modern critics of capitalism, such as C.B. Macpherson and Jürgen Habermas. The classic goal of the liberal democratic tradition, argues Macpherson, is freedom within diversity – the equal freedom of all for self-actualization. But rather than consider what human "freedom" and "self-actualization" really mean (liberals charily avoid such substantive questions), the burden of Macpherson's critique is that liberal capitalism's market processes are unequal, in terms of both opportunities and outcomes. See Macpherson, *Democratic Theory: Essays in Retrieval; The Rise and Fall of Economic Justice and Other Essays.* For Jürgen Habermas' similar argument concerning the formal ideal of an "undistorted speech situation" and political economic realities that contradict this, see *Legitimation Crisis,* 89ff., 107ff.; Habermas and Luhmann, *Theorie der*

Gesellschaft oder Sozialtechnologie – Was leistet die Systemforschung?, 101ff.

35 Kenneth Burke asserts: "After a society has thoroughly adapted its ways to an economy in which money figures as an end rather than means, you may expect its members to carry on a maximum percentage of activities that would seem irrational in any other context." The efficacy of money is in the realm of social motives what Occam's Razor is in the realm of physical motives (Burke, *A Grammar of Motives*, 95). Cf. notes 5 above and 39 below.

36 Borgmann, *Technology and the Character of Contemporary Life*, 80.

37 See Hirsch, *Social Limits to Growth*, especially part 2; Leiss, *The Limits to Satisfaction: An Essay on the Problem of Needs and Commodities*.

38 This term is used by Connolly, *Appearance and Reality in Politics*.

39 That is, "free rider" problems arise precisely in times when the social order requires sacrificial commitment and allegiance to its structures and policy objectives. See Connolly, "The Dilemma of Legitimacy," *Legitimacy and the State*: "We publicly call upon the state to promote growth, eliminate superfluous public programmes, control inflation, and discipline those who siphon off public resources; and we privately resist the specific sacrifices it would impose upon us" (231). See also Cohen and Rogers, *On Democracy*, chapter 3, who point out how the structures of capitalist democracy encourage individual agents and groups to apply a utilitarian calculus and rational economic motivation to all goods, including collective ones.

40 Burke, *Grammar of Motives*, chapter 3.

41 Eric Voegelin observes: "The expansion of the will to power from the realm of phenomena to that of substance, or the attempt to operate in the realm of substance pragmatically as if it were the realm of phenomena – that is the definition of magic. The interrelation of science and power, and the consequent cancerous growth of the utilitarian segment of existence, have injected a strong element of magic culture into modern civilization" (Voegelin, "The Origins of Scientism," 488).

42 See ibid., 462–94; Voegelin, "Industrial Society in Search of Reason," 31–46.

43 Sheldon Wolin notes that these widely shared methodological assumptions associated with scientific positivism lead modern social and political theorists to search for the scientific "laws" of social organization and change in order to address the very problems of social solidarity and meaning created by the rise of industrial society based on and oriented by the application of such laws. The science of society in the nineteenth and twentieth centuries is modelled after the natural sciences and is directed toward a similar functional application of ideas and values as hypotheses whose validity is determined

by their social and political utility. The root belief is that communal solidarity and meaning in the industrial age will be restored scientifically, via rational organization and technical planning. See Wolin, *Politics and Vision*, chapter 10.

44 Kenneth Burke traces the reduction of circumference in the history of modern thought from God's design to natural law and naturalism to the materialism of evolutionary and historicist views to "economic factors" and narrow monetary and technological rationalisms: "And when we have arrived at the stage where the sheer symbols of exchange are treated as the basic motives of human relations, when we have gone from 'God's law' to 'natural law,' and thence to the 'market law' that had become a 'second nature' with those raised in a fully developed capitalist ethic, we find many pious apologists of the *status quo* who would deduce human freedom itself from the free market, as the only scene from which a free social act could be drawn. They thus attribute to the mechanics of price the position in the genealogy of action once held by no less distinguished a personage than God Himself, formerly defined as the ground of all possibility." Burke, *Grammar of Motives*, 92.

45 The contrast is developed in Job 28, where human knowledge of things and the technical ability to use them – "Man puts his hand to the flinty rock, and overturns mountains by the roots. He cuts out channels in the rocks, and his eye sees every precious thing. He binds up the streams so they do not trickle, and the thing that is hid he brings forth to light" (vv.9–11) – is distinguished from wisdom, which is not an object of human knowledge under human control: "But where is wisdom to be found? And where is the place of understanding? Man does not know the way to it, and it is not found in the land of the living ... It cannot be gotten for gold, and silver cannot be weighed as its price" (vv.12–15). Wisdom is linked to the divine purposes of the Creator in fashioning the creation, and it has a moral quality: "God understands the way to it [wisdom], and he knows its place ... When he gave to the wind its weight, and meted out the waters by measure ... then he saw it and declared it; he established it and searched it out. And he said to man, 'Behold, the fear of the Lord, that is wisdom; and to depart from evil is understanding'" (23–8). Wisdom, unlike knowledge, is not a possession, which is why it is personified in wisdom literature and stands in intimate relation to the divine purposes it mediates. We will return to this link between creation and wisdom in the concluding chapter.

46 Owen Barfield calls this the "idolatry of literalism," which can be overcome only through historical imagination, a historical remembering of the development of the images by which we think and act in

the world. See Barfield, *Saving the Appearances: A Study in Idolatry*; and *History, Guilt, and Habit.*

47 Barfield, "The Rediscovery of Meaning," *The Rediscovery of Meaning and Other Essays*, 14.

48 Albert Camus, *La peste* (Paris: Gallimard, 1947), 67.

CHAPTER TWO

1 For an account of the economic recession and consequent social struggles, see McConnell, *The Decline of Agrarian Democracy*; and Gordon, Edwards, and Reich, *Segmented Work, Divided Workers: The Historical Transformation of Labor in the United States*, chapter 3.

2 Walter Rauschenbusch argues that under early twentieth-century economic conditions "ordinary integrity becomes an heroic virtue"; *Christianizing the Social Order*, 206.

3 See Rauschenbusch, *Christianity and the Social Crisis*, 26; *The Social Principles of Jesus*, 28, 144; and *A Theology for the Social Gospel*, 184ff.

4 See, for example, Rauschenbusch, *Social Principles of Jesus*, 59–60.

5 Offe, *Contradictions of the Welfare State*, 259.

6 See Charles Taylor's critique of this in "Neutrality in Political Science," *Philosophy and the Human Sciences*, 58–90.

7 Bottomore, *Critics of Society: Radical Thought in North America.*

8 Cook, *The Regenerators: Social Criticism in Late Victorian English Canada*. This thesis is repeated in Allen Mills' study of Woodsworth's political thought, *Fool for Christ*, 253ff.

9 Cook, *The Regenerators*, 223.

10 Camus, "The Artist and His Time: Create Dangerously," *Resistance, Rebellion, and Death*, 250.

11 See Rauschenbusch, "The Influence of Historical Studies on Theology," especially the conclusion.

12 Rauschenbusch, *Christianity and the Social Crisis*, xiii.

13 Rauschenbusch, *A Theology for the Social Gospel*, 37.

14 See ibid., 167, 174.

15 Ibid., chapter 15.

16 Ibid., 146.

17 Rauschenbusch, *Christianizing the Social Order*, 97. Indeed, says Rauschenbusch, "The social gospel is concerned about a progressive social incarnation of God" (*Theology for the Social Gospel*, 148; cf. 223).

18 Rauschenbusch, *Christianity and the Social Crisis*, 22ff.

19 Rauschenbusch, *Theology for the Social Gospel*, 140.

20 Ibid., 174ff.

21 In all of Rauschenbusch's writings these three central values provide the criteria for a just or "Christian" social order as well as for an ade-

quate conception of God. See *Theology for the Social Gospel*, 187; *Christianizing the Social Order*, 104. He states at one point: "The splendid parole of the French Revolution: 'Liberty, equality, fraternity,' contains the social principles of the church." *The Righteousness of the Kingdom*, 173.

22 See Rauschenbusch, *The Social Principles of Jesus*, chapter 2; *Theology for the Social Gospel*, 270ff.

23 Rauschenbusch, *Christianizing the Social Order*, 44; cf. 332ff.

24 Rauschenbusch, *Christianity and the Social Crisis*, 421.

25 "This identification of the interest of God and man is characteristic of the religion of Jesus" (Rauschenbusch, *Theology for the Social Gospel*, 50). Christianity is most Christian when "the consciousness of God and the consciousness of humanity blend completely" (14). Jesus represents a new stage in the evolution of humanity and society in his consciousness of "the absolute unity of human and divine life" (152). Rauschenbusch's interpretation of the Atonement is based on Jesus' complete God-consciousness, his awareness of God's universal, cooperative solidarity with humankind (chapter 19).

26 Rauschenbusch, *The Social Principles of Jesus*, 128 (cf. 60, 141). The centrality of this "hinge" as Rauschenbusch's ultimate warrant for moving freely between theology and ethics, Scripture and experience, is elucidated by James Gustafson, "From Scripture to Social Policy and Social Action."

27 See Rauschenbusch, *Christianizing the Social Order*, 47; *Theology for the Social Gospel*, 11ff.; *Social Principles of Jesus*, chapter 9.

28 See Rauschenbusch, *Social Principles of Jesus*, chapters 1–3.

29 Rauschenbusch, *Christianity and the Social Crisis*, chapter 4.

30 See Rauschenbusch, *Christianizing the Social Order*, 83ff.; *Social Principles of Jesus*, 74ff.

31 See H.R. Niebuhr, *Christ and Culture*, chapter 3.

32 Rauschenbusch, *Social Principles of Jesus*, 35, 50; *Christianity and the Social Crisis*, 90ff.; *Theology for the Social Gospel*, chapters 10 and 11.

33 Note, for example, the dubious assertion that Jesus' religion is distinctive for its "happy and sunny character" (Rauschenbusch, *Social Principles of Jesus*, 54), and the inordinate confidence frequently expressed in the rational and moral capacities of society's elites (Rauschenbusch, *Christianity and the Social Crisis*, 220, 285, 409ff.).

34 Rauschenbusch, *Social Principles of Jesus*, part 4; *Theology for the Social Gospel*, chapters 4–11, 19.

35 Rauschenbusch, *Social Principles of Jesus*, chapter 11; *Theology for the Social Gospel*, chapter 19.

36 H.R. Niebuhr, *Christ and Culture*, chapter 6.

37 Rauschenbusch, *Social Principles of Jesus*, 196.

38 Rauschenbusch, *Christianizing the Social Order*, part 4; *Christianity and the Social Crisis*, chapter 5.
39 See Rauschenbusch, *Social Principles of Jesus*, 75–6.
40 Rauschenbusch, *Christianizing the Social Order*, 326.
41 Ibid., 194, 237.
42 See ibid., 200, 293ff.; *Theology for the Social Gospel*, chapters 8 and 11.
43 Ibid., 180ff.
44 Ibid., 194ff.
45 For recent social theoretical discussions of this problem, see Macpherson, *The Life and Times of Liberal Democracy*, 98ff.; Bernstein, *Beyond Objectivism and Relativism: Science, Hermeneutics, and Praxis*, 225ff.
46 Rauschenbusch states: "Social institutions are the slow growth of centuries; they will not rise ready-made from the ground when we stamp our foot. Even religion is not powerful enough to make a break in the continuity of history. All we can do is to take our social relations and institutions as we find them, and mold them whenever we find them at all plastic" (*Christianizing the Social Order*, 328).
47 See Rauschenbusch, *Christianity and the Social Crisis*, 190; *Christianizing the Social Order*, 100.
48 Rauschenbusch asserts: "For the first time in religious history we have the possibility of so directing religious energy by scientific knowledge that a comprehensive and continuous reconstruction of social life in the name of God is within the bounds of human possibility" (*Christianity and the Social Crisis*, 209).
49 Rauschenbusch, *Christianizing the Social Order*, 323.
50 Rauschenbusch, *Christianity and the Social Crisis*, 195.
51 Ibid., 350–1.
52 Ibid., 229, 254.
53 See Marx, "The German Ideology," *The Marx-Engels Reader*, 186ff.
54 Rauschenbusch, *Christianizing the Social Order*, 197; cf. 412ff.
55 Ibid., 394ff., 448ff.; *Christianity and the Social Crisis*, 407ff.
56 Ibid., 397.
57 Ibid., 457; *Christianity and the Social Crisis*, 409ff.
58 Further examples of the affinity between Rauschenbusch and Marxist social theory are Rauschenbusch's view of the dialectical historical movement toward socialist communitarianism (*Christianity and the Social Crisis*, 388ff.), his understanding of the formation of class consciousness and solidarity (ibid., 403ff.; *Christianizing the Social Order*, 394ff.), and his belief that capitalism cannot be reformed but must be abolished along with the class structure in order to realize a cooperative society in which there is a collective ownership of the means of production (ibid., 408; *Christianizing the Social Order*, 240ff.).

59 See Rauschenbusch, "The Ideals of the Social Reformers" and "Dogmatic and Practical Socialism," *The Social Gospel in America*, ed. Handy, part 3.

60 Here I disagree with Donald Meyer, who appears to ignore the predominance of Rauschenbusch's religio-ethical appeal. "The insights of modern social science were the logical foundations of Rauschenbusch's optimism. It was new knowledge that opened the way to a Christianized social order" (*The Protestant Search for Political Realism, 1918–41*, 17). As I have tried to show, Rauschenbusch's optimism and hopes for a Christian social order were rooted in his theology of history centred in the concept of the kingdom of God, a perspective which also includes the social sciences and their insights but is not logically founded on them. It is only as the economic and social sciences are employed in the service of a religious and moral vision of the true spiritual ends of life – the *human* good – that they attain their real object and function. The rest he calls external "scaffolding" (Rauschenbusch, *Social Principles of Jesus*, 124). Cf. Harlan Beckley's account of Rauschenbusch's religious theory of justice in Beckley, *Passion for Justice*, chapter 2.

61 See Rauschenbusch, *Christianity and the Social Crisis*, 285, 409ff.; *Christianizing the Social Order*, 468ff.; *Social Principles of Jesus*, chapter 7.

62 Or at least by "Marxist" and "Weberian" social theorists. On Marx, see note 58 above. Evidence of Weberian influence can be found in Rauschenbusch's statements on the inevitable forces of routinization, institutionalization, and formalization of the animating principles of a charismatic leader (*Christianity and the Social Crisis*, chapters 3 and 4) and his discussion of the unintended social consequences of religion in the link between Calvinism and capitalism (*Christianizing the Social Order*, 211ff.).

63 Rauschenbusch asserts: "Science has given us directive powers, and we can now make Nature make us. As we are comprehending the great laws of social life, the time for large directive action is coming, and we shall make Society make its members. My appeal is to Christian men to use the prophetic foresight and moral determination which their Christian discipleship ought to give them in order to speed and direct this process" (*Christianizing the Social Order*, 331; cf. 40ff.). "The race must increasingly turn its own evolution into a conscious process. It owes that duty to itself and to God who seeks an habitation in it. It must seek to realize its divine destiny ... It combines religion, social science, and ethical action in a perfect synthesis" (*Social Principles of Jesus*, 76). "Theology ought to be the science of redemption and offer scientific methods for the eradication of sin" (*Theology for the Social Gospel*, 57).

64 Lears, *No Place of Grace: Antimodernism and the Transformation of American Culture, 1880–1920*, 7, 64, and passim.

65 See Rauschenbusch, *Christianity and the Social Crisis*, 308, 409ff.

66 In *Social Principles of Jesus*, 77 (cf. 107ff.), Rauschenbusch explicitly calls this an ethic of *noblesse oblige*.

67 Rauschenbusch, *Christianity and the Social Crisis*, 274–5.

68 See Rauschenbusch, *Christianizing the Social Order*, 277ff.; Woodsworth, *Strangers Within Our Gates*, and the good discussion of this issue in Marilyn Barber's introduction to the volume. See also Mills, *Fool for Christ*, 42ff.

69 Woodsworth, *Strangers Within Our Gates*; *My Neighbor*.

70 Woodsworth, *My Neighbor*, 5.

71 Allen, *The Social Passion: Religion and Social Reform in Canada, 1914–28*, 4. This is true also of the radical Christian social activism of Nellie McClung, whose popular writings and novels represented an (often ignored) attempt to address social questions and bring about social reform from a feminist social gospel perspective. See Nellie L. McClung, *In Times Like These*, introduction by Veronica Strong-Boag (Toronto: University of Toronto Press, 1972).

72 See Woodsworth, *My Neighbor*, 14, 24, 127.

73 Woodsworth, *The First Story of the Labor Church and Some Things for Which It Stands*, 12.

74 Ibid., 13.

75 Ibid., 15.

76 Woodsworth, *My Neighbor*, 214.

77 Ibid., 109. An interesting parallel to this way of thinking is found in the writings of Ernst Troeltsch: "Modern protestantism no longer believes in the idea of revelation as held in early protestantism and catholicism .... It believes in the elevation, deepening, purification and empowering of human life through the personal powers which proceed from Jesus ... This is why the real life of protestantism is to be found outside the church" (Troeltsch, *Protestantisches Christentum und Kirche in der Neuzeit*, as cited in *Ernst Troeltsch: Writings on Theology and Religion*, ed. and trans. Morgan and Pye, 45).

78 For a detailed account of Woodsworth's transition from church to politics, and for a superb biography by an important Canadian historian, see McNaught, *A Prophet in Politics: A Biography of J.S. Woodsworth* (Toronto: University of Toronto Press, 1959). For an important study of Woodsworth's political thought, see Mills, *Fool for Christ*.

79 See Woodsworth, *My Neighbor*, 10ff., 127, 211ff. McNaught, commenting on Woodsworth's first speech in the Canadian House of Commons as the first Independent Labor Party member of Parliament, states: "Here was the linking of various themes into a total pattern of

responsibility – the voice of a conscience that would dog the cautious constitutionalists until Woodsworth's last days in the House. The insistence on accepting moral responsibility was to lead to bitter debates over the nature and purposes of the b.n.a. Act, the purposes of armaments, and Canadian foreign policy, as well as the functioning of class institutions and the profit motive" (*A Prophet in Politics*, 167).

80 Woodsworth, *My Neighbor*, 126.

81 See Woodsworth, *The First Story of the Labor Church*, 13.

82 The League for Social Reconstruction – the Canadian equivalent of the British Fabian Society – which made Woodsworth its honorary president, was a socialist think tank that produced the socio-economic analysis and research necessary for the policy planning of the ccf. See the important study by the Research Committee for the League for Social Reconstruction, *Social Planning for Canada*.

83 See Tawney, *The British Labor Movement*; McNaught, *A Prophet in Politics*, chapter 9; and the opening statement of the ccf's charter document, the "Regina Manifesto," in Young, *The Anatomy of a Party: The National ccf, 1932–61*, Appendix A, 304.

84 Note the eclecticism of Woodsworth's proposed solutions for labour conflict in *My Neighbor*, 54ff.

85 Woodsworth, quoted in Young, *The Anatomy of a Party*, 45.

86 Woodsworth said of the Federated Labor Party, a forerunner of the ccf: "The Labor Party leaves the 'scientific orthodox' groups and the revisionist groups to fight out their theories, but takes the great underlying principle stressed by Marx, viz., the collective ownership and democratic control of the means of wealth production. Men may differ widely in theory and yet unite to fight a common foe" (quoted in Penner, *The Canadian Left: A Critical Analysis*, 183).

87 For a classic expression of Fabian ideas on political economy, see Tawney, *The Acquisitive Society*.

88 See Macpherson, *The Life and Times of Liberal Democracy*, chapter 3; Held, *Models of Democracy*, chapter 4.

89 For a historical political analysis of this problem (which exists for all democratic socialist movements), see Przeworski, *Capitalism and Social Democracy*, chapters 1–3.

90 Rauschenbusch, *Theology for the Social Gospel*, 84–6.

91 See Troeltsch, "Was heisst 'Wesen des Christentums'?" in *Gesammelte Schriften*, Bd. 2, *Zur religiösen Lage, Religionsphilosophie und Ethik*, 386–451.

92 Troeltsch states: "Das Wesen ist ein Idealgedanke, der zugleich die Möglichkeit neuer Verknüpfungen mit dem konkreten Leben der Gegenwart bildet ... Es ist nichts anderes, als die der Gegenwart entsprechende Gestaltung des christlichen Gedankens, die sich an

frühere Gestaltungen anfugt, indem sie den Wachstrieb frei legt, aber auch ihn sofort in neue Blätter und Blüten schiessen lasst. Wesensbestimmung ist Wesensgestaltung" (ibid., 431). Defining the "essence" of Christianity is, to borrow a Tillichian term, a matter of "religiöse Verwirklichung" (religious realization). See Tillich, *Gesammelte Werke*, Bd. 2: *Christentum und Soziale Gestaltung: Frühe Schriften zum Religiösen Sozialismus.*

93 Rauschenbusch, *Theology for the Social Gospel*, 152.

94 Ibid., 145.

95 See Taylor, "Legitimation Crisis?" *Philosophy and the Human Sciences*, chapter 10.

96 This combination of technical control and the individual quest for fulfilment has given rise to a consumer culture vision of the "good life," with contradictory consequences: commodification of goods leads to enforced lifestyle needs; the high mobility and bureaucratization of social and economic life undermine kinship ties, community stability and citizenship participation; the imperatives of economic growth and productivity lead to the ruination of nature and require the sacrifice of creative work. The liberal outlook is captive to what Albert Borgmann calls the "irony of technology": the technological promise to provide access to liberating human self-realization for all by making available the instruments of control over nature leads rather to disengagement from reality in the production and consumption of commodities, the undermining of the very goods sought in classical liberalism, namely, liberty, equality, and fraternity.

97 Rauschenbusch identifies the economic system as "the strategic key to the spiritual conquest of the modern world" (*Christianizing the Social Order*, 458; cf. chapter 5 of the same book, ("The Last Entrenchment of Autocracy," which deals with capitalism.)

98 Rauschenbusch, *Theology for the Social Gospel*, 117.

CHAPTER THREE

1 For a concise statement of Niebuhr's critique see Niebuhr, "Walter Rauschenbusch in Historical Perspective."

2 It is necessary to add an immediate proviso here: first, that the approach of the FCSO was not uniform, and I shall develop the argument with reference (for the most part) to particular members of the FCSO. I also wish to make it clear that my argument focuses on the adequacy of the respective religious social theories of Niebuhr and the FCSO. Certainly Niebuhr's theological anthropology and theology of history are far more profoundly developed and related to the full range of Christian theological symbols than are the views of the

FCSO. The constraints of this study necessarily limit our attention to those aspects of Niebuhr's theological ethic that render his social theory less illuminating than the FCSO's model on matters of political economy.

3 See, for example, Reinhold Niebuhr, "Faith and the Empirical Method in Modern Realism" and "Ideology and the Scientific Method," in *Christian Realism and Political Problems*, chapters 1 and 6.

4 "This essential homelessness of the human spirit is the ground of all religion; for the self which stands outside itself and the world cannot find the meaning of life in itself or the world" (Reinhold Niebuhr, *The Nature and Destiny of Man*, 1:14; cf. *Moral Man and Immoral Society: A Study in Ethics and Politics*, 81–2; and *An Interpretation of Christian Ethics*, chapter 2).

5 Niebuhr, *Nature and Destiny*, 1:1.

6 Ibid., 1:16; cf. 1:chapter 7.

7 See Arendt, *The Human Condition*, 273ff.; Bernstein, *Beyond Objectivism and Relativism*, 16ff. On the Cartesian project of epistemologically grounding an "absolute conception of reality," see Williams, *Descartes: The Project of Pure Inquiry*.

8 Niebuhr, *Nature and Destiny*, 1:182f. Cf. Kierkegaard, *The Concept of Anxiety: A Simple Psychologically Orienting Deliberation on the Dogmatic Issue of Hereditary Sin*.

9 Niebuhr, *Nature and Destiny*, 1:257. One may recall here Martin Buber's critique of Kierkegaard precisely on this point: "This [God] relation is an exclusive one, the exclusive one, and this means, according to Kierkegaard, that it is the excluding relation, excluding all others; more precisely, that it is the relation which in virtue of its unique, essential life expels all other relations into the realm of the unessential" (Buber, "The Question to the Single One," *Between Man and Man*, 71).

10 Niebuhr, *Nature and Destiny*, 1:260.

11 For Kant's position, see Kant, *Foundations of the Metaphysics of Morals*, especially sections 2 and 3; and *Kritik der Praktischen Vernunft*.

12 This runs counter to Kant's approach, represented in the following passage from *Foundations of the Metaphysics of Morals*: "Nor could one give poorer counsel to morality than to attempt to derive it from examples. For each example of morality which is exhibited to me must itself have been previously judged according to principles of morality to see whether it is judged worthy to serve as an original example ... Even the Holy One of the Gospel must be compared with our ideal of moral perfection before He is recognized as such ... Imitation has no place in moral matters, and examples serve only for encouragement ... But they can never justify our guiding ourselves

by examples and our setting aside their true original which lies in reason" (25). However, the tension between is and ought, real and ideal, the endless quest for impossible perfection, is as powerful and permanent for Kant as it is for Niebuhr, despite having a different focus (rational law rather than revealed love): "Die völlige Angemessenheit des Willens aber zum moralischen Gezetze ist Heiligkeit, eine Vollkommenheit, deren kein vernünftiges Wesen der Sinnenwelt in keinem Zeitpunkte seines Daseins fähig ist. Da sie indessen gleichwohl als praktisch notwendig gefordert wird, so kann sie nur in einem ins Unendliche gehenden Progressus zu jener völligen Angemessenheit angetroffen werden" (Kant, *Kritik der Praktischen Vernunft*, 140–1).

13 Niebuhr, *Nature and Destiny*, 1:123–5.

14 Ibid., 1:147.

15 Ibid., 1:60. Paul Lehmann lucidly delineates the central importance of Christology in Niebuhr's theology in "The Christology of Reinhold Niebuhr," in *Reinhold Niebuhr: His Religious, Social and Political Thought*, ed. Charles Kegley, 327–56.

16 See Barth, *Church Dogmatics*, vol. 3, part 2: *The Doctrine of Creation*, 132–202.

17 See Barth, *Church Dogmatics*, vol. 2, part 2: *The Doctrine of God*, 509–51.

18 Niebuhr, *Nature and Destiny*, 2:63ff.; "The Truth in Myths," *Faith and Politics: A Commentary on Religious, Social and Political Thought in a Technological Age*, 15–31; "Coherence, Incoherence and Christian Faith," *Christian Realism and Political Problems*, chapter 11; *Faith and History: A Comparison of Christian and Modern Views of History*, chapter 10.

19 See Gordon Harland's insightful exposition in *The Thought of Reinhold Niebuhr*, part 1.

20 Niebuhr, *Nature and Destiny*, 1:26; 2:1ff.; *Faith and History*, chapter 11. Richard Wrightman Fox (*Reinhold Niebuhr: A Biography*) asserts: "[Niebuhr's] stance was naturalistic in the sense that his ultimate appeal in both politics and theology was always to the observed facts of human experience. His starting point was the community of concrete human beings confronted by the paradoxically free yet finite character of their nature" (217). My reading of Niebuhr calls this interpretation into question; I am arguing that Niebuhr's ultimate appeal is to transcendent revelation which illuminates (and is validated in, not derived from) human experience, and that his starting point is not "the community of concrete human beings" but rather the human self in the dialectic between its essential and existential dimensions.

21 Niebuhr, *Faith and History,* 19. His approach can be contrasted here with that of his brother, H. Richard Niebuhr, *The Meaning of Revelation.*

22 Niebuhr, *Interpretation of Christian Ethics,* chapter 1 and 50f.; *Faith and History,* 24ff.

23 Niebuhr states that the doctrine of the Atonement "is an absolutely essential presupposition for the understanding of human nature and human history" (*Nature and Destiny,* 1:148; cf. ibid., 2:chapter 2; and *Faith and History,* chapter 9).

24 See Niebuhr, *Interpretation of Christian Ethics,* chapter 2.

25 Niebuhr, *Moral Man and Immoral Society,* 74.

26 "[The Christian faith] must derive ... insights for collective action which are drawn only from individual religious experience. They are applicable because the collective life of mankind conforms to the ultimate laws of God, as surely as does individual life. But they are not ascertained by the collective conscience, if indeed there is such an entity. They are mediated by the individual conscience to the collectivity" (Reinhold Niebuhr, "Christian Faith and Social Action," *Faith and Politics,* 133).

27 Niebuhr, *Moral Man and Immoral Society,* 81; *Interpretation of Christian Ethics,* chapter 7; *The Children of Light and the Children of Darkness: A Vindication of Democracy and a Critique of Its Traditional Defense,* 61; "Christian Faith and Social Action," *Faith and Politics* 133ff.

28 Niebuhr, *Nature and Destiny,* 2:49.

29 See ibid., 2:125–6, 211–12, 284.

30 See ibid., 2:chapter 3; "Love and Law in Protestantism and Catholicism," *Christian Realism and Political Problems,* chapter 10.

31 Niebuhr, *Nature and Destiny,* 2:74.

32 Ibid., 2:69.

33 See ibid., 2:88; *Faith and History,* 184ff.

34 Niebuhr, *Nature and Destiny,* 1:219–27.

35 Ibid., 1:226.

36 See Reinhold Niebuhr, *Reflections on the End of an Era,* 230.

37 See Niebuhr, "Christian Faith and Social Action," 136.

38 Niebuhr, "Love and Law," *Christian Realism and Political Problems,* 168.

39 See Niebuhr, "Christian Faith and Social Action," 135. Cf. Niebuhr "Augustine's Political Realism," *Christian Realism and Political Problems,* 135; *Nature and Destiny,* 2:95ff.

40 Tillich, "Reinhold Niebuhr's Doctrine of Knowledge," *Reinhold Niebuhr,* ed. Charles Kegley, chapter 4; Wieman, "A Religious Naturalist Looks at Reinhold Niebuhr," ibid., chapter 17.

41 See Williams, "Niebuhr and Liberalism," *Reinhold Niebuhr,* ed. Charles Kegley, chapter 10.

42 Niebuhr, *Reflections on the End of an Era*, 93.

43 Ramsey, "Love and Law," in *Reinhold Niebuhr*, ed. Charles Kegley, 168f.

44 See Outka, *Agape: An Ethical Analysis*, 34ff., 174ff.

45 Ibid., 177.

46 Beverly Wildung Harrison makes a related argument of Niebuhr's approach to social ethics in her book *Making the Connections: Essays in Feminist Social Ethics*. She states: "Reinhold Niebuhr gained a following for predicating his entire social ethical approach on a presumed discontinuity between the dynamics of power existing in social, economic, and political life and the dynamics of power in interpersonal interactions, in face to face groups like the family. Like many a male ethicist, Niebuhr romanticized the family ... Niebuhr, who is often cited as a critic of theological liberalism, was on this point a typical theological liberal. He never questioned the dualism embedded in liberal political ideology between the 'private' sphere, that is, the arena of those interpersonal, humane relations of the family, and the 'public' sphere, those 'impersonal relations' of institutions and collectivities. He did not notice that this private\public split legitimized both a capitalist mode of political-economic organization and female subjugation in personal or domestic life" (27–8). Harrison also criticizes Niebuhr's dualistic account of self-sacrificial love (as the 'ideal') and the self-interested love that characterizes all public action (as political 'realism') as rooted in an inadequate theological anthropology. For other critical discussions of Niebuhr's approach from feminist perspectives, see Judith Plaskow, *Sex, Sin and Grace: Women's Experience and the Theologies of Reinhold Niebuhr and Paul Tillich* (Lanham, MD: University Press of America, 1980); Judith Vaughan, *Sociality, Ethics and Social Change* (Lanham, MD: University Press of America, 1983).

47 Niebuhr, *Moral Man and Immoral Society*, 90.

48 On Niebuhr's changing views of the New Deal, from a "palliative which cannot cure the problem" to a much more positive evaluation, compare his editorial "New Deal Medicine," with "Marxists are Taking Stock." See also the article by Becker, "Reinhold Niebuhr: From Marx to Roosevelt."

49 See Niebuhr's essay, "Liberty and Equality," *Faith and Politics*, especially 197–8.

50 For various (similar) accounts of these changes in Niebuhr's social and political thought, see Bennett, "Reinhold Niebuhr's Social Ethics," *Reinhold Niebuhr*, ed. Charles Kegley, chapter 5; Arthur Schlesinger, Jr, "Reinhold Niebuhr's Role in American Political Thought and Life," ibid., chapter 7; Kenneth Thompson, "The Political Philosophy of Reinhold Niebuhr," ibid., chapter 8.

51 Niebuhr, "Ideology and the Scientific Method," *Christian Realism and Political Problems*, 89–90.

52 Niebuhr, *Interpretation of Christian Ethics*, 131; cf. *Nature and Destiny*, 1:chapter 4.

53 This is so because religious understanding gives one access to the organic harmony in the ideal of love, which provides a sense of wholeness and *Gemeinschaft* unattainable in mechanistic, bourgeois society, a reminder that human fulfilment and unity lies beyond politics and social life. This underlying notion of organic equilibrium is present already in the early writings of Reinhold Niebuhr (see *Reflections on the End of an Era*, chapters 8 and 9, passim) and it explains in part – with Burke's argument that we should work for pragmatic reforms within the limits prescribed by the positive institutions of constitutional government because there is no higher rationality by which they can be judged – Niebuhr's later attraction to the conservative social theory of Edmund Burke.

54 *Interpretation of Christian Ethics*, 74.

55 See, for example, Niebuhr, *Moral Man and Immoral Society*, 4, 214; *Children of Light and Children of Darkness*, 50f., 114f.

56 See Niebuhr, *Moral Man and Immoral Society*, 7, 89–90, 210; *Interpretation of Christian Ethics*, 112–13; idem, *Reflections on the End of an Era*, chapter 2.

57 It is abundantly clear, even from his early writings, that Niebuhr never was a Marxist. See Beverly Wildung Harrison, "The Role of Social Theory in Religious Social Ethics: Reconsidering the Case for Marxian Political Economy," in *Making the Connections*, 54–80. Harrison also offers a critical analysis of Weber's methodological dualism between "ideal" and "real" factors in social process and relates this to Niebuhr's political liberalism. For a cogent demonstration of the incompatibility of Niebuhr's early thought with Marxist social theory, see Louis H. Tietje, "Was Reinhold Niebuhr Ever a Marxist? An Investigation into the Assumptions of His Early Interpretation and Critique of Marxism."

58 Indeed, while Niebuhr rejects any notion of *moral* progress in history, he does hold to an evolutionary view of social relations: "History obviously moves toward more inclusive ends, towards more complex human relations, towards the technical enhancement of human powers and the cumulation of knowledge" (*Nature and Destiny*, 2:315).

59 Niebuhr, *Children of Light and Children of Darkness*, 38ff.; *Reflections on the End of an Era*, 99ff.; *Nature and Destiny*, 2:244.

60 Niebuhr, *Children of Light and Children of Darkness*, 45. Cf. *Nature and Destiny*, 1:43–53, 65ff.; *Reflections on the End of an Era*, chapters 7–9.

61 See Niebuhr, *Interpretation of Christian Ethics*, 120; *Children of Light and Children of Darkness*, 10ff., 46–58, 103.

62 See Niebuhr, *Nature and Destiny*, 1:56.

63 Rawls, *A Theory of Justice*. For an excellent alternative analysis of Niebuhr's conception of justice see Beckley, *Passion for Justice*, chapters 3, 6, and 7.

64 Niebuhr, *Faith and History*, 193.

65 Niebuhr, *Children of Light and Children of Darkness*, 53.

66 Benne, *The Ethic of Democratic Capitalism: A Moral Reassessment*, part 1. Harlan Beckley, in "A Christian Affirmation of Rawls's Idea of Justice as Fairness – Part I"; "A Christian Affirmation – Part II," ibid., argues that the Christian ideal of love (understood in Gene Outka's language as "equal regard") can embrace the minimal or "thin" moral beliefs undergirding Rawls' theory of justice, namely, that all people are rational, free, and equal. These moral beliefs, however, remain excessively formal, and indeed (as Beckley seems to admit, "Part I," 225) trade heavily on the theoretical claims of neo-classical economics: in understanding practical rationality as instrumental calculus, freedom as the pursuit of private interests through contracts, and equality as differential entitlements.

   While Niebuhr, like Rawls, seeks stability rooted in some measure of public consensus mediated procedurally by the state, he is far more aware than is Rawls of the conflictual realities of political power and ideology, and far less sanguine about the "fairness" of principles of justice rooted in an abstract rational consensus. My point (as I hope will become clear) is that Niebuhr's theological anthropology renders the problem of social justice far more acute and complex than can be accounted for or illuminated by Rawls' "original position," or any other formal, procedural theory of justice. It is more important, says Niebuhr against John Dewey, to preserve the spirit of forgiveness than to seek islands of neutrality (*Interpretation of Christian Ethics*, 145).

67 See Rawls, *A Theory of Justice*, section 41, and chapter 3.

68 Sandel, *Liberalism and the Limits of Justice*, 175.

69 Ibid., 154ff.

70 Sandel asserts: "The morally diminished status of the good must inevitably call into question the status of justice as well. For once it is conceded that our conceptions of the good are morally arbitrary, it becomes difficult to see why the highest of all (social) virtues should be the one that enables us to pursue these arbitrary conceptions 'as fully as circumstances permit'" (ibid., 168; cf. 178).

71 Niebuhr, *Children of Light and Children of Darkness*, 61.

72 Niebuhr, *Nature and Destiny*, 2:257–8.

73 See Niebuhr, "Liberty and Equality," *Faith and Politics*, 185–98.

74 Niebuhr, *Children of Light and Children of Darkness*, 10. Emphasis mine.

75 Macpherson, *The Life and Times of Liberal Democracy*, chapter 4. See also his *Democratic Theory*, chapter 10; Held, *Models of Democracy*, chapter 6; Margolis, "Democracy: American Style," in *Democratic Theory and Practice*, ed. Duncan, chapter 8.

76 See Niebuhr, *Nature and Destiny*, 2:262ff; "Coercion, Self-Interest, and Love," in Boulding, *The Organizational Revolution: A Study in the Ethics of Economic Organization*, 228–44; "The Christian Faith and the Economic Life of Liberal Society," in Ward, ed., *Goals of Economic Life*, 433–59. Carole Pateman points out that the pluralist model of democracy is characterized by a preoccupation with stability and an oversimplified contrast between procedural democracy and totalitarianism as the only two political alternatives. See Pateman, *Participation and Democratic Theory*, chapter 1.

77 Niebuhr, *The Irony of American History*, 103; cf. 86ff.; "Liberty and Equality," 198. C.B. Macpherson avers: "The [equilibrium] analysis rests on the extreme pluralist assumption that the politically important demands of each individual are diverse and are shared with varied and shifting combinations of other individuals, none of which combinations can be expected to be a numerical majority of the electorate. This position is most nearly approached in a prosperous and expanding capitalist society: where the economy provides or promises a share of affluence to everybody, class interest will not outrank all the other divisions of interest. But in any other case the model is not appropriate" (*Democratic Theory*, 190).

78 See, for example, Skocpol, "Legacies of New Deal Liberalism"; Wolfe, *America's Impasse*, chapter 2.

79 For examples, see Niebuhr, *Moral Man and Immoral Society*, 113ff.; *Nature and Destiny*, 2:261ff.

80 Niebuhr, "Christian Politics and Communist Religion," *Christianity and the Social Revolution*, ed. Lewis, Polanyi, Kitchen, 462. See also *Moral Man and Immoral Society*, 125, 189. In *Reflections on the End of an Era*, Niebuhr puts forth this thesis even more forcefully: "Mass production requires mass consumption; and capitalism is unable to provide mass consumption. From this basic ill of modern society all other defects seem to spring" (24).

81 See Niebuhr, *Reflections on the End of an Era*, chapter 2 and passim.

82 On Keynesian underconsumption theory and compromise policies, see Hirsch, *Social Limits to Growth*, chapters 8 and 9; O'Connor, *Accumulation Crisis*, chapter 7; Przeworski, *Capitalism and Social Democracy*, chapter 6; Offe, *Contradictions of the Welfare State*, chapter 8.

83 The Keynesian solution is to *displace* class conflict from mode of production (supply side structures) to the volume of distribution and

growth (i.e., it provides a demand side solution), and this gives rise to an interclass, growth-security alliance which seeks to appease all interests through the technical management of economic growth and expansion of productivity, thus avoiding the need to make political choices. As Alan Wolfe points out, the success of this method is the very reason for its failure – a lack of political vision and consensus – so that when the rising social costs and supply side problems of such policies result in stagflation, the alliance and the compromise break down. See Wolfe, *America's Impasse*, chapters 2–4.

84 See Niebuhr, "The Christian Faith and the Economic Life of Liberal Society," 455ff.

85 Ibid., 457.

86 Niebuhr's critique of Marx effectively exploits the economistic assumptions in Marx's strategy of making the proletariat the absolute, universal agent of social change, and of solving the social crisis through economic reorganization. The class struggle is not, Niebuhr correctly argues, merely the result of economic conditions and therefore cannot be addressed simply by transforming the relations of production. But Niebuhr's understanding of the class struggle as the result of the universal human spiritual condition abstracts too much from particular historical forms of socio-economic relations and the common social meanings that inform the motivations and actions of individual agents.

87 The best secondary study of the FCSO is Roger Hutchinson, "The Fellowship for a Christian Social Order: A Social Ethical Analysis of a Christian Socialist Movement."

88 *Towards the Christian Revolution*, ed. Scott and Vlastos.

89 Research Committee for the LSR, *Social Planning for Canada* (Toronto: University of Toronto Press, 1975), originally published in 1935.

90 Note the titles of two reviews of *Towards the Christian Revolution*: "Marxist Christians Nail Their Theses to the Door," by Garrison, in *The Christian Century*; and "Christians on the Marxian Road," by Nixon in *Christendom*.

91 Niebuhr's review appeared in *Radical Religion*.

92 Ibid., 44.

93 See, for example, Line, "The Theological Principles," in Scott and Vlastos, *Towards the Christian Revolution*, 39ff.

94 Ibid., chapter 2.

95 Ibid., 46. Line asserts that the theology of "radical Christianity" or "religious radicalism" will share the "Barthian realism" about the plight of a world that has turned from God and "it will agree that man has not the means to save himself but must look to forces in the universe and in history that are not his to command" (ibid., 48).

Clearly this is a different concept of God than one finds in the social gospel.

96 Vlastos, "The Ethical Foundations," in ibid., 70.

97 Ibid., 70–1. Elsewhere Vlastos defines religion in similar language: " Religion is man's conscious relating of his own life to the reality that creates, sustains, and outlasts his own life and every life … I mean by reality the world in which we live and move and have our being. Its characteristic feature is that it is 'there,' whether we like it or not, whether we recognize it or not, whether we accept it or not. It resists our wishes; it survives our doubts; it cuts across our illusions and mashes them in its own good time with the effortless, irresistable advance of a glacier or a tide. Religion is man's opportunity to come to terms with this reality, discover his oneness with it, and find through it meaning and value" (*Christian Faith and Democracy*, 9). The language here is clearly similar to that used in places by H. Richard Niebuhr: for example in "A Communication: The only Way into the Kingdom of God," *The Christian Century*, 6 April 1932, 447; and *Radical Monotheism and Western Culture*, 122.

98 Vlastos, "The Ethical Foundations," 51–3. Cf. Marx, "Theses on Feuerbach," in *The Marx-Engels Reader*, 145. Jesus' ethic is also built on material foundations, as are all "spiritual" values, argues Vlastos. Love is also a material activity (Vlastos, "The Ethical Foundations," 57ff.), contra Hegel's definition in *Philosophy of Right* as "*consciousness of unity.*" See *Hegel's Philosophy of Right*, trans. with notes by Knox (Oxford: Oxford University Press, 1967), 110ff.

99 Vlastos, "The Ethical Foundations," 52–7.

100 Vlastos, "Sin and Anxiety in Niebuhr's Religion," is a review of Niebuhr, *Nature and Destiny*, vol. 1.

101 Avineri, *The Social and Political Thought of Karl Marx*, 87.

102 See Vlastos, "The Impossible Possibility." This is a review of Niebuhr, *An Interpretation of Christian Ethics*.

103 Vlastos, "Religious Foundations of Democracy: Fraternity and Liberty," 2ff.

104 Vlastos, "Sin and Anxiety in Niebuhr's Religion," 1203. The question remains, what kind of community is required? This will be considered below.

105 Vlastos, "The Ethical Foundations," in Scott and Vlastos, *Towards the Christian Revolution*, 62ff. On the need for a social and dynamic conception of the self, see also Line, "The Philosophical Background."

106 See Vlastos, "Religious Foundations of Democracy: Fraternity and Liberty," 12ff.; Scott, "The Biblical Basis," in Scott and Vlastos, *Towards the Christian Revolution*, chapter 4.

107 Scott, "The Biblical Foundations," in ibid., 77.

108 Vlastos, "Reclaim the Gospel of Solidarity," 246; "The Religious Foundations of Democracy: Fraternity and Equality," 154–5; *Christian Faith and Democracy*, 66.

109 Connolly, *Appearance and Reality in Politics*, 117.

110 Vlastos, *Christian Faith and Democracy*, 64.

111 Cf. Scott's well-known book on *The Relevance of the Prophets*, which also takes this view. Social injustice for the prophets of ancient Israel is a religious problem, a lack of discernment concerning the purposes of God (evident in concrete experience) that leads to a failure to align one's will and the life of the community with those divine purposes.

112 Ibid., 76. But God is not simply the "universe." God is defined as the "whole good" in the structure of the world. "God is the power of good in all its various forms: in the order and structure of inorganic matter, in the process of growth and sensitivity in the realm of life, in the conditions of intelligence, cooperation, appreciation and creative love on the human level" (Vlastos, *The Religious Way*, 8).

113 Vlastos, "What is Love?".

114 Ibid., 121.

115 Ibid., 127–8.

116 Ibid., 131.

117 Vlastos, *Christian Faith and Democracy*, 10ff.

118 Ibid., chapter 3. Vlastos states that "history presents me with a limited number of real choices" and this means that "reality justifies the means and the end and everything else. It means that I have renounced idealist longings and purist daydreams and magic, and am working with the limited possibilities of the only world in which action is possible – the real world" (75). We might recall here Buber's distinction between faith and magic: "Magic wants to be effective without entering into any relationship and performs its arts in the void" (*I and Thou*, 131).

119 Vlastos, "The Religious Foundations of Democracy: Fraternity and Equality," 145–8.

120 Vlastos, "The Ethical Foundations," in Scott and Vlastos, *Towards the Christian Revolution*, 73.

121 Vlastos, *Christian Faith and Democracy*, 77.

122 See Vlastos, "The Meaning of Commitment," in *The Religious Way*, 17ff.

123 See Gordon, "The Political Task," in Scott and Vlastos, *Towards the Christian Revolution*, 152.

124 Vlastos, "Love and the Class Struggle," 26. Cf. Vlastos, *Christian Faith and Democracy*, 69–75.

125 Line, "The Philosophical Background," in Scott and Vlastos, *Towards the Christian Revolution*, 15ff. Vlastos tersely asserts: "Human life is human relatedness" ("The Ethical Foundations," in ibid., 63).

126 Vlastos, "The Ethical Foundations," in ibid., 65.

127 This same point has more recently been made by Michael Ignatieff, *The Needs of Strangers*: "Yet we recognize our mutual humanity in our differences, in our individuality, in our history, in the faithful discharge of our particular culture of obligations. There is no identity we can recognize in our universality ... The problem is not to defend universality, but to give these abstract individuals the chance to become real, historical individuals again, with the social relations and the power to protect themselves ... Woe betide any man who depends on the abstract humanity of another for his food and protection. Woe betide any person who has no state, no family, no neighbourhood, no community that can stand behind to enforce his claim of need" (52–3).

128 See Vlastos, "The Ethical Foundations," in Scott and Vlastos, *Towards the Christian Revolution*, 67ff.; *Christian Faith and Democracy*, chapter 4; "Religious Foundations of Democracy: Fraternity and Equality," 139ff.

129 See Vlastos, "The Ethical Foundations," in Scott and Vlastos, *Towards the Christian Revolution*, 138–9; *Christian Faith and Democracy*, 53–4; and Arendt, *The Origins of Totalitarianism*, part 3, *Totalitarianism*, chapter 1. Arendt states: "The truth is that the masses grew out of the fragments of a highly atomized society whose competitive structure and concomitant loneliness of the individual had been held in check only through membership in a class. The chief characteristic of mass man is not brutality and backwardness, but his isolation and lack of normal social relationships" (15; cf. 21ff., 50). As Albert Camus puts it, "Tyranny dominates a crowd of solitudes" ("Create Dangerously," *Resistance, Rebellion, and Death*, 269).

130 Vlastos, "The Ethical Foundations," in Scott and Vlastos, *Towards the Christian Revolution*, 67. This conception of the relationships of reciprocity between individuals and their communities also provides an implicit critique of socialist totalitarianism, which also reduces individuals to the functional (usually economic) needs of the social totality.

131 See Scott, "The Biblical Basis," in ibid.; Vlastos, *Christian Faith and Democracy*, 20ff.; and "Religious Foundations of Democracy: Fraternity and Liberty," *Journal of Religion* 12ff.

132 See Vlastos' "Religious Foundations of Democracy" articles. For more recent discussions of the relationship between covenant and democracy in Christian social ethics, cf. H.R. Niebuhr, "The Idea

of Covenant and American Democracy"; Lovin, "Covenantal Relationships and Political Legitimacy."

133 Vlastos, "Religious Foundations of Democracy: Fraternity and Liberty."

134 See Berlin, "Two Concepts of Liberty," *Four Essays on Liberty,* chapter 3. Cf. Taylor, "What's Wrong With Negative Liberty," *Philosophy and the Human Sciences,* chapter 8.

135 Vlastos, "Religious Foundations of Democracy: Fraternity and Liberty," 17.

136 See Vlastos, "The Religious Foundations of Democracy: Fraternity and Equality."

137 Vlastos, *Christian Faith and Democracy,* 19ff.

138 See Pateman, *Participation and Democratic Theory; The Problem of Political Obligation: A Critique of Liberal Theory;* Macpherson, *The Life and Times of Liberal Democracy,* chapter 5; Held, *Models of Democracy,* 254ff.

139 Gordon, "The Political Task," and Havelock, "The New Society," both in Scott and Vlastos, *Towards the Christian Revolution.*

140 See Pateman, *Participation and Democratic Theory,* chapter 2; *The Problem of Political Obligation,* chapter 2; Macpherson, *Essays in Democratic Theory,* chapter 2; Walzer, *Spheres of Justice,* chapters 2, 3, 12; Connolly, *Appearance and Reality in Politics,* chapter 4.

141 Vlastos, "Religious Foundations of Democracy: Fraternity and Liberty," 15ff. For a discussion of this idea of property or "goods" as part of a cultural information system that links people together in an intelligible universe of social meanings, see Mary Douglas and Baron Isherwood, *The World of Goods: Towards an Anthropology of Consumption* (New York: Basic Books, 1979; New York: W.W. Norton & Co., 1982). The problem with conventional economic rationality, these authors argue, is that it abstracts goods, work and consumption out of the whole scheme of social relationships, and this damages the possibility for understanding these crucial aspects of our life. In order to develop an adequate model of economic rationality, the individual and goods/consumption must be set back into the context of social obligations and the social process. Within such a communicative system of social purposes and goods, the rightful measure of poverty and wealth, of economic justice and rationality, is not possessions but social involvement and access to participation in the life of the community. Cf. Walzer, *Spheres of Justice,* chapter 4; Cohen and Rogers, *On Democracy.* As I shall argue in the next chapter, however, such an economic understanding of participation remains problematic.

142 Vlastos, "The Religious Foundations of Democracy: Fraternity and Equality," 153.

143 Forsey, "The Economic Problem," in Scott and Vlastos, *Towards the Christian Revolution*, 101.

144 Gordon, "The Political Task," in ibid., 152.

145 See ibid., 156ff.; Havelock, "The New Society," in ibid., 242ff. See also the discussion of the FCSO's economic policies by Mel Watkins, "Economics, Politics and the Relevance of Social Democracy," in *A Long and Faithful March: 'Towards the Christian Revolution' 1930's/1980's*, ed. Harold Wells and Roger Hutchinson (Toronto: United Church Pub. House, 1989): 73–81.

146 Forsey, "The Economic Problem," in Scott and Vlastos, *Towards the Christian Revolution*, 119.

147 In making this judgment, Forsey, who had a graduate degree in economics from Oxford, and who taught economics and political science at McGill University, cites the work of the British Marxist, John Strachey, *The Nature of Capitalist Crisis*. The concept of the state and its relationship to society remains of course an unsettled and controversial issue, not only in Marxist social theory. For a recent discussion of this issue see Carnoy, *The State and Political Theory*.

148 Forsey, "A New Economic Order," in Scott and Vlastos, *Towards the Christian Revolution*, chapter 6. It should be noted that there was not a consensus on this judgment in the FCSO, some of whom affirmed the cooperative movement strategy of J.S. Woodsworth and the earlier social gospel; see, for example, Gordon, "The Political Task," 156ff.

149 Forsey, "A New Economic Order," *Towards the Christian Revolution*, ed. Scott and Vlastos, 139. Przeworski provides an insightful and relevant observation on this point: "Marx's theory provided a useful threefold analysis: first, capitalism is based on exploitation (the source of profit is surplus value); second, the private property of the means of production is the source simultaneously of the injustice and the irrationality of capitalism; third, the falling rate of profit is the source of crises. The theory has been politically useful only as a justification of revolutionary goals, specifically of the program of nationalization of the means of production. Marx's economics, even its most sophisticated version, is not a helpful tool for addressing workers' distributional claims within capitalism and it is useless as a framework for administering capitalist economies" (*Capitalism and Social Democracy*, 206). One can see the policy dilemmas this creates for socialist movements who seek to gain power democratically in capitalist societies. It is not surprising that many embraced Keynesian economics as a pragmatic compromise.

150 Forsey, "A New Economic Order," in Scott and Vlastos, *Towards the Christian Revolution*, 141. This is not to deny the ambiguities present in Forsey's view of the state. He is not altogether clear about the

relationship of the state to the economy and to civil society, and there are hints of naïve "fellow-travelling" with the Soviet model of state socialism (ibid., 144). On this point, Reinhold Niebuhr is undoubtedly right to argue that the social problem cannot be reduced to private ownership, and therefore cannot be resolved simply by economic reorganization. Furthermore, Niebuhr's emphasis on a pluralism of power centres rather than on centralization is important, although I have criticized the procedural form that this pluralism takes in his work.

151 See Horn, *The League for Social Reconstruction: Intellectual Origins of the Democratic Left in Canada, 1930–1942*.

152 Avineri, *The Social and Political Thought of Karl Marx*, 86ff.; cf. Carol C. Gould, *Marx's Social Ontology: Individuality and Community in Marx's Theory of Social Reality* (Cambridge, MA: MIT Press, 1978).

153 Michael Joseph Smith also criticizes political realists for taking advantage of the ambiguity between theoretical and normative aspects of their analyses, turning descriptive analyses into normative exhortation in a rather uncritical fashion. See Smith, *Realist Thought from Weber to Kissinger*, chapter 9.

154 Forsey, "The Economic Problem," in Scott and Vlastos, *Towards the Christian Revolution*, 116.

155 Scott, "The Biblical Basis," in ibid., 84–90.

156 Line, "The Philosophical Background," in ibid., 17ff.

157 Havelock, "The New Society," in ibid., passim.

158 Vlastos, "The Religious Foundations of Democracy: Fraternity and Equality," 145.

159 See Walzer, *Spheres of Justice*; Taylor, "The Nature and Scope of Distributive Justice," in *Philosophy and the Human Sciences*.

160 "So far from being inherently materialistic, the machine is, with the one exception of language, the greatest instrument of cooperative community that men have yet discovered. It binds men in ever closer interdependence and forces them to work together or be destroyed. There is nothing wrong with its multiplication of goods. The more material goods, the better. The only questions are how those goods are produced and how they are distributed" (Vlastos, "The Ethical Foundations," in Scott and Vlastos, *Towards the Christian Revolution*, 60–1). The Marxist overtones here are unmistakeable, and although the question of who controls technology and for what purposes is of fundamental importance, the uncritical belief in the inherent "goodness" of the technological multiplication of material products is highly problematic. The difficulty here is rooted in a flawed religious understanding of anthropology, one that pays insufficient attention to the symbol of creation and its moral implications.

CHAPTER FOUR

1 It should also be noted that language of crisis is far more prominent in the Canadian document, appearing even in the title, and appears (undefined) in the U.S. statement only with reference to the "farm crisis," "debt crisis," and the global economy (NCCB, *Economic Justice For All*, 218ff., 272ff., 290).

2 On this point the U.S. bishops – whose statement is generally much more comprehensive than the Canadian document (it is more than ten times longer) – are more helpfully explicit than the Canadian bishops. The Canadians simply cite two "fundamental gospel principles," whereas the former U.S. bishops point out that, while their ethical principles and norms are rooted in the Bible, their reading of Scripture is shaped by the Catholic social tradition. This is obviously true of the Canadian statement as well. The advantage of the Canadian statement is the succinct clarity of its argument. Hence the two fundamental principles featured in the Canadian bishops' letter represent an accurate distillation also of the basic ethical principles informing the U.S. letter.

3 CCCB, "Ethical Reflections," 3.

4 Calvez and Perrin, *The Church and Social Justice: The Social Teaching of the Popes from Leo XIII to Pius XII*; Dorr, *Option for the Poor: A Hundred Years of Vatican Social Teaching*; Gremillion, ed., *The Gospel of Peace and Justice: Catholic Social Teaching Since Pope John*; Hollenbach, *Claims in Conflict: Retrieving and Renewing the Catholic Human Rights Tradition*.

5 See Pope John XXIII, *Mater et Magistra*, 219. All references to the Roman Catholic social documents, listed here in chronological order, will hereafter appear in brackets and with paragraph numbers in the body of the text: Leo XIII, *Rerum Novarum* (1891); Pius XI, *Quadragesimo Anno* (1931); John XXIII, *Mater et Magistra* (1961), *Pacem in Terris* (1963); Vatican II, *Gaudium et Spes* (1965); Paul VI, *Populorum Progressio* (1967), *Octogesima Adveniens* (1971); John Paul II, *Redemptor Hominis* (1979), *Redemptoris Mater* (1979), *Laborem Exercens* (1981), *Solicitudo Rei Socialis* (1987), *Centesimus Annus* (1991).

6 See the discussion of these periods of economic crisis in Gordon, Edwards, and Reich, *Segmented Work, Divided Workers: The Historical Transformation of Labor in the United States*; Samuel Bowles, David Gordon, and Thomas Weisskopf, *Beyond the Wasteland: A Democratic Alternative to Economic Decline* (Garden City, NY: Anchor Press/Doubleday, 1983), chapter 11.

7 Hollenbach, *Claims in Conflict*, 131ff.

8 George H. Williams, *The Mind of John Paul II: Origins of His Thought and Action* (New York: Harper & Row, 1981), 17.

9 In an insightful theological ethical analysis of *Laborem Exercens*, David Hollenbach shows that its biblical theological interpretation of the Genesis narratives is inadequate and partial. Hollenbach, "Human Work and the Story of Creation: Theology and Ethics in *Laborem Exercens*," in *Co-Creation and Capitalism: John Paul II's Laborem Exercens*, ed. Houck and Williams, 59–77. John Paul's emphasis on human creativity and the organic unity of the social world is more representative of the Priestly creation accounts and ignores the more ambiguous view of human possibilities and social integration present in the Yahwistic narratives, where sin and conflict and the potential for destruction in all areas of life are more prominently featured. Thus the danger in John Paul's ontological analysis of human personhood and work, says Hollenbach, is that "it will lack the categories which are necessary to guide action in non-ideal circumstances" (ibid., 75).

10 This language also occurs in NCCB, *Economic Justice for All*, 32.

11 In *Centesimus Annus* (11) John Paul II gives the following interpretation of the *imago Dei* as a divinely imprinted image and likeness: "Man ... is the only creature on earth which God willed for itself."

12 Arendt, *The Human Condition*.

13 Baudrillard, *The Mirror of Production*, 54–5. Baudrillard, as does Arendt, attributes the most definitive form of this anthropology of *animal laborans* to Karl Marx, who defined human beings in terms of labour and production. Baudrillard states: "Radical in its *logical* analysis of capital, Marxist theory nonetheless maintains an *anthropological* consensus with the options of Western rationalism in its definitive form acquired in eighteenth century bourgeois thought ... It [Marxist theory] generalizes the economic mode of rationality over the entire expanse of human history, as the generic mode of human becoming" (32–3). Cf. Arendt, *The Human Condition*, 101. On the growing predominance of economic discourse and technological production as the constitutive and generally unquestioned paradigm in making political judgements about public policy, see Wolin, "Contract and Birthright"; "Democracy and the Welfare State: The Political and Theoretical Connections Between Staatsräson and Wohlfahrtsstaatsräson."

14 Cf. Baudrillard, *The Mirror of Production*, chapter 5; Arendt, *The Human Condition*, 126ff. I am not suggesting (*pace* Arendt) that work is *necessarily* to be defined only in utilitarian terms, but that it *is* so reduced in a capitalist political economy. We will return to this point in the analysis of the U.S. bishops' statement.

15 Arendt, *The Human Condition*, 153–8.

16 See, for example, Macpherson, *The Rise and Fall of Economic Justice*, 51; and Marx, *Grundrisse: Foundations of the Critique of Political Economy*, 415ff.

17 Cf. Arendt, *The Human Condition*, 305ff.

18 It is revealing, I think, that Catholic theologians both from the left and the right have claimed *Laborem Exercens* as supporting their socio-economic perspectives. Cf. Baum, *The Priority of Labor: A Commentary on Laborem Exercens, Encyclical Letter of Pope John Paul II*; and Novak, "Creation Theology," *Co-Creation and Capitalism*, ed. Houck and Williams, 17–41.

19 Shades of this flawed notion are also present in the CCCB's most recent statement on economic policy: "Indeed, human work has the power, in and of itself, to create human community and social solidarity." CCCB, "A Statement on Social Policy," *Dissent* (Summer 1988):319.

20 Albert Borgmann argues this point strenuously against instrumentalist theories of technology, while also avoiding the monolithic conception of someone like Jacques Ellul. See especially Borgmann, *Technology and the Character of Contemporary Life*, Part 2.

21 CCCB, "Ethical Reflections," 17.

22 Ibid., 4.

23 Gregory Baum, in a commentary on the CCCB statement, argues that it is part of a shift to the left in official Catholic social teaching, a shift marked by *Octogesima Adveniens* and *Justice in the World* and endorsed by John Paul II's *Laborem Exercens*, which affirms and incorporates the perspective of liberation theology. See Baum, "The Shift in Catholic Social Teaching," in Baum and Cameron, *Ethics and Economics*. I disagree with Baum's interpretation for a number of reasons. First, although the language of liberation is certainly present in *Octogesima Adveniens*, this is rooted in a different theological understanding of the incarnation than is present in liberation theology. The immediate source of liberation language in this encyclical is a theological anthropology (classically expressed in Karl Rahner's formula that Christologically all theology is anthropology) that affirms that at the heart of human experience is found the mysterious presence of God which transcends all human comprehension and gives infinite meaning and dignity to human life, calling it always to transcend itself in love and trust. It is in the context of this theological anthropology that one should interpret Pope Paul VI's discussion of utopias (*Octogesima Adveniens*, 37), which is quite different in meaning and socio-political implication from the eschatological utopianism of liberation theology. Liberation theology appeals to a biblical theology of history in which the historical process of socio-political liberation is eschatologically identified with salvation and the definitive self-creation of a "new humanity" by means of a "permanent cultural revolution." See Gustavo Gutierrez, *A Theology of Liberation: History,*

Politics and Salvation (Orbis Books, 1973), 32. In liberation theology, this biblical theology of history is linked to a revolutionary class struggle of the oppressed against their oppressors, to which humanity must be converted in order to experience liberation-salvation. This is in sharp contrast to the calls in the official Catholic documents for recognition of the human rights and dignity of the marginalized, for international cooperation in social and economic development, and for public dialogue concerning social justice alternatives. Hence, contrary to Baum, I think it is important to note that the principle of the preferential option for the poor and marginalized has a different theological foundation and assumptions in official Catholic social teaching than it has in liberation theology, and this leads to a different model for social analysis and change.

I am not suggesting by this that the Canadian bishops evince an abstract neutrality on social issues. As I argue, the bishops do take a stand on economic policy and call for alternative strategies and priorities opposed to the economic status quo, which could be called "leftist." I am simply pointing out that the theological and social model in which the Canadians ground this stand is different from liberation theology in some important ways. In my view, it is quite obvious (one need only read their footnotes) that the Canadian bishops ground their position more in official Catholic social thought than in the texts of liberation theology, and this has theological and socio-political implications that should be recognized.

24 CCCB, "Ethical Reflections," 5; John Paul II, *Laborem Exercens*, 26.
25 That is, the New Testament writers nowhere attribute theological significance to the fact that Jesus was a carpenter. In my view, this attempt to ground the principle in the life of Jesus also belies a mistaken understanding of Christological authority, but that is another matter.
26 The bishops assert: "In order to forge a true community out of the present crisis, people must have a chance to choose their economic future rather than have one forced upon them. What is required, in our judgment, is a real public debate about economic visions and industrial strategies involving choices about values and priorities for the future direction of this country" (CCCB, "Ethical Reflections," 16).
27 Ibid., 6.
28 Hollenbach, *Claims in Conflict*, 204.
29 In this section I expand on the CCCB statement with additional materials that help to elaborate and clarify the basic analysis and policy proposals the Canadian bishops provide. The bishops' own theoretical sources are cited extensively in note 9 of "Ethical Reflections." Their analysis is admittedly controversial ("We recognise that these

proposals run counter to some current policies or strategies advanced by both governments and corporations," ibid., 8) and stands in opposition to other models of socio-economic analysis and policy proposals. It is not possible to discuss these conflicting models and interpretations in detail here, although it will be necessary to locate the CCCB statement within the strategic policy debates.

30 CCCB, "Ethical Reflections," 8–9.

31 Ibid., 13. For analyses of modern corporate life that support the bishops' concerns, see Herman, *Corporate Control, Corporate Power*; Lindblom, *Politics and Markets*; Barry Bluestone and Bennett Harrison, *The Deindustrialization of America: Plant Closings, Community Abandonment, and the Dismantling of Basic Industry* (New York: Basic Books, 1982).

32 Ibid., 9.

33 The bishops refer to this as the "survival of the fittest" doctrine of international economic competition ("Ethical Reflections," 10–11).

34 Ibid., 12.

35 Gonick, *Out of Work*, 53.

36 CCCB, "Ethical Reflections," 11–12; Gonick, *Out of Work*, 74ff.; *Inflation or Depression: The Continuing Crisis of the Canadian Economy*, 60ff.

37 For a good survey of these trends in the Canadian economy, see Wolfe, "The Rise and Demise of the Keynesian Era in Canada," in *Modern Canada: 1930's–1980's*, ed. Cross and Kealey, 46–80.

38 CCCB, "Ethical Reflections," 12–13. Cf. Przeworski, *Capitalism and Social Democracy*, 179.

39 CCCB, "Ethical Reflections," 9.

40 Ibid., 13ff.

41 Ibid., 13.

42 Ibid., 14–16.

43 Clarkson, *Canada and the Reagan Challenge: Crisis and Adjustment, 1981–85*; Clement, *Continental Corporate Power: Economic Elite Linkages Between Canada and the United States*; Levitt, *Silent Surrender: The Multinational Corporation in Canada*; Safarian, *Foreign Ownership of Canadian Industry*; Williams, *Not for Export: Toward a Political Economy of Canada's Arrested Industrialization*.

44 See Clarkson, *Canada and the Reagan Challenge*, part 4; Mahon, *The Politics of Industrial Restructuring: Canadian Textiles*, chapter 8.

45 Mahon, *The Politics of Industrial Restructuring*, 130ff.

46 CCCB, "Ethical Reflections," 13–15.

47 Ibid., 15.

48 Ibid., 14.

49 In their recent "A Statement on Social Policy," the Canadian Conference of Catholic Bishops call for a "people-oriented" rather than a "market-oriented" economy. We will return to this below.

50 In effect, the Canadian bishops wish to redefine the public sector: "The public sector itself needs to be reorganized, strengthened, and revitalized as the engine for economic and social development in Canada" (CCCB, "A Statement on Social Policy," 320).

51 Ibid., 315.

52 It is interesting to note that in their most recent statement on social policy, the Canadian bishops call upon several social movements advocating different causes – feminist, aboriginal, environmental, religious – to join together to revitalize the public realm against the domination of market priorities. But they do not define the substantive meaning of "vitality" for public life.

53 Paul Hawkin, "Nothing Fails Like Success," *The CoEvolution Quarterly* (Summer 1982):66. This is also the message of William Leiss, *The Limits to Satisfaction*: "Taken together, the conceptions of mastery over nature and insatiable desire are the abstract expressions of a concrete, developing social practice. They express a particular orientation of human activity in its relationship to the natural environment which, in more explicit terms, encourages individuals to regard nature exclusively as a support system for human wants. This perspective establishes the provisioning of our material demands as the single organizing principle for our relationship to the rest of nature" (39). Thus, "by exclusively directing our energies outward in the search for additional resources, in the course of which non-human nature becomes nothing but a means for the satisfaction of human needs, we are diverted from examining the character and objectives of our material demands" (43).

54 As Fred Hirsch's illuminating analysis of the structural characteristics of modern economic growth reveals, there are also important social limits to consumption and economic growth which are obscured in the frameworks of conventional economic analysis, causing us to lose sight of our social and communal needs and leading to adverse "externalities." See Hirsch, *Social Limits to Growth*.

55 My point here is not simply to say "nature too" must be considered. Environmental and ecological concerns are evident in some of the earlier social statements (see especially CCCB, "Northern Development: At What Cost?" in Baum and Cameron, *Ethics and Economics*, 151–61). My point is that these concerns are not adequately linked to and rooted in a theological perspective in which the whole God-world relationship is considered. This is not a mere abstract claim which depoliticizes the discussion. It is a *theological* consideration that critically and constructively informs the way in which political and economic issues are reflected upon and addressed, and is therefore highly relevant to ethical deliberation on matters of public policy.

Indeed one of the things the bishops have so clearly demonstrated by their statements is that theological ethical principles do contribute to public debates on economic theory and practice. I am here trying to push the theological considerations and implications further.

56 Ferkiss, "Individual Needs and Social Consensus," 142.

57 NCCB, *Economic Justice For All,* 22ff. Further references to this document (citing paragraph numbers) in this section of the chapter will hereafter appear in brackets in the text.

58 Hollenbach, "Liberalism, Communitarianism, and the Bishops' Pastoral Letter on the Economy."

59 Prominent current representatives of liberalism (whose positions are by no means homogeneous, or even closely compatible) include John Rawls, Ronald Dworkin, and Robert Nozick; of communitarianism, Michael Sandel, Alasdair MacIntyre, and Michael Walzer.

60 Hollenbach, "Liberalism," 36–7.

61 Borgmann, *Technology and the Character of Contemporary Life,* chapter 14 and passim.

62 Hollenbach *en passant* and uncritically identifies Aristotle and Thomas Aquinas with the modern communitarians (26), implicitly assuming, I take it, that the synthesis brings together not only contemporary social theories but traditional and modern ones as well. Although there is no room here to consider the views of Aristotle and Aquinas on the common good, human nature, and the virtues, I hope to make clear that the substantive content of these meanings changes considerably when they are placed into a modern liberal communitarian context of thought, practice, and institutions.

63 Borgmann, *Technology,* 92.

64 The bishops employ the Vatican II definition of the common good, stated in *Gaudium et Spes* (26) as "the sum of those conditions of social life which allow social groups and their individual members relatively thorough and ready access to their own fulfillment" (*Economic Justice For All,* 79).

65 See John Paul II, *Laborem Exercens,* 3.

66 See Connolly, *Appearance and Reality in Politics,* 97.

67 Borgmann, *Technology,* 80.

68 Gorz, *Farewell to the Working Class,* 1.

69 Keane and Owens, *After Full Employment.*

70 Bertil Ohlin, cited in Przeworski, *Capitalism and Social Democracy,* 37. Jean Baudrillard also points out this implication of the Keynesian response to the 1929 economic crisis: "Consumption became the strategic element; the people were henceforth mobilized as consumers; their 'needs' became as essential as their labor power … But something else is at play in the strategy of consumption. By allowing for

the possibility of expanding and consuming, by organizing social redistribution ... the system created the illusion of a symbolic participation (the illusion that something that is taken and won is also redistributed, given, and sacrificed). In fact, this entire symbolic simulation is uncovered as leading to super-profits and super-power" (*Mirror of Production*, 144). Ironically, to participate in such a system is to be caught in a web of economic necessity.

71 On the logic of participation and cooperation under capitalist conditions, see the illuminating studies of Przeworski, *Capitalism and Social Democracy*, chapters 4 and 5.

72 While the bishops understand that the virtues of citizenship require particular institutional relationships (296), they feel it is enough simply to call generally for the cultivation of virtues. Indeed, in a footnote on this point, they simply list a collection of diverse, incompatible social analyses and theories (see NCCB, *Economic Justice for All*, 296, note 2). Another example of the same thing is the bishops' response to the breakdown of family values. While they seem to recognize the important impact of socio-economic structures on the family (206, 344), they call primarily for a revival of personal responsibility and commitment to traditional family values to counter their destruction (209, 345).

73 Edward S. Herman, in *Corporate Control, Corporate Power*, thoroughly examines the dominance of the profit goal as the key to corporate behaviour, and the enormous power of the large corporations to resist any reforms incompatible with profitable growth – tendencies also enshrined in legal constraints upon corporate actions (e.g., protecting stockholders' investments), as well as North American business structure, culture, and political traditions. See also Lindblom, *Politics and Markets: The World's Political-Economic Systems*, chapters 12–14.

74 It might be said that whereas Reinhold Niebuhr's pluralist equilibrium model subordinates the question of rational political legitimation to the central "reality" of power struggle in all political relationships, the U.S. bishops presume the basic rational legitimacy of current political economic structures and therefore call for more cooperative attitudes and a cultural consensus on values to render those structures more functionally stable.

75 Panitch, "Recent Theorizations of Corporatism: Reflections on a Growth Industry," 160.

76 See Panitch, 162–73; Carnoy, *The State and Political Theory*, 39–42. The societies closest to being corporatist social systems, for socio-cultural as much as particular economic reasons, are Austria, Sweden, and Germany. See Peter Gerlich, Edward Grande, and Wolfgang C.

Muller, "Corporatism in Crisis: Stability and Change of Social Partnership in Austria," *Political Studies* 36 (1988): 209–23; Scharpf, "Economic and Institutional Constraints of Full-Employment Strategies: Sweden, Austria, and West Germany, 1973–1982," in *Order and Conflict in Contemporary Capitalism*, ed. Goldthorpe, chapter 11. While the bishops point toward structures of participation and representation characteristic of European forms of corporatism, their policy proposals for piecemeal reform and attitudinal change ("cultural consensus") are located within the quite different – decentralized, pluralist or "segmented," market-based, firm-centred – institutional and political structures of American political economy. In such a context, corporatist appeals can more easily be understood as a strategy designed to integrate the organized working class into the market-based decisions and disciplines necessary to foster economic growth. The language of sacrifice for the common good and the call for attitudes of cooperation are prominent in such corporatist programs, which seek to stabilize capitalist economic relations (as part of a microeconomic, "reactive" approach to policy making) in a context of growing conflict and a lack of cultural consensus (see studies in Goldthorpe, *Order and Conflict*).

77 Robert E. Lane explains the difference in these two realms in terms of the divergent criteria of justice in (and therefore people's justice assessments of) market and political institutions. Market justice, understood in terms of the "earned deserts" of individuals seeking the material satisfaction of individual wants, generates fewer conflicts and is perceived to be more "fair" than political justice, based on equality and need in the domain of collective goods. This perception can be attributed to the widespread acceptance of market *procedures* of allocation and desert as "natural," fair, and productive (hence the perception of a harmony of interest, i.e., the material production of commodities), whereas in the political realm people are more attentive to the distributive *outcomes*, where considerations of equality and conflicting social interests are more significant. (Lane, "Market Justice, Political Justice").

78 Even the most "democratic" liberal corporatists, such as Lester Thurow and Robert Reich, are concerned primarily with finding ways to integrate citizens and social groups into a more efficient national economic machine that can compete in a global market. Collective goods, such as environmental concerns, are simply given a consumption value on the "acquisitive agenda" and are understood to be available on the zero-sum market, if enough consumers register preferences for them and direct energies more efficiently toward the production of economic growth.

79 The bishops state: "The development of effective new forms of partnership between private and public agencies will be difficult in a situation as immensely complex as that of the United States in which various aspects of national policy seem to contradict one another. On the theoretical level, achieving greater coordination will make demands on those with the technical competence [as if this were only a technical matter] to analyze the relationship among different parts of the economy. More practically, it will require the various subgroups within our society to sharpen their concern for the common good and moderate their efforts to protect their own short-term interests" (NCCB, *Economic Justice for All*, 318; cf. 321, 324–5).

80 The current technological cast of both politics and labour render such foci for reform impotent, as Albert Borgmann argues. Concerning democracy: "The calls for participatory democracy which are oblivious to the substance of politics and merely recommend new forms of transaction are pointless and will remain inconsequential. One may as well call for participation in pocket calculators" (*Technology*, 113). Concerning labour: "If reliability and productivity are basic to technological production, then even what limited humanization of the work place is possible remains no more secure than the consonance of humanization with the basis of production" (123).

81 This is the moral imperative James M. Gustafson gives in volume 1 of his *Ethics From a Theocentric Perspective*, 113. It is an imperative found also in the work of H. Richard Niebuhr, and in Soren Kierkegaard, who states the principle in terms of "the simultaneous maintainance of an absolute relationship to the absolute and a relative relationship to the relative." See Kierkegaard, *Concluding Unscientific Postscript*, 386. To make the relative absolute leads to "bad infinity," that is, an absolute and idolatrous dependence upon *external* patterns and processes in which the spiritual, inner meaning of life is obscured and ignored, leading to disorder.

CHAPTER FIVE

1 Wolin, "Contract and Birthright," 189; cf. his "Democracy and the Welfare State: The Political and Theoretical Connections Between Staatsräson and Wohlfahrtsstaatsräson," 471ff.

2 See Psalms 14 and 53 where the foolishness of atheism, not as an intellectual position but as a spiritual and moral condition, is contrasted with the wisdom of those who seek after God (cf. Psalm 111:10; Proverbs 14:8).

3 Heller, *The Disinherited Mind*, 210.

4 Ibid., 213.

5 In Book VIII of *De Civitate Dei* Augustine (here following Cicero) credits Socrates and the Platonists with making the transition in philosophy from physics to ethics (*mores*), from natural science to wisdom, from an analysis of external causality to an analysis of the inner life of human beings and the purification of the intellect required for insight into the nature of the *summum bonum*, "the necessary condition of human happiness" (VIII, 3). They furthermore recognize this as the loving enjoyment of the supreme Good, that is, God. Only the natural theology of Platonic philosophy is therefore truly religious, based on rational insight into the hidden spiritual principles of existence, knowledge, and love.

6 Guthrie identifies the Greek Sophists of fifth and fourth centuries B.C. with positivism in the classical battle over the relation between *nomos* and *physis*. See Guthrie, *The Sophists*, chapters 4 and 7 in particular.

7 Voegelin, *The New Science of Politics*, 5.

8 The influence of Galileo on Hobbes is emphasized by C.B. Macpherson in his "Introduction" to Hobbes' *Leviathan*. Galileo provided Hobbes with a new mechanistic "master-philosophy which would explain nature, man and society in terms of motion" (19). Basil Willey's excellent discussion of Hobbes' mechanico-materialist philosophy includes the following apposite but unreferenced quotation: "Fear and reverence Nature no longer; she is no mystery, for she 'worketh by motion,' and Geometry, which is the mother of the sciences, and indeed the *only* science God has yet vouchsafed to us – Geometry can chart these motions. Feel, then, as if you lived in a world which can be measured, weighed, and mastered; and confront it with due audacity." Cited in Willey, *The Seventeenth Century Background*, 101. For Hobbes' discussion of scientific reason, see *Leviathan*, chapter 5; for his disparagement of classical philosophy, see ibid., chapter 46.

9 Hobbes, *Leviathan*, 81.

10 Ibid., Introduction.

11 See ibid., 150ff., 185–8.

12 Ibid., 160–1.

13 Ibid., 186.

14 Ibid., 223.

15 "For where no Covenant hath preceded, there hath no Right been transferred, and every man has the right to every thing; and consequently no action can be Unjust." And further: "Therefore before the names of Just and Unjust can have place, there must be some coercive Power, to compel men equally to the performance of their Covenants ... Therefore where there is no Common-wealth, there nothing

is Unjust. So that the nature of Justice consisteth in keeping of valid Covenants: but the Validity of Covenants begins not but with the Constitution of a Civill Power, sufficient to compel men to keep them" (ibid., 202–3).

16 "The only way to erect such a Common Power, as may be able to defend them from the invasion of Forraigners, and the injuries of one another, and thereby to secure them in such sort, as that by their owne industrie and by the fruites of the Earth, they may nourish themselves and live contentedly; is, to conferre all their power and strength upon one Man, or upon one Assembly of men, that may reduce all their Wills, by plurality of voices, unto one Will ... This done, the Multitude so united into one Person, is called a COMMON-WEALTH, in latine CIVITAS. The is the Generation of that great LEVIATHAN or rather (to speak more reverently) of that *Mortall God*, to which wee owe under the *Immortall God*, our peace and defense ... And in him consisteth the Essence of the Common-wealth; which (to define it) is *One Person, of whose Acts a great Multitude, by mutuall Covenants one with another, have made themselves every one the Author, to the end he may use the strength and means of them all, as he shall think expedient, for their Peace and Common Defense*" (ibid., 227–8).

17 Ibid., 362.

18 Augustine, *De Civitate Dei*, see especially books XIV and XIX.

19 Ibid., XIV, 4, 13.

20 These representive sins, depicted in the temptations of Jesus (Luke 4; Matthew 4) and catalogued in I John 2:16, are elaborated by Augustine in the *Confessions*, X, 29–41. On *superbia* as the perverse imitation of God that leads to the disordered injustice of *libido dominandi* in the earthly city, see also *De Civitate Dei*, XIX, 12. These sins represent the chief motivational principles of Hobbesian anthropology. See especially *Leviathan*, chapters 11 and 13.

21 Cf. the statement by Augustine in *City of God*: "And if [God] were to withdraw what we may call his constructive power [*potentiam ... fabricatoriam*] from existing things, they would cease to exist" (XII, 26; cf. also XXII, 24; V, 9). Augustine links this hidden creative power to divine Wisdom and the providential ordering of all reality.

22 The religious maxim, "Love of money is the root of all evil," is not the expression of a merely moralistic insight. It expresses the awareness that money can become the reductive sign that publicly mediates and assigns meaning or "value" to all goods, actions, occupations, and even motivations (as a rationale of conduct and choice). As Kenneth Burke points out, money can become a "god-term" that grounds social cohesion and purpose: "Money endangers religion in that money can serve as universal symbol, the unitary ground of all

action. And it endangers religion not in the dramatic, agonistic way of a 'tempter,' but in its quiet, rational way as a *substitute* that performs its mediatory role more 'efficiently,' more 'parsimoniously,' with less 'waste motion' as regards the religious or ritualistic conception of 'works'" (*Grammar of Motives*, 112). It is a sign of the times in North American society that University of Chicago economist Gary Becker can write a convincing book on *The Economic Approach to Human Behavior* (Chicago: University of Chicago Press, 1975), explaining even such private, intimate decisions as relate to marriage and family life on an economic rationality model.

23 See Augustine, *De Doctrina Christiana*, I; *De Civitate Dei*, XI, 16, 25; XV, 7.

24 Augustine, *De Doctrina Christiana*, I, xxvii. Translations mine unless otherwise noted.

25 See Augustine, *De Trinitate*, VIII, 4.

26 Ibid., XIV, 18. Translation based on John Burnaby's in *Augustine: Later Works*, Library of Christian Classics (Philadelphia: Westminster Press, 1955).

27 Augustine, *De Civitate Dei*, XV, 5. Translation based on *The City of God*, ed. V. Bourke, trans. G. Walsh, D. Zema, G. Monahan, and D. Honan (Garden City: Image Books, 1958).

28 Augustine, *Confessions*, XIII, 34. Two other passages from Book XIII help us understand Augustine's meaning here: "But when people by your Spirit see these works, it is you who sees in them. Therefore when they see that these works are good, it is you who sees that they are good, and wherever because of you these things please us, it is you who pleases us in them; and whatever things by your Spirit please us, please you in us" (XIII, 31). "Laudant te opera tua, ut amemus te, et amamus te, ut laudent te opera tua" ("Your works praise you, so that we may love you, and we love you so that your works may praise you," XIII, 33).

29 Burke, *The Rhetoric of Religion: Studies in Logology*, chapter 3; *The Grammar of Motives*, chapter 3.

30 Burke, *The Rhetoric of Religion*, 202. Cf. Burke's similar formulation on 212: "The explicit statement that man is made in God's image would be logologically translated: 'God and man are characterized by a common motivational principle,' which we would take to be the principle of personality that goes with skill at symbol-using."

31 Niebuhr, "Augustine's Political Realism," *Christian Realism and Political Problems*, 120–1.

32 See *De Civitate Dei*, II, 21; XIX, 20ff. I will discuss this definition and Augustine's corrective below.

33 Niebuhr, "Augustine's Political Realism," 127.

34 Ibid., 128–9, 132ff.
35 On this point see also the two chapters that follow Niebuhr, "August-ine's Political Realism" at the end of *Christian Realism and Political Problems*, "Love and Law in Protestantism and Catholicism" and "Coherence, Incoherence, and Christian Faith."
36 Niebuhr, "Coherence, Incoherence, and Christian Faith," 197ff.
37 Ibid., 201–2.
38 Ibid., 181.
39 Niebuhr, *Nature and Destiny,* 1:16; cf. "Love and Law in Protestantism and Catholicism," 171.
40 Niebuhr, "Augustine's Political Realism," 138ff.
41 Ibid., 140.
42 Two especially useful book-length treatments are Burnaby, *Amor Dei: A Study of the Religion of St Augustine*; and O'Donovan, *The Problem of Self-Love in St Augustine*. Both authors provide extensive critical analy-sis of and response to influential modern misinterpretations of Augustine's views, such as Anders Nygren's *Agape and Eros*, cited favourably by Niebuhr in "Augustine's Political Realism."
43 See the excellent treatment of this point by Cochrane, *Christianity and Classical Culture*, chapter 11; Burnaby, *Amor Dei*, chapter 5; O'Dono-van, *The Problem of Self-Love in Augustine*, chapter 6.
44 See Augustine, *De Civitate Dei*, XI, 24; XII; *Confessions*, XIII, 4.
45 See *De Civitate Dei*, XI, 28; *Confessions*, XIII, 9.
46 See *De Civitate Dei*, XII, 1ff.
47 See especially *De Civitate Dei*, XIV.
48 See ibid., XIV, 13.
49 In the Preface to Book I of *De Civitate Dei*, Augustine speaks of the *civitas terrena* as "a city that aims at domination" but is "itself domi-nated by the lust for domination [*libido dominandi*]," which is the most furious [*saeuissimo*] domination that enslaves and devastates human hearts (ibid., XIX, 15).
50 See ibid., XIX.
51 Ibid., XII, 28.
52 Ibid., XI, 2.
53 See ibid., X, 23ff.; XI, 15ff.
54 Ibid., XI, 2.
55 See ibid., X, 3ff. (and especially 25); XII, 1; and passim. Also *Confes-sions*, VII, 11; XIII, 2–3; and passim.
56 *De Civitate Dei*, X, 3; XIX, 14. Burnaby's criticism of Nygren's interpre-tation on this point is worth citing: "According to Nygren, the for-mula by which Augustine intended to provide for the relative love of the creature, while reserving absolute love for God, in fact makes *all* love, even the love of God, relative to the self and its enjoyment. But

this conclusion is merely the consequence of Nygren's false restriction of *amor* to desire ... To 'enjoy' is to cleave to something *in* the love which is enjoyment, not *by means* of the love which is desire" (*Amor Dei*, 109).

57 Ibid., XV, 22. See also Augustine's theocentric definition of "true virtue" as that virtue which "refers all goods of which it makes good use" to that end (*fine*) wherein peace finds its perfection and true greatness (XIX, 10).

58 Ibid., XV, 22.

59 Gilson clarifies Augustine's view of *caritas* in a manner that addresses Niebuhr's flawed understanding: "It is obvious that the man who loves another in charity does not cease to love his own good simply because he wills the good of another. Loving another with one's whole soul does not mean disowning or sacrificing oneself; it means loving another as oneself, on the basis of perfect equality ... But in the case of God, we no longer love *a* good but *the* Good, whereas we are not *the* Good but merely one good among many. How, then, could we possibly treat Him on a basis of equality? To love such a good as it deserves to be loved, we must love it unreservedly, without equality" (Gilson, *The Christian Philosophy of Saint Augustine*, 137–8).

60 *De Civitate Dei*, X, 3ff.; XII, 1; XIX, 23–4.

61 Ibid., XIV, 1–4; XV, 8. It is precisely the attempt to measure the eternal mind of God by the temporal, mutable standards of the human intellect that provokes Augustine's scathing attack on cyclical cosmological theories in XII, 18.

62 Ibid., XI, 16.

63 See Niebuhr, "Augustine's Political Realism," 126ff., 130.

64 For an excellent account of how these are related in Augustine's thought see Cochrane, *Christianity and Classical Culture*, chapter 12.

65 See Cochrane's illuminating comparison of Herodotus, Thucydides, and Augustine in ibid., chapter 12; cf. Eric Voegelin's comparison of Herodotus, Thucydides, and Plato on the same question of how to account philosophically for the history of political conflict and disorder in the ancient world. *Order and History*, volume 2; *The World of the Polis* (Baton Rouge: Louisiana State University Press, 1957).

66 *De Civitate Dei*, II, 21; XIX, 21.

67 Ibid., XIX, 21. Note the definition of "true virtue" in XIX, 10.

68 Ibid., XIX, 23.

69 Ibid., XIX, 24.

70 Ibid., XV, 5.

71 Ibid., XV, 7, 22.

72 Ibid., XV, 5ff.

73 Ibid., XV, 17, 21.

74 Ibid., XIX, 12.

75 Ibid., XIX, 13.

76 Ibid., XIX, 14.

77 Ibid., XIX, 17.

78 Ibid., XIX, 24. This is far from being a "morally neutral definition of political cohesion" that fails to make distinctions between different forms of political and social community, as Niebuhr's interpretation has it (*Nature and Destiny*, 2:273–4).

79 See Augustine's description of this in *De Civitate Dei*, XXII, 29–30.

80 Ibid., XXII, 29. Cf. Philippians 4:7.

81 Cochrane expresses this Augustinian approach to wisdom in the following formulation: "As truth it may be described as reason irradiated by love; as morality, love irradiated by reason" (*Christianity and Classical Culture*, 506). Such a view rejects Niebuhrian dualisms; see ibid., 510ff.

82 See p. 170, note 160.

83 See the profound philosophical and moral meditation on this by Kohak, *The Embers and the Stars*

Bibliography

Allen, Richard. *The Social Passion: Religion and Social Reform in Canada, 1914–28.* Toronto: University of Toronto Press, 1971.

Arendt, Hannah. *Between Past and Future: Eight Exercises in Political Thought.* New York: Viking Press, 1968.

– *The Human Condition.* Chicago: University of Chicago Press, 1958.

– *The Origins of Totalitarianism*, part 3, *Totalitarianism.* New York: Harcourt Brace Jovanovich, 1951; 1968.

Augustine, Aurelius. *De Civitate Dei.* Corpus Christianorum: Series Latina, vols. 47, 48. Turnholt: Brepols, 1955.

– *Confessions*, 2 vols. Loeb Classical Library. Cambridge: Harvard University Press, 1912.

– *De Doctrina Christiana.* Corpus Christianorum: Series Latina, vol. 32. Turnholt: Brepols, 1962.

– *De Trinitate.* Corpus Christianorum: Series Latina, vol. 50. Turnholt: Brepols, 1968.

Avineri, Schlomo. *The Social and Political Thought of Karl Marx.* Cambridge: Cambridge University Press, 1968.

Barfield, Owen. *History, Guilt, and Habit.* Middletown, CT: Wesleyan University Press, 1979.

– *The Rediscovery of Meaning and Other Essays.* Middletown, CT: Wesleyan University Press, 1977.

– *Saving the Appearances: A Study in Idolatry.* New York: Harcourt Brace Jovanovich, 1957.

– *Speaker's Meaning.* Middletown, CT: Wesleyan University Press, 1967.

Barth, Karl. *Church Dogmatics*, II/2, III/2. Ed. G.W. Bromiley and T.F. Torrance. Edinburgh: T.&T. Clark, 1957; 1960.

Baudrillard, Jean. *The Mirror of Production*. Trans. Mark Poster. St Louis: Telos Press, 1975.

Baum, Gregory. *The Priority of Labor: A Commentary on Laborem Exercens, Encyclical Letter of Pope John Paul II*. New York: Paulist Press, 1982.

– and Duncan Cameron. *Ethics and Economics: Canada's Catholic Bishops on the Economic Crisis*. Toronto: James Lorimer, 1984.

Becker, William. "Reinhold Niebuhr: From Marx to Roosevelt." *The Historian* 35 (August 1973):539–50.

Beckley, Harlan. "A Christian Affirmation of Rawls's Idea of Justice as Fairness – Part I." *Journal of Religious Ethics* 13, no. 2 (Fall 1985):210–42.

– *Passion for Justice: Retrieving the Legacies of Walter Rauschenbusch, John A. Ryan, and Reinhold Niebuhr*. Louisville, KY: Westminster/John Knox Press, 1992.

Bellah, Robert, and Norma Haan, eds. *Social Science as Moral Inquiry*. New York: Columbia University Press, 1983.

Benne, Robert. *The Ethic of Democratic Capitalism: A Moral Reassessment*. Philadelphia: Fortress, 1981.

Berlin, Isaiah. *Four Essays on Liberty*. Oxford: Oxford University Press, 1969.

Bernstein, Richard J. *Beyond Objectivism and Relativism: Science, Hermeneutics, and Praxis*. Philadelphia: University of Pennsylvania Press, 1983.

Borgmann, Albert. *Technology and the Character of Contemporary Life*. Chicago: University of Chicago Press, 1984.

Bottomore, T.B. *Critics of Society: Radical Thought in North America*. New York: Pantheon Books, 1968.

Buber, Martin. *Between Man and Man*. Trans. Ronald Gregor Smith. Glasgow: Collins, 1947.

– *I and Thou*. Trans. Walter Kaufmann. New York: Scribner's, 1970.

Burke, Kenneth. *A Grammar of Motives*. New York: Prentice-Hall, 1945.

– *The Rhetoric of Religion: Studies in Logology*. Berkeley: University of California Press, 1970.

Burnaby, John. *Amor Dei: A Study of the Religion of St Augustine*. London: Hodder & Stoughten, 1938.

Calvez, Jean-Yves, and Jacques Perrin. *The Church and Social Justice: The Social Teaching of the Popes from Leo XIII to Pius XII*. Chicago: Henry Regnery, 1961.

Calvin, Jean. *Institutes of the Christian Religion*, 2 vols. Ed. John T. McNeill, trans. Ford Lewis Battles. Philadelphia: Westminster Press, 1960.

Camus, Albert. *Resistance, Rebellion, and Death*. Trans. Justin O'Brien. New York: Vintage Books, 1960.

Canadian Conference of Catholic Bishops. "Ethical Reflections on the Economic Crisis." In Gregory Baum and Duncan Cameron, *Ethics and Econom-*

ics: Canada's Catholic Bishops on the Economic Crisis. Toronto: James Lorimer, 1984, 3–18.

– "A Statement on Social Policy." Dissent (Summer 1988):314–21.

Carnoy, Martin. The State and Political Theory. Princeton: Princeton University Press, 1984.

Clarkson, Stephen. Canada and the Reagan Challenge: Crisis and Adjustment, 1981–85. Toronto: James Lorimer, 1985.

Clement, Wallace. Continental Corporate Power: Economic Elite Linkages Between Canada and the United States. Toronto: McClelland & Stewart, 1977.

Cochrane, Charles N. Christianity and Classical Culture: A Study of Thought and Action From Augustus to Augustine. New York: Oxford University Press, 1957.

Cohen, Joshua, and Joel Rogers. On Democracy. New York: Penguin, 1983.

Connolly, William E. Appearance and Reality in Politics. Cambridge: Cambridge University Press, 1981.

Cook, Ramsey. The Regenerators: Social Criticism in Late Victorian English Canada. Toronto: University of Toronto Press, 1985.

Cort, John C. Christian Socialism: An Informal History. Maryknoll, NY: Orbis, 1988.

Cross, Michael, and Gregory Kealey, eds. Modern Canada: 1930's–1980's, vol. 5, Readings in Canadian Social History. Toronto: McClelland and Stewart, 1984.

Dombrowski, James. The Early Days of Christian Socialism in America. New York: Octagon Books, 1966.

Dorr, Donal. Option for the Poor: A Hundred Years of Vatican Social Teaching. Maryknoll, NY: Orbis Books, 1983.

Douglass, R. Bruce, ed. The Deeper Meaning of Economic Life: Critical Essays on the U.S. Catholic Bishops' Pastoral Letter on the Economy. Washington, DC: Georgetown University Press, 1986.

Dufort, Jean-Marc. "Le discours social récent des évêques du Canada: analyse théologique." Science et esprit 38, no. 1 (1986):49–79.

Duncan, Graeme, ed. Democratic Theory and Practice. Cambridge: Cambridge University Press, 1983.

Edwards, Richard. Contested Terrain: The Transformation of the Workplace in the Twentieth Century. New York: Basic Books, 1979.

Ferkiss, Victor. "Individual Needs and Social Consensus." Zygon 17, no. 2 (June 1982):133–150.

Fox, Richard Wrightman. Reinhold Niebuhr: A Biography. New York: Pantheon Books, 1985.

Gannon, Thomas M., S.J. The Challenge to the American Economy: Reflections on the U.S. Bishops' Pastoral Letter on Catholic Social Teaching and the U.S. Economy. New York: Macmillan, 1987.

Garrison, W.E. "Marxist Christians Nail Their Theses to the Door." Review of *Towards the Christian Revolution*, R.B.Y. Scott and Gregory Vlastos, eds. *The Christian Century* 24 (February 1937):249–50.

Gilson, Etienne. *The Christian Philosophy of Saint Augustine*. Trans. L.E.M. Lynch. New York: Random House, 1960.

Goldthorpe, John H., ed. *Order and Conflict in Contemporary Capitalism*. Oxford: Oxford University Press, 1984.

Gonick, Cy. *Inflation or Depression: The Continuing Crisis of the Canadian Economy*. Toronto: James Lorimer, 1975.

– *Out of Work*. Toronto: James Lorimer, 1978.

Gordon, David M., Richard Edwards, and Michael Reich. *Segmented Work, Divided Workers: The Historical Transformation of Labor in the United States*. Cambridge: Cambridge University Press, 1982.

Gorz, Andre. *Farewell to the Working Class*. Trans. Michael Sonnenscher. Boston: South End Press, 1982.

Gremillion, Joseph, ed. *The Gospel of Peace and Justice: Catholic Social Teaching Since Pope John*. Maryknoll, NY: Orbis Books, 1976.

Gustafson, James M. *Ethics From a Theocentric Perspective*, 2 vols. Chicago: University of Chicago Press, 1981, 1984.

– "From Scripture to Social Policy and Social Action." *Andover Newton Quarterly* 9, no. 3 (1969):160–9.

Guthrie, W.K.C. *The Sophists*. Cambridge: Cambridge University Press, 1971.

Habermas, Jürgen. *Legitimation Crisis*. Trans. Thomas McCarthy. Boston: Beacon Press, 1975.

– *Technik und Wissenschaft als "Ideologie."* Frankfurt am Main: Suhrkamp Verlag, 1968.

– and Niklas Luhmann, *Theorie der Gesellschaft oder Sozialtechnologie – Was leistet die Systemforschung?* Frankfurt: Suhrkamp Verlag, 1971.

Harland, Gordon. *The Thought of Reinhold Niebuhr*. New York: Oxford University Press, 1960.

Harrison, Beverly Wildung. *Making the Connections: Essays in Feminist Social Ethics*. Ed. Carol Robb. Boston: Beacon Press, 1985.

Held, David. *Models of Democracy*. Stanford: Stanford University Press, 1987.

Heller, Erich. *The Disinherited Mind*. New York: Meridian Books, 1959.

Herman, Edward S. *Corporate Control, Corporate Power*. Cambridge: Harvard University Press, 1981.

Hirsch, Fred. *Social Limits to Growth*. Cambridge, MA: Harvard University Press, 1976.

Hobbes, Thomas. *Leviathan*. Ed. C.B. Macpherson. Harmondsworth: Penguin Books, 1968.

Hollenbach, David. *Claims in Conflict: Retrieving and Renewing the Catholic Human Rights Tradition*. New York: Paulist Press, 1979.

– "Liberalism, Communitarianism, and the Bishops' Pastoral Letter on the Economy." *The Annual of the Society of Christian Ethics* (1987):19–40.

Horn, Michiel. *The League for Social Reconstruction: Intellectual Origins of the Democratic Left in Canada, 1930–1942.* Toronto: University of Toronto Press, 1980.

Houck, John, and Oliver Williams, eds. *Co-Creation and Capitalism: John Paul II's Laborem Exercens.* Washington, DC: University Press of America, 1983.

Hutchinson, Roger. "The Fellowship for a Christian Social Order: A Social Ethical Analysis of a Christian Socialist Movement." Th.D. diss., Toronto School of Theology, 1975.

– and Harold Wells, eds. *A Long and Faithful March: "Towards the Christian Revolution" 1930's/1980's.* Toronto: United Church Publishing House, 1989.

Ignatieff, Michael. *The Needs of Strangers.* Harmondsworth: Penguin, 1984.

Jonas, Hans. *The Phenomenon of Life: Toward a Philosophical Biology.* New York: Dell, 1966.

– *Philosophical Essays: From Ancient Creed to Technological Man.* Englewood Cliffs, NJ: Prentice-Hall, 1974.

Kant, Immanuel. *Foundations of the Metaphysics of Morals.* Trans. Lewis White Beck. Library of Liberal Arts. Indianapolis: Bobbs-Merrill, 1959.

– *Kritik der Praktischen Vernunft.* Philosophische Bibliothek 38. Hamburg: Felix Meiner Verlag, 1929.

Keane, John, and John Owens. *After Full Employment.* London: Hutchinson Press, 1986.

Kegley, Charles, ed. *Reinhold Niebuhr: His Religious, Social and Political Thought.* New York: Pilgrim Press, 1984.

Kierkegaard, Søren. *The Concept of Anxiety: A Simple Psychologically Orienting Deliberation on the Dogmatic Issue of Hereditary Sin.* Ed. and trans. Reidar Thomte, with A. Anderson. Princeton: Princeton University Press, 1980.

– *Concluding Unscientific Postscript.* Trans. D. Swenson and W. Lowrie. Princeton: Princeton University Press, 1941.

Kohak, Erazim. *The Embers and the Stars: A Philosophical Inquiry into the Moral Sense of Nature.* Chicago: University of Chicago Press, 1984.

Kroeker, P. Travis. "Canada's Catholic Bishops and the Economy: A Theological Ethical Analysis." *Toronto Journal of Theology* 2 (Spring 1986):3–18.

– "Ethics, Economics and Christian Realism: Religious Social Theories of Reinhold Niebuhr and Gregory Vlastos." *The Annual of the Society of Christian Ethics* (1988):77–89.

– "Theology, Ethics and Social Theory: The Social Gospel Quest for a Public Morality." *Studies in Religion/Sciences Religieuses* 20, no. 2 (1991):181–99.

Lane, Robert. "Market Justice, Political Justice." *American Political Science Review* 80, no. 2 (1986):383–402.

League for Social Reconstruction. *Social Planning for Canada.* Toronto: University of Toronto Press, 1975.

Lears, T.J. Jackson. *No Place of Grace: Antimodernism and the Transformation of American Culture, 1880–1920*. New York: Pantheon Books, 1981.

Leiss, William. *The Limits to Satisfaction: An Essay on the Problem of Needs and Commodities*. Toronto: University of Toronto Press, 1976.

Levitt, Kari. *Silent Surrender: The Multinational Corporation in Canada*. Toronto: Macmillan, 1970.

Lindblom, Charles E. *Politics and Markets: The World's Political-Economic Systems*. New York: Basic Books, 1977.

Lipset, Seymour M. *Agrarian Socialism: The Cooperative Commonwealth Federation in Saskatchewan*. Berkeley: University of California Press, 1950.

Lovin, Robin W. "Covenantal Relationships and Political Legitimacy." *The Journal of Religion* 60, no. 1 (January 1980):1–16.

Löwith, Karl. *Max Weber and Karl Marx*. Trans. Hans Fantel. London: George Allen & Unwin, 1982.

Lukes, Steven. *Essays in Social Theory*. New York: Columbia University Press, 1977.

McConnell, Grant. *The Decline of Agrarian Democracy*. Berkeley: University of California Press, 1959.

McNaught, Kenneth. *A Prophet in Politics: A Biography of J.S. Woodsworth*. Toronto: University of Toronto Press, 1959.

Macpherson, C.B. *Democratic Theory: Essays in Retrieval*. Oxford: Oxford University Press, 1973.

– *The Life and Times of Liberal Democracy*. Oxford: Oxford University Press, 1977.

– *The Rise and Fall of Economic Justice and Other Essays*. Oxford: Oxford University Press, 1985.

Mahon, Rianne. *The Politics of Industrial Restructuring: Canadian Textiles*. Toronto: University of Toronto Press, 1984.

Marx, Karl. *Grundrisse: Foundations of the Critique of Political Economy*. Trans. Martin Nicolaus. New York: Random House, 1973.

– *The Marx-Engels Reader*, 2nd ed. Ed. Robert Tucker. New York: Norton, 1978.

Merkley, Paul. *Reinhold Niebuhr: A Political Account*. Montreal: McGill-Queen's University Press, 1975.

Meyer, Donald. *The Protestant Search for Political Realism, 1918–41*. Berkeley: University of California Press, 1961.

Mills, Allen. *Fool for Christ: The Political Thought of J.S. Woodsworth*. Toronto: University of Toronto Press, 1991.

Minus, Paul M. *Walter Rauschenbusch: American Reformer*. New York: Macmillan, 1988.

National Conference of Catholic Bishops. *Economic Justice for all: Pastoral Letter on Catholic Social Teaching and the u.s. Economy*. Washington, DC: National Conference of Catholic Bishops/United States Catholic Conference, 1986.

Niebuhr, H. Richard. *Christ and Culture*. New York: Harper & Row, 1951.
– "The Idea of Covenant and American Democracy." *Church History* 23, no. 2 (June 1954):126–35.
– *The Meaning of Revelation*. New York: Macmillan, 1941.
– *Radical Monotheism and Western Culture: With Supplementary Essays*. New York: Harper & Row, 1960.
– *The Responsible Self: A Study in Moral Philosophy*. New York: Harper & Row, 1963.
Niebuhr, Reinhold. *The Children of Light and the Children of Darkness: A Vindication of Democracy and a Critique of its Traditional Defense*. New York: Charles Scribner's Sons, 1944.
– "The Christian Faith and the Economic Life of Liberal Society." In *Goals of Economic Life*, ed. A.D. Ward. New York: Harper & Brothers, 1953, 433–59.
– "Christian Politics and Communist Religion." In *Christianity and the Social Revolution*, ed. John Lewis, Karl Polanyi, and Donald Kitchen. London: Victor Gollancz, 1935, 442–72.
– *Christian Realism and Political Problems*. New York: Charles Scribner's Sons, 1953.
– "Coercion, Self-Interest, and Love." In Kenneth E. Boulding, *The Organizational Revolution: A Study in the Ethics of Economic Organization*. New York: Harper & Brothers, 1953, 228–44.
– *Faith and History: A Comparison of Christian and Modern Views of History*. New York: Charles Scribner's Sons, 1949.
– *Faith and Politics: A Commentary on Religious, Social and Political Thought in a Technological Age*. Ed. Ronald Stone. New York: George Braziller, 1968.
– *An Interpretation of Christian Ethics*. New York: Harper & Row, 1935.
– *The Irony of American History*. New York: Charles Scribner's Sons, 1952.
– "Marxists are Taking Stock." *Christianity and Society* 5, no. 2 (Spring 1940):8–9.
– *Moral Man and Immoral Society: A Study in Ethics and Politics*. New York: Charles Scribner's Sons, 1932.
– *The Nature and Destiny of Man*, 2 vols. New York: Charles Scribner's Sons, 1941, 1943.
– "New Deal Medicine." *Radical Religion* 4, no. 2 (Spring 1939):1–3.
– *Reflections on the End of an Era*. New York: Charles Scribner's Sons, 1932.
– "Review of *Towards the Christian Revolution*." *Radical Religion* 2, no. 2 (Spring 1937):42–4.
– "Walter Rauschenbusch in Historical Perspective." *Religion in Life* 27, no. 4 (Autumn 1958):527–36.
Nixon, Justin Wroe. "Christians on the Marxian Road." Review of *Towards the Christian Revolution*, R.B.Y. Scott and Gregory Vlastos, eds. *Christendom* 1, no. 3 (Summer 1937): 482–5.

O'Connor, James. *The Fiscal Crisis of the State*. New York: St Martin's Press, 1973.

O'Donovan, Oliver. *The Problem of Self-Love in St Augustine*. New Haven: Yale University Press, 1980.

Offe, Claus. *Contradictions of the Welfare State*. Ed. John Keane. Cambridge, MA: MIT Press, 1984.

– "Democracy Against the Welfare State? Structural Foundations of Neoconservative Political Opportunities." *Political Theory* 15, no. 4 (November 1987):501–37.

Outka, Gene. *Agape: An Ethical Analysis*. New Haven: Yale University Press, 1972.

Panitch, Leo. "Recent Theorizations of Corporatism: Reflections on a Growth Industry." *British Journal of Sociology* 31, no. 2 (June 1980):159–87.

Pascal, Blaise. *Pensées*. Trans. A.J. Krailsheimer. Harmondsworth: Penguin, 1966.

Pateman, Carole. *Participation and Democratic Theory*. Cambridge: Cambridge University Press, 1970.

– *The Problem of Political Obligation: A Critique of Liberal Theory*. Berkeley: University of California Press, 1985.

Penner, Norman. *The Canadian Left: A Critical Analysis*. Scarborough, Ont: Prentice-Hall, 1977.

Plato. *The Republic*, 2 vols. Loeb Classical Library. Cambridge: Harvard University Press, 1937.

Przeworski, Adam. *Capitalism and Social Democracy*. Cambridge: Cambridge University Press, 1985.

Rauschenbusch, Walter. *Christianity and the Social Crisis*. New York: Macmillan, 1907.

– *Christianizing the Social Order*. New York: Macmillan, 1914.

– "The Influence of Historical Studies on Theology." *The American Journal of Theology* 11 (January 1907):111–27.

– *The Righteousness of the Kingdom*. Ed. Max Stackhouse. Nashville: Abingdon Press, 1968.

– *The Social Principles of Jesus*. New York: Association Press, 1917.

– *A Theology for the Social Gospel*. New York: Macmillan, 1917.

Rawls, John. *A Theory of Justice*. Cambridge: Harvard University Press, 1971.

Safarian, A.E. *Foreign Ownership of Canadian Industry*. Toronto: University of Toronto Press, 1973.

Sandel, Michael. *Liberalism and the Limits of Justice*. Cambridge: Cambridge University Press, 1982.

Scott, R.B.Y. *The Relevance of the Prophets*. New York: Macmillan, 1944.

– and Gregory Vlastos, eds. *Towards the Christian Revolution*. New York: Willett, Clark, 1936.

Skocpol, Theda. "Legacies of New Deal Liberalism." *Dissent* (Winter 1983):33–44.

Smith, Michael Joseph. *Realist Thought from Weber to Kissinger.* Baton Rouge: Louisiana State University Press, 1986.

The Social Gospel in America, 1870–1920. Ed. Robert Handy. New York: Oxford University Press, 1966.

Stackhouse, Max. *Public Theology and Political Economy.* Grand Rapids, MI: Eerdmans, 1986.

Strain, Charles R. "Toward a Generic Analysis of a Classic of the Social Gospel: An Essay Review of Walter Rauschenbusch, *Christianity and the Social Crisis.*" *Journal of the American Academy of Religion* 46 (1978): 525–43.

Tawney, R.H. *The Acquisitive Society.* New York: Harcourt, Brace, 1921.

– *The British Labor Movement.* New Haven: Yale University Press, 1925.

Taylor, Charles. *Human Agency and Language. Philosophical Papers,* vol. 1. Cambridge: Cambridge University Press, 1985.

– *Philosophy and the Human Sciences. Philosophical Papers,* vol. 2. Cambridge: Cambridge University Press, 1985.

Thurow, Lester C. *The Zero-Sum Society: Distribution and the Possibilities for Economic Change.* New York: Penguin, 1980.

Tietje, Louis H. "Was Reinhold Niebuhr Ever a Marxist? An Investigation into the Assumptions of his Early Interpretation and Critique of Marxism." Ph.D. diss., Union Theological Seminary, New York, 1984.

Toulmin, Stephen. *The Return to Cosmology: Postmodern Science and the Theology of Nature.* Berkeley: University of California Press, 1982.

Troeltsch, Ernst. *Gesammelte Schriften.* Bund II: *Zur Religiösen Lage, Religionsphilosophie und Ethik.* Tübingen: J.C.B. Mohr, 1913. Reprint, Tübingen: Scientia Verlag Aalen, 1962.

– *Writings on Theology and Religion.* Ed. and trans. Robert Morgan and Michael Pye. Atlanta: John Knox Press, 1977.

Vlastos, Gregory. *Christian Faith and Democracy.* New York: Hazen Books, 1939.

– "The Impossible Possibility." Review of *An Interpretation of Christian Ethics,* by Reinhold Niebuhr. *Christendom* 1, no. 2 (Winter 1936):390–4.

– "Love and the Class Struggle." *Radical Religion* 3, no. 2 (Spring 1938):26–8.

– "Reclaim the Gospel of Solidarity." *The Christian Century,* 25 February 1942: 245–7.

– "Religious Foundations of Democracy: Fraternity and Liberty." *The Journal of Religion* 22, no. 1 (January 1942):1–19.

– "The Religious Foundations of Democracy: Fraternity and Equality." *The Journal of Religion* 22, no. 2 (April 1942):137–55.

– *The Religious Way.* New York: The Woman's Press, 1934.

– "Sin and Anxiety in Niebuhr's Religion." *The Christian Century,* 1 October 1941:1202–4.

– "What is Love?" *Christendom* 1 (Autumn 1935):117–31.

Voegelin, Eric. "Industrial Society in Search of Reason." *World Technology and Human Destiny,* ed. R. Aron. Ann Arbor: University of Michigan Press, 1963.

– *The New Science of Politics.* Chicago: University of Chicago Press, 1952.

– "The Origins of Scientism." *Social Research* 15, no. 4 (1948):462–94.

Walzer, Michael. *Spheres of Justice: A Defense of Pluralism and Equality.* New York: Basic Books, 1983.

Weber, Max. *From Max Weber: Essays in Sociology.* Ed. and trans. H.H. Gerth and C. Wright Mills. New York: Oxford University Press, 1946.

– *Gesammelte Aufsatze zur Wissenschaftslehre.* Tübingen: J.C.B. Mohr/Paul Siebeck, 1968.

– *Gesammelte Politische Schriften.* 3rd ed. Auflage. Tübingen: J.C.B. Mohr/ Paul Siebeck, 1971.

– *The Methodology of the Social Sciences.* Ed. and trans. E.A. Shils and H.A. Finch. New York: Free Press, 1949.

– *The Protestant Ethic and the Spirit of Capitalism.* Trans. Talcott Parsons. New York: Charles Scribner's Sons, 1958.

– *The Sociology of Religion.* Trans. Ephraim Fischoff. Boston: Beacon Press, 1963.

Willey, Basil. *The Seventeenth Century Background.* Garden City: Doubleday, 1953.

Williams, Bernard. *Descartes: The Project of Pure Inquiry.* Harmondsworth: Penguin, 1978.

Williams, George. H. *The Mind of John Paul II: Origins of his Thought and Action.* New York: Harper & Row, 1981.

Williams, Glen. *Not for Export: Toward a Political Economy of Canada's Arrested Industrialization.* Toronto: McClelland and Stewart, 1986.

Wolfe, Alan. *America's Impasse: The Rise and Fall of the Politics of Growth.* New York: Pantheon Books, 1981.

– "Inauthentic Democracy: A Critique of Public Life in Modern Liberal Society." *Studies in Political Economy* 21 (Autumn 1986):57–81.

Wolfe, David. "The Rise and Demise of the Keynesian Era in Canada." *Modern Canada: 1930–1980's.* Readings in Canadian Social History, vol. 5. Ed. Michael Cross and Gregory Kealey. Toronto: McClelland and Stewart, 1984, 46–80.

Wolin, Sheldon. "Contract and Birthright." *Political Theory* 14, no. 2 (May 1986):179–93.

– "Democracy and the Welfare State: The Political and Theoretical Connections Between Staatsräson and Wohlfahrtsstaatsräson." *Political Theory* 15, no. 4 (November 1987):467–500.

– "Max Weber: Legitimation, Method, and the Politics of Theory." In *Legitimation and the State,* ed. William Connolly. New York: New York University Press, 1984, 63–87.

– *Politics and Vision: Continuity and Innovation in Western Political Thought.*
Boston: Little, Brown, 1960.

Woodsworth, James Shaver. *The First Story of the Labor Church and Some Things
for Which It Stands.* Winnipeg: Labor Church Offices, 1920.

– *My Neighbor.* Toronto: University of Toronto Press, 1972.

– *Strangers Within Our Gates.* Toronto: University of Toronto Press, 1972.

Young, Walter. *The Anatomy of a Party: The National* CCF, *1932–61.* Toronto:
University of Toronto Press, 1971.

Index

Allen, Richard, 36
Anthropocentric, 34, 44;
  utilitarianism, 6–7, 13–
  14, 17–18, 48, 86–8,
  101–3, 110–11, 120–1,
  122
Arendt, Hannah, xii–xiii,
  12, 49, 78, 167n.129,
  102–3
Augustine, 181n.5, 123,
  130, 131–2, 133–43
Avineri, Schlomo, 85

Bacon, Francis, 12, 124,
  129
Barfield, Owen, 149–
  50n.46, 150n.47
Barth, Karl, 50–1
Baudrillard, Jean, 102,
  172n.13, 177–8n.70
Baum, Gregory, 173–4n.23
Beckley, Harlan, 153n.60,
  162n.66
Benne, Robert, 8, 63
Bernstein, Richard, 49
Borgmann, Albert, 12,
  112, 173n.20, 180n.80
Bottomore, T.B., 20
Burke, Edmund, 58,
  161n.53

Burke, Kenneth, 14, 133,
  148n.35, 149n.44, 182–
  3n.22
Burnaby, John, 184nn.43,
  56

Calvin, John, 10, 146–
  7n.27; Calvinism,
  146n.11, 153n.62
Capitalism, xi; and Catholic bishops, 105–11,
  114–20; and Christian
  realism, 59–60, 65–8,
  76–7, 80–5, 86; and
  Pope John Paul II, 100–
  4; and Protestantism, 3–
  9; and social gospel, 19,
  26, 29–31, 38–40, 42. *See
  also* Class conflict; Corporatism, Liberalism
Catholic bishops, 142–3;
  Canadian, 104–11; u.s.,
  111–20
Catholic social tradition,
  92–8
Christology: Augustine,
  137–8; Catholic, 96–
  100, 104–5, 115; Rein-
  hold Niebuhr, 51–5;
  social gospel, 23–6, 31

Class conflict, 27, 30, 65–
  6, 76–7, 82–3, 93, 100,
  117–18
Cochrane, C.N., 184n.43,
  185nn.64, 65, 186n.81
Common good: August-
  ine on, 138–43 *passim*;
  Catholic view of, 93–8
  passim, 103–5, 110–12,
  114–20 *passim*; FCSO
  on, 89; social gospel
  on, 25, 29, 33, 41, 43
Connolly, William, 73,
  148n.39
Cook, Ramsey, 20–2
Cooperative Common-
  wealth Federation
  (CCF), 35–40 *passim*, 67,
  68
Corporatism: Christian,
  94–5; liberal, 113, 114–
  20. *See also* Capitalism;
  Liberalism; Policy;
  Socialism
Covenant community:
  FCSO on, 47, 72–3, 75,
  77–81, 90; u.s. bishops
  on, 113–14
Creation theology: and
  Catholicism, 99–104

passim, 113–14, 120–1;
and cosmology, 4, 9–
12, 14–18, 131–6, 143;
and moral wisdom, 14–
18, 88–90, 122–43
passim

Democracy: and capital-
ism, 18, 19, 26, 29–31,
66, 76–7, 88–9; develop-
mental, 39–40, 42–3;
economic, 31,34, 38–9,
111–12; participatory,
18, 79–83, 109; plural-
ist equilibrium, 47, 62–
5, 118, 178n.74; and
technology, 113, 115–
16, 119; and theology,
23–6, 32, 34
Descartes, René, 10, 11;
Cartesianism, 9, 11–12,
49–50

Fellowship for a Chris-
tian Social Order
(FCSO), 46–7, 67–90,
142. *See also* Vlastos,
Gregory
Ferkiss, Victor, 110
Forsey, Eugene, 68, 83–5,
86
Fox, Richard, 158n.20

Galileo, Galilei, 10, 128,
181n.8
Gilson, Etienne, 185n.59
Gordon, J. King, 68, 81,
83
Gorz, Andre, 116
Gustafson, James,
151n.26, 180n.81

Habermas, Jürgen, 147–
8n.34
Harland, Gordon, 158n.19
Harrison, Beverley W.,
160n.46, 161n.57
Havelock, Eric, 68, 81, 86
Hegel/Hegelian, 5, 20,
21–2, 43–4, 70, 165n.98
Heller, Erich, 123
Herman, Edward, 178n.73
Hirsch, Fred, 176n.54

Hobbes, Thomas, 123,
128–30
Hollenbach, David, 98,
172n.9, 105, 111–12

Ideal/Idealism: criticism
of, 69–71, 73, 89, 141–2;
in Reinhold Niebuhr,
45–6, 49–58 *passim*; in
social gospel, 25, 29,
30, 32–4, 42, 44
Idolatry, 16–17, 44, 124,
133, 138
Imago Dei, 25, 88, 90, 92–
3, 96, 99–104 *passim*,
113, 120–1. *See also*
Creation theology;
Nature, human

John XXIII, Pope, 94–6
John Paul II, Pope, 98–
105, 110, 114, 121
Jonas, Hans, 11, 146n.26
Justice, xi–xii, 12–13, 15;
Augustine on, 130–43
passim; and democracy,
79–83; Hobbes on, 128–
9; liberal theories of,
111–13; and love, 53–6,
59, 60–5, 74–5, 131–2;
Plato on, 125–7

Kant, Immanuel, 11, 50–1
Keynesian economics, 60,
66, 84, 91, 106, 116,
163nn.82, 83
Kierkegaard, Soren, 49–
50, 157n.9, 180n.81
Kingdom of God, 7, 22–
34 *passim*, 41–4 *passim*,
45, 70, 104, 114, 142
Kohak, Erazim, 146n.25,
186n.83

Lane, Robert E., 179n.77
League for Social Recon-
struction (LSR), 67–8,
85, 155n.82
Lears, Jackson, 33
Leiss, William, 176n.53
Leo XIII, Pope, 93–4, 118
Liberalism, 8, 12–18
passim, 22, 33–4, 104,

120–1; Catholic cri-
tique of, 93–5; and
communitarianism,
111–13; FCSO critique
of, 71–4, 77–82, *passim*;
and modern identity,
42–4; Reinhold Nie-
buhr's critique of, 59,
60–5. *See also* Capital-
ism; Progressivism;
Spiritual crisis
Line, John, 69, 164–5n.95
Love: Augustine on, 130–
43 *passim*; and justice,
53–6, 60–4, 74–6; law
of, 49–58, 67; as mutu-
ality, 57, 71–6; and
social movement, 24;
and solidarity, 99, 104–
5, 114–15

Macpherson, C.B., 65,
147–8n.34, 163n.77
Marx, Karl/Marxism, 5;
and Christian realism,
59, 60, 66, 68, 70, 76,
82, 85–8, 164n.86; and
social gospel, 30, 32,
38, 152n.58. *See also*
Socialism, scientific
Meyer, Donald, 153n.60

Nature: domination of, 9,
12, 16, 18, 43, 67, 88, 92,
101–4, 110, 129–30; hu-
man, 49–56, 60–4, 67,
71–3, 77–8, 85–90, 93–
104 *passim*, 116, 131–43
passim; and scientism,
9–14, 16, 33–4, 40, 43–4,
122–33. *See also* Cre-
ation theology; Technol-
ogy, and mastery
Niebuhr, H. Richard, 26,
159n.21, 167–8n.132
Niebuhr, Reinhold, 45–
67; and Augustine,
134–43 *passim*; and
Catholic bishops, 118,
178n.74; and FCSO, 68–
74, 81, 83, 84, 85, 88–90
Nygren, Anders, 184n.42,
184–5n.56

O'Donovan, Oliver,
    184nn.42, 43
Offe, Claus, 20
Outka, Gene, 57, 160n.44

Pascal, Blaise, 10, 147n.28
Pateman, Carole, 81,
    163n.76
Paul VI, Pope, 96–7,
    173n.23
Pius XI, Pope, 93–4, 118
Plato, 70, 123, 125–6, 128
Policy: Canadian bish-
    ops, 105–11; and ethics,
    15, 17, 42–4, 122, 127–8,
    142–3; FCSO, 83–5; Rein-
    hold Niebuhr, 65–7;
    social gospel, 29, 37–40;
    U.S. bishops, 114–20
Productivist paradigm,
    xi, xiv, 13, 16–18, 88,
    101–4, 110–11, 115, 120–
    1, 143
Progressivism, 12–13, 25,
    33–4, 40, 43–4, 113,
    114, 115, 117, 121. See
    also Liberalism, Tech-
    nology
Przeworski, Adam,
    155n.89, 169n.149

Ramsey, Paul, 57, 160n.43
Rawls, John, 62, 63,
    162n.66
Rauschenbusch, Walter,
    22–34, 35, 43, 48, 156n.1

Reason/rationality:
    Augustine on, 136–43
    passim; public, 4–8, 14,
    89–90, 93, 123–8; and
    revelation, 47, 51–4, 56–
    7, 75–6, 96, 142

Sandel, Michael, 63,
    162n.70
Scott, R.B.Y., 68, 72, 78–9
Smith, Michael J., 170
    n.153
Social gospel, 19–44, 142;
    and Christian realism,
    45–7, 59, 67, 69, 86
Socialism: Canadian, 35–
    40, 83–5; Christian, 30,
    67–8; scientific, 27, 29–
    31, 42, 93–4
Social theory, 17; Augus-
    tinian, 139–43; Catho-
    lic, 92–104, 111–13,
    114–20; Christian realis-
    tic, 47, 48, 58–67, 76–
    85, 88–9; Hobbesian,
    128–30; social gospel,
    20, 27, 28–34, 39–40
Spiritual crisis, 9–14, 21,
    44, 90, 120–1, 122–33
Stackhouse, Max, 8
Subject-object dualism,
    11–12, 147n.32, 16, 47–
    8, 99–100, 110–11
Symbol, xii-xiii, 14–18
    passim, 42–3, 114–15,
    123–33, 142–3

Taylor, Charles, 42–3
Technology: liberal prom-
    ise of, 104, 112–13, 115;
    and mastery, 7–9, 12–
    13, 43–4. See also Pro-
    gressivism
Theology: Catholic bish-
    ops, 104–5, 113–14;
    FCSO, 69–76; Reinhold
    Niebuhr, 48–58, 134–8
    passim; social gospel,
    22–8, 36–7, 42–4. See
    also Christology, Cre-
    ation theology
Tillich, Paul, 56, 159n.40
Troeltsch, Ernst, 40–1,
    154n.77

Vatican II, 96–8
Vlastos, Gregory, 46, 69–
    88 passim, 142
Voegelin, Eric, 9, 128,
    148n.41, 185n.65

Weber, Max, 3–9, 10, 32,
    153n.62, 143
Wieman, Henry Nelson,
    56, 69, 159n.40
Willey, Basil, 181n.8
Williams, Daniel Day, 57,
    159n.41
Williams, George, 98
Wolin, Sheldon, 122,
    145n.1, 148–9n.43
Woodsworth, James
    Shaver, 35–40